WITHDRAWN

The Entrepreneur's Guide to Financial Statements

The Entrepreneur's Guide

CJ Rhoads, Series Editor

The Entrepreneur's Guide to Financial Statements

David Worrell

 PRAEGER

AN IMPRINT OF ABC-CLIO, LLC

Santa Barbara, California • Denver, Colorado • Oxford, England

Copyright 2014 by ABC-CLIO, LLC

All rights reserved. No part of this publication may be reproduced, stored in a retrieval system, or transmitted, in any form or by any means, electronic, mechanical, photocopying, recording, or otherwise, except for the inclusion of brief quotations in a review, without prior permission in writing from the publisher.

Library of Congress Cataloging-in-Publication Data

Worrell, David.
   The entrepreneur's guide to financial statements / David Worrell.
     pages cm. — (The entrepreneur's guide)
   Includes bibliographical references and index.
   ISBN 978–1–4408–2935–2 (hardback) — ISBN 978–1–4408–2936–9 (ebook)
   1. Small business—Finance. 2. Financial statements. I. Title.
HG4027.7.W675   2014
658.15′12—dc23   2013033748

ISBN: 978–1–4408–2935–2
EISBN: 978–1–4408–2936–9

18 17 16 15 14   2 3 4 5

This book is also available on the World Wide Web as an eBook.
Visit www.abc-clio.com for details.

Praeger
An Imprint of ABC-CLIO, LLC

ABC-CLIO, LLC
130 Cremona Drive, P.O. Box 1911
Santa Barbara, California 93116-1911

This book is printed on acid-free paper ∞

Manufactured in the United States of America

Contents

PART 4   RATIOS AND ANALYSIS

PART 5   MANAGING BY THE NUMBERS

Tables and Figures

TABLES

FIGURES

Preface

Life is full of opportunities to create, accomplish, and build. We humans have a limitless ability to imagine things that do not yet exist and to pursue them with passion and conviction. At heart, each of us is looking to leave our mark on the world. For some of us, that passion inevitably leads to a new chapter in our careers and suddenly we find ourselves building a company around activities that started as a simple hobby. The baker starts a bakery. The pilot launches an airline. The engineer builds a machine shop. It happens every day, in every city.

It seems natural enough, but when a passion turns into a business, something funny occurs: Suddenly, the business takes on a life of its own. Before long, the company is making demands that have nothing to do with our vision or our original passion. Bakeries have payroll; airlines need capital; a machine shop deals with inventory; and they all worry about cash flow.

Unfortunately, as business owners, we don't always possess the skills (or the time to develop the skills) to feed both our passion and the demands of our business. Hopefully, a practical hands-on business book like this one can fill in the gap and provide entrepreneurs with deeper insight into the most critical aspects of their business—in this case, understanding financial statements and using them to guide the growth of a business.

A strong and growing business can mean greater opportunity to do the kind of work that we love—but we need to understand the financial foundation that makes it all possible. Financial statements are the key to this understanding and to making the kind of business decisions that will assure a long and prosperous career as an entrepreneur.

There are several reasons why we, as business owners, must take full responsibility for the financial statements—and financial health—of our business. Let's get going and start with a look at four of these reasons: Speaking the Language, Finding Our Direction, Managing through Change, and Spotting Opportunities and Trends.

FINANCE IS THE LANGUAGE OF BUSINESS

Businesses speak in numbers. Even an art gallery or a cupcake shop tells its story in numbers: how many cupcakes are made, how many paintings are sold, how much profit is returned to the owner, and so on. The life story of a business is best understood when it is quantified.

Sure, marketers and human resource experts will tell you that a company "is all about the people" or "nothing without the brand." And of course, that is true in a way. But even "people" and "brands" have to be counted, measured, and controlled. A company cannot hire an unlimited number of people; a marketing campaign cannot run on an unlimited budget. Even human resources and marketing must make decisions that produce real economic results, or the very fabric of a company quickly unravels. Fortunately, finance is a discipline that can help us make better decisions across the entire company—from purchasing and sales to marketing and HR.

Finance—and particularly the use of financial statements—is the practice of understanding exactly how a business works, from the inside out.

- Did the marketing campaign result in more profit than expense? (Should we do it again?)
- Does our union contract leave enough money to buy new machines when the current equipment breaks?
- Can we open a second location with more staff?
- How many customers do we need to make the new location profitable?

These are just a few of the real business questions that finance can answer. Asking and answering these kinds of questions is vital to the success and sustainability of a business.

It is not enough to have a powerful vision, great products, or even smart people. Only a deeper dive into finance can show whether the effort is, and will be, successful at creating profits that will keep the business operating for years to come.

WHERE IS THE COMPANY GOING?

Sometimes entrepreneurs are so busy building their business that they don't stop to see where they are heading. Like sailing alone across the ocean without a compass or a map, building a company without knowing the financial direction is unnecessarily risky. There are, of course, waypoints and weather to guide us: the rising and setting of the sun; gentle trade winds that can push us in the right direction; maybe even a few lighthouses along the way to keep us from the worst dangers. But a few days lost at sea will convince the hardiest soul of the value of a compass and map.

Just as a strong breeze can be either a helpful trade wind or the start of a disastrous storm, a change in cash flow can be caused by both good conditions and bad. It is a business owner's job to know which is which. Without understanding finance, it is difficult for an owner to know whether she is sailing her company into a safe harbor or into the raging winds of a hurricane. A foundation in basic finance, however, will make the health and welfare of the company crystal clear.

MANAGE BY THE NUMBERS

Becoming familiar with finance is the key to unlocking the secrets of our business success. Fortunately, learning to use finance to guide our business is not as complex as it may seem, once someone explains the basics. The best part about using finance to understand our business is that the results are dynamic: the picture can change—and our actions can change it!

Watching the financial numbers change over time gives us the feedback we need to take actions that will improve the financial health of our business. Every decision and action we take in our business—from raising prices or dropping them, to spending more or saving more—will impact the numbers going forward.

Managing business "by the numbers" means not only finding and understanding the current financial health of the company, but also taking action and observing the impact it has on future financial reports.

NUMBERS + TIME = TREND

Finance works best when it is comparative. A single number or ratio by itself can be important, but the whole story comes from looking at the same number over time: past, present, and future. Is today's number a fluke, or part of a trend? A business has so many moving parts that—without comparing past, present, and future—it is impossible to know for sure whether one day's problem is a temporary annoyance or the symptom of a chronic issue.

Fortunately, every business generates enough data to paint a meaningful, multidimensional picture. The trick of course, is to identify, collect, and organize the data in a meaningful way.

BOOK OBJECTIVES AND ORGANIZATION

This book is a combination of real-world examples and lessons I've learned from many years of experience. Small business owners across the country have helped to fill this book with interesting stories of how they use financial statements and metrics to solve important business problems. This book and its companion workbook (available at http://www.rocksolidfinance.com/workbook) are designed to help business owners:

- *Understand complex financial terminology.* We will define terms in ways that relate directly to everyday life: connecting finance concepts not only to business operations, but also to common life events that will make these concepts crystal clear.
- *See the big picture.* We will examine the parts of the financial statements and how they work together to present a complete picture of the business, its current health, and its future prospects.
- *Know themselves and their business better.* We will illustrate how simple math can be applied to financial statements to answer more in-depth questions about profits, cash flow, growth prospects, and personal goals.
- *Predict the future.* We will present tools to "see the future," including simple equations and charts that can literally predict disaster (or wealth) before it happens.
- *Make better decisions.* Along the way, we will learn to "tell the story" of our own businesses based on the numbers. This uncovers weaknesses and strengths in the company, which empowers better strategic decision-making.
- *Beat the competition.* Using the same tools, we will learn how to evaluate *other* businesses to determine their competitive position and our potential advantages. These lessons will guide us as we make bold moves to trump competitors.
- *Grow!* Finally, we will reveal new insights into what drives our own business growth, what is necessary to fuel that growth, what is limiting growth (or will limit it in the future), and—most important—we will learn to communicate all of this to investors, bankers, vendors, and other business partners who can help us grow.

This book is organized into five major parts: the income statement, the balance sheet, the cash flow statement, key ratios, and dashboards and planning. The book's mix of real-world examples, stories, fill-in-the-blank exercises, and highly structured writing will help the business owner find exactly the help needed, at exactly the right time. You can get additional help and practice by using the companion workbook, available at http://www.rocksolidfinance.com/workbook.

Ready to go? Let's start by looking at the data flowing through your company, as shown in the income statement.

Acknowledgments

It's no use writing a book that no one reads, so my sincere thanks to you who are about to embark upon this challenge. A healthy business can be exciting, financially rewarding, and just plain fun. I hope the tools you'll find here will help you make your business something that enriches your life and the lives of others.

In preparing this book I've called upon the experience of hundreds of entrepreneurs and financial executives who have graciously shared their stories with me. Their imagination, tenacity, and drive have inspired me. Thanks to all of you who have shared these important lessons.

In particular, thanks to those business owners who have graciously allowed their stories to appear in this book. The names and details have been changed a great deal, but the fact that these illustrations were inspired by actual business situations is invaluable. Sincere appreciation goes out to my favorite entrepreneurs: Jim Worrell, Marc Pitre, Michael Shapiro, Ralph Concepcion, Darrin Brockelbank, Heather Brockelbank, Jenni Lough Watson, Caroline Walker, Bill Manby, George Spears, Chris Younger, Greg Rose, and Steve Lenhart.

Of course, no book is truly written by just one person. There are many more to recognize for their contributions: Jim Horan for getting the ball rolling; CJ Rhoads for her unflappable guidance; Brian Romer and Hilary Claggett for making it easy; John Steffen, Steve MacPherson, Danielle Phinney, Debbie Renshaw, and Therese Shoborg for keeping me on task . . .

. . . and to my wife Tracey for, well, everything else.

Part 1

THE INCOME STATEMENT

1

Income Statement Basics

Most people intuitively understand that a business must make more money than it spends. In that sense, running a business is really no different than what we try to do in our personal life: we add up our paychecks, subtract our bills, and hope that at the end of the month there is money left over.

Companies track their income (sales) and expense (spending) in a similar way. The tally we use to do this is called an Income Statement, or sometimes a "Profit and Loss Statement." In this book we will use the common abbreviation, "P&L."

The P&L is the single most important measure of a company's health and sustainability. Only a P&L can tell us whether our overall operations are resulting in profits, which will help our company continue. Of course, the P&L might tell us that the results are losses, which will spell doom on a long-term basis.

Overall, a P&L may look like a simple tabulation of income and expenses, but there is more here than meets the eye. In fact, the P&L does have a standard layout format with four sections—but also an endless opportunity for creativity.

A STANDARD FORMAT

Every P&L shares a common top-to-bottom organization. The structure of a P&L follows a simple concept: You have to make money before you can spend it. So every P&L starts with a list of the income sources, followed by the expenses.

It does not matter what industry we are in, or how we earn our money—the fundamental organization of a P&L stays the same. Compare Table 1.1 and Table 1.2. The first is an example P&L from a preschool, while the second is from a manufacturing business.

Table 1.1. P&L from a Preschool

Rockabye Baby Day Care
Profit & Loss
January

Income	
4000 - Tuition Income	46,307
Total Income	46,307
Cost of Sales	
5010 - Food Supplies	581
5020 - Student Supplies	621
Total Cost of Sales	1,202
Gross Profit	45,105
Expenses	
6020 - Auto & Gas	450
6030 - Bank Charges	
6035 - Credit Card Fees	606
6030 - Bank Charges - Other	137
Total 6030 - Bank Charges	742
6040 - Insurance Expense	793
6050 - Laundry & Cleaning	640
6060 - License Expense	375
6070 - Legal & Professional Fees	250
6080 - Meals and Entertainment	243
6090 - Office Expense	448
6100 - Rent	6,459
6120 - Repair & Maintenance	60
6130 - Utilities	624
6600 - Payroll Expenses	15,752
Total Expenses	26,836
Other Income & Expense	0
Net Income	18,270

Table 1.2. P&L from a Manufacturer

Rock Solid Manufacturing
Profit & Loss
January

Income	
4000 - Sales - Manufactured Goods	35,256
Total Income	35,256
Cost of Goods Sold	
5100 - Cost of Goods	5,982
5200 - Direct Labor (Payroll)	7,568
5400 - Equipment, Fuel, & Fees	3,521
Total Cost of Goods Sold	17,071
Gross Profit	18,185
Expense	
6100 - Advertising & Promotion	398
6200 - Automobiles	795
6300 - Bank Charges	159
6450 - Employee Services	283
6500 - Tools & Equipment (Not Rentals)	599
6600 - Facilities, Storage & Office	195
6700 - Payroll Expenses (Office Staff)	2,325
6900 - Uniforms	2,057
6950 - Utilities	492
Total Expense	7,303
Net Ordinary Income	10,882
Other Income & Expense	
Other Income	
7100 - Gain on Sale of Asset	5,926
Total Other Income	5,926
Other Expense	
8100 - Depreciation	628
8300 - Taxes	396
Total Other Expense	1,024
Net Other Income	4,902
Net Income	15,784

Notice how in both tables, these example P&Ls are each divided into four major sections. Even though Table 1.1 shows the results from a preschool business and Table 1.2 is from a cabinet-making operation, the sections are the same:

1. Income
2. Cost of Sales
3. Expenses
4. Other Income and Expenses

The order of these sections will always be the same (although the names may change slightly, as we will see later). The Income section shows the money the company makes from sales. The Cost of Sales section shows those expenses that are directly attributable to the sales themselves. The Expenses section lists everything else a company purchases. And the Other Income and Expenses section is a handy spot for unusual items and transactions that require additional explanation or calculation.

TOTALS THAT TELL A STORY

Notice that each section ends with a subtotal from the section and a cumulative or running total for the statement as a whole. The subtotal for Cost of Sales, for example, is the sum of all expenses within that section. The running total that follows the Cost of Sales shows the tally of all income and cost of sales, which is called the gross margin.

There are four cumulative or running total lines that have important functions shown in Table 1.3.

DEFINITIONS

These totals are more than just mathematical sums, however. Each total is a kind of signpost that gives the owner vital information about the business, particularly when examined over a period of time. Let's drill down and get some specific definitions out of the way.

Total Revenue

Total revenue is a pretty simple number—the sum of all the categories of sales—but it's a helpful way to look at the big picture, particularly for companies that have several different kinds of revenue.

Table 1.3. Running Totals from the P&L

Name of Line	What It Means	How It's Calculated
Total Revenue	The total sales of the company	Add up all of the income categories
Gross Profit	The difference between what customers paid to buy goods from the business and what the business paid to buy or make the same goods (or services)	Total Revenue minus Total Cost of Goods Sold
Operating Profit	What is left after paying all normal business expenses	Gross Profit minus Total Expenses
Net Profit	What is left after *all* business expenses *and other costs* (or other income) are counted, even if those other amounts are not directly related to the normal business operations	Operating Profit plus Other Income minus Other Expenses (Note that Other Income and Other Expenses are commonly grouped together as "Other Income and Expense")

It may be that sales have fallen in one area and increased in another. Tracking total revenue (instead of just one kind of sales revenue) helps to smooth out random or even seasonal shifts in customer buying patterns.

Gross Profit

Gross profit, also called gross margin (when expressed as a percentage) or gross margin dollars, is what's left of our revenue after deducting those costs that are directly associated with the production of our product or delivery of our service. Gross profit tells us only the difference between what we paid for our goods and what we sold them for. (A negative gross profit, of course, means that we are selling for less than we buy!)

Gross profit is one of the most useful numbers on the P&L for businesses that make or resell products. Manufacturers, retailers, resellers, and contractors are examples of businesses that must keep a close eye on gross profit. A business owner can't always control every expense in their business, but by looking at gross profit, they will quickly know whether key expense items might be creeping up too high, or whether prices might be too low.

Operating Profit

Operating profit is what's left of gross profit after deducting all other normal expenses associated with our operations. "Normal" expenses include anything that is needed to stay in business, such as rent, wages, and marketing. It does not include unusual or one-time expenses, such as paying a legal judgment or replacing a building that burned down.

Operating profit is a pretty good proxy for the health of a company. Steady and consistent operating profits are the sign of a business that is able to control costs and to charge for the value it creates at every step.

Net Profit

Net profit is most commonly a measure of what is left after a company pays taxes and accounts for other nonoperating expenses (including depreciation and amortization, which we will address in Chapter 3). As the true "bottom line" of a business, net profit is the ultimate way of measuring the financial success of a business.

These simple definitions are true for all businesses and all P&Ls. The basic relationships between the sections of a P&L and their corresponding "totals" are the same for coffee shops and copper mines. But clearly there will be differences, too.

DIFFERENCES BY INDUSTRY AND FUNCTION

As we've seen, every P&L for every business has a few things in common: four sections, a strict order, and common names for the lines that calculate profits and losses.

There can also be some differences. Often, as in Tables 1.1 and 1.2, the difference reflects the nature of the business. For example, the cabinet maker in Table 1.2 is able to show that most of his costs are directly related to the goods produced. In this case, producing more cabinets takes more hours from a carpenter, more wood, more nails and glue, etc. That's far different from the preschool business shown in Table 1.1. There, the costs for things such as labor (i.e., teachers) are largely the same, no matter how many children show up for class.

The result is that the manufacturer can easily list a great deal of expenses in the "Cost of Sales" category, while the preschool operator cannot. The majority of expenses for the cabinet maker are captured in the Cost of Sales section of the P&L. The majority of expenses for the preschool operator fall into the general Expense section of the

P&L. This is a common difference between businesses that sell products and those that sell services.

Tables 1.4 and 1.5 show another pair of P&L statements. This time, we see a restaurant and a retailer. Like the preschool, both the restaurant and the retail shop must have staff ready to serve customers

Table 1.4. Restaurant P&L

Rocky's Pizzeria Profit & Loss January	
Ordinary Income/Expenses	
Income	
4000 - Food	9,500
4030 - Beer	2,536
4040 - Soft Beverages	78
Total Income	12,114
Cost of Goods Sold	
5000 - Food	3,300
5010 - Beer	535
5040 - Soft Beverages	33
5050 - Labor	2,962
Total Cost of Goods Sold	6,830
Gross Profit	5,284
Expenses	
6030 - Bank Charges	235
6040 - Insurance Expense	125
6050 - Laundry & Cleaning	300
6060 - Rent	1,425
6310 - Labor-Managers	427
6320 - Waste Removal	125
Total Expenses	2,637
Operating Profit	2,647
Other Income & Expense	0
Net Income	2,647

whether customers show up or not, but these P&Ls look a bit different. In both cases, these businesses have chosen to list certain kinds of labor in the Cost of Sales category, and others in the Expense category.

Table 1.5. Retail P&L

Rockin' Robin Toy Store	
Profit & Loss	
January	
Ordinary Income/Expenses	
Income	
4000 - Board Games	1,752
4010 - Children's Games	1,578
4020 - Computer Games	2,500
Total Income	5,830
Cost of Sales	
5000 - Board Games	876
5010 - Children's Games	720
5020 - Labor-Cashier	975
Total Cost of Sales	2,571
Gross Profit	3,259
Expenses	
6030 - Credit Card Charges	159
6050 - Insurance Expense	175
6060 - Office Supplies	52
6060 - Rent & CAM	595
6070 - Repair & Maintenance	75
6200 - Payroll Expenses	350
6310 - Labor-Managers	427
Total Expenses	1,833
Operating Income	1,426
Other Income & Expense	
7300 - Income Tax Accrued	157
Total Other Income & Expense	157
Net Income	1,269

This seems like a good idea, since a busy store (or restaurant) will need more cashiers (or servers), but not necessarily more managers or executives.

Review and compare these P&L statements to others in the Appendix. In all of them, the basic structure is the same; but how the business owner uses the P&L differs in order to better reflect the underlying business.

There are, of course, guidelines for deciding how to record the income and expense in a business, depending on its general industry. Most restaurants have a P&L that looks something like Table 1.4. Most manufacturers will recognize the P&L from the cabinet maker shown in Table 1.2.

With practice we can even begin to describe the underlying business simply by looking at the P&L. How a company categorizes sales and expenses, what they call those categories, how they use the Cost of Sales section, and how much gross profit they make can all provide clues about their operations.

In the next chapters, we'll start looking at each section more closely, beginning with the Revenue section. As we work from the top line toward the bottom, we'll look at the deeper meaning and impact of how, when, and why to mold and shape a P&L statement to suit the business it serves.

SUMMARY

- ☑ The Income Statement, or P&L, is one of the three main financial statements used by business owners to manage a company.
- ☑ Every P&L has four sections: Income, Cost of Sales, Expenses, and Other Income and Expenses.
- ☑ The business structure, industry, and practices may shape the way some items are recorded on the P&L.
- ☑ Looking at a P&L can reveal a lot about the business and how the business owner measures and monitors his results.

2

Revenue

Even though the four sections of a P&L are standard for all businesses, what falls into each section is not standard at all. How we organize the contents of each section are largely up to us, the business owners. In fact, P&Ls are a bit like snowflakes—no two companies' P&Ls are ever the same.

The flexibility and customization available to business owners is helpful in many ways. When an owner or manager needs to make a decision based on financial facts, the flexibility to craft a P&L that reflects the reality of the business is vital. By matching the financial statements to the "on the ground" business model, we can better understand what is really happening and see what decisions we need to make to affect change.

If we were locked into a single P&L format, it would be terribly difficult to create reports that would guide our action. For example, a car dealer might calculate both sales and expenses very differently from a company that makes cupcakes. And well they should.

No matter how it is recorded, every business has some kind of revenue, so let's decipher the language of income first.

REVENUE AND INCOME

The first section of a P&L is always Income, which is also known as revenue. The fact that revenue is first reflects the common saying, "Nothing happens until you make a sale." Having income at the top keeps business owners focused squarely on the reason they are in business—to sell something.

What goes into the Income section is, as we've said, completely up to you—well, almost completely.

Within the Income section, companies generally have line items like "Revenue from Sales" or perhaps several lines that show revenue from various kinds of sales. (For example, the retail toy store in Table 1.5 chose to break out the sale of each kind of game—kids' games, computer games, and board games.) As we will see, there are many kinds of income that may or may not belong in the Income section.

For example, a car dealer is going to have a very different Income section from that of a cupcake shop. A car dealer in particular makes an interesting case. Let's take a closer look.

EXAMPLE: WHAT IS INCOME FOR A CAR DEALER?

Consider my friend Kim, who owns a car dealership. Besides selling cars to consumers, Kim receives rebates and incentives from the manufacturer. Kim might also make loans on the cars he sells and collect interest payments from buyers.

When Kim sells a car, how do you think he calculates what the car cost him to buy, and the price at which he sold it? Imagine how different ways of recording a sale might change how Kim thinks about his business. For example, he sold a car for $20,000. But he also received a rebate from the manufacturer for that car. Additionally, he made the loan to the buyer. Finally, when the buyer paid for the car, the buyer also gave Kim the money for the taxes and tags. Table 2.1 shows all of the possible income sources Kim has when selling a car.

Table 2.1. Kim's Possible Income Items

Kim's Cars Profit & Loss January	
Income	
4000 - Car Sales	20,000
4010 - Sales Tax	1,000
4020 - Manufacturer's Rebate	5,000
4030 - Loan Origination Fee	1,000
4040 - Lifetime Value of Interest on Car Loan	6,563
4050 - Fees for Registration, Title, & Tag	2,500
Total Income	36,063

Table 2.2. The Wrong Way to Show Kim's Income

Kim's Cars Profit & Loss January	
Income	
4000 - Car Sales	36,063
Total Income	36,063

When all is said and done, Kim will have received cash, a rebate, loan fees, interest payments, and taxes. Kim *could* call all of these sources of money "income." In fact, he might be tempted to record this one transaction as shown in Table 2.2.

If Kim thought that he was actually selling cars for more than $36,000 each, he might imagine that his business is doing quite well and start making bad decisions. Maybe he would offer his salespeople a large bonus on each sale, redecorate the showroom, or start planning his retirement.

Whoa! Not so fast! Showing income in this way will clearly lead his business in the wrong direction. Let's look at why he should *not* call some of these things income.

DEFINING INCOME

Deciding what to put in the Income section of the P&L is ultimately up to us, the business owners. But there are rules that will help us decide what is—and what is not—income. If Kim considered all the money income, he would have broken almost all the rules.

Remember, we want a P&L that describes and guides the operation of a business. The P&L must reflect the realities of the business—showing the difference between those things that business owners can control, and those that they cannot control. A P&L should help business owners segment and prioritize their business—preventing less important things from obscuring the more important items.

Simply stated, there are four rules for deciding what goes into the Income section of the P&L:

1. *Control*: Did the business control the terms of the income?
2. *Customers*: Did the income come from people you want to describe as customers?

3. *Transaction*: Did the company sell a product or service in exchange for the revenue?
4. *Timing*: Did the sale happen during the time period measured by the P&L?

There is always room for argument in these matters, but let's look at each of these criteria separately to evaluate Kim's income categories.

CONTROL

The Income portion of a P&L gives us the opportunity to separate revenue that we control from revenue that might be considered indirect or ancillary. Why? The P&L should help you see what is *most important* in your business and compare the related revenue and expenses for *that activity*. Income you control by the direct action of your staff, your business model, your website, or your sales teams are clearly important to measure and track.

Collecting tax on a sale, for example, is clearly *not* something you control. The government sets the rates and rules; the business is simply stuck in the middle. On the other hand, you control the sale of a product or service by setting the price, the hours you are open for business, the number of salespeople selling it, the amount of advertising you do, and how well you treat customers coming in the door. Watching the income you "control" might help you adjust your effort in each of these activities.

> Warning! Don't jump to the conclusion that collecting taxes or government fees is not a kind of income. A business must certainly account for every dollar collected—whether it meets the three criteria for top line income or not. Title fees collected by our car dealer, however, should certainly be separated from the income from selling cars. We'll explore how to do this a bit later.

CUSTOMERS

Every dollar that comes into a business comes from somewhere else, but not all of it comes from customers. Rebates, commissions, royalties, and interest payments are just a few of the kinds of income a company might earn from sources that are clearly not customers. When deciding what to show as "top line" revenue, income from noncustomer sources probably does not qualify. (Remember, these are guidelines, and your specific circumstances might warrant something different.)

Just as we want to measure the income that we can control, we also want to know that the income came from customers and not from some third party. Why? A business exists to serve its customers. Properly defining who is a customer (and who is not) can have a profound impact on a company's organization, operation, and outlook. *Financial statements and reports should reflect that decision.* So reports should carefully emphasize income from clients over all other sources.

If Kim had combined rebates and loan fees into one big category of income from the sale of a car, he would have clearly flunked the test. Rebates are obviously paid by a manufacturer (not a customer). Loan origination fees are likely paid by a bank. There are better ways to categorize all of these things.

TIMING

Timing is one of the most important aspects of qualifying and recording revenue. For our purposes, we simply want to be sure that our P&L includes only the income created during the period the P&L measures. In other words, last month's sales do not belong in this month's P&L.

To keep things straight, remember that there are several steps to every sale. Record each action when it happens: When something is sold, record a sale; when a payment is received, record the receipt; when money is deposited, record the deposit. This may sound like it complicates a simple sales transaction, but if the sale, payment, and deposit happen on different days—or in different months or years—it becomes very important to track the actual dates of each step.

A proper P&L captures all the transactions that happen within a set of dates. Typically we look at a monthly P&L, but sometimes we want to know our profit or loss for the week, quarter, or year. Income should be recorded only when it actually occurs—and recording the sale separately from the payment is a good first step toward proper *accrual accounting*.

There are, of course, many situations when it is difficult to pinpoint the exact day when a sale is made. Long-term contracts, construction projects, and other types of revenue can force us to think carefully about when we record the sale. This complex task is beyond the scope of this book, but readers are encouraged to learn more about the topic called "revenue recognition."

> *Definition*: Accrual accounting is the method we use to record revenue and expenses when we incur them, regardless of when the payments change hands. Accrual accounting helps us measure the business activity during a period. The alternative method, called cash basis accounting, measures the exchange of payments.

TRANSACTION: EXCHANGING VALUE FOR VALUE

Finally, even if our income meets all of the above criteria, it must also be the result of a legitimate sale transaction. In other words, the company must have exchanged something of value—goods or services—for the income.

Sometimes a company will receive money that is completely unrelated to a sale or transaction. If a company receives cash because of a bank loan, for example, it clearly is not income. (In Part 2, we will discuss how these transactions are reported on the Balance Sheet.)

Bank loans are not the only example. A landlord might receive a security deposit from a renter. This transaction appears to satisfy our other criteria—the money is from a customer, and the landlord controlled the transaction—but no actual product or service was involved, so no sale was completed. A refundable deposit like this is another example of money received that is not income.

In Kim's case, I would argue that only the actual sale price of the car is income. Everything else fails at least one of our four criteria.

EXCEPTIONS TO THE RULES

If these criteria are not enough to decide whether revenue should be counted as top line income, we could also consider the impact that the revenue will have on reporting. Good management reporting is the reason for good accounting practices. If measuring and tracking a particular kind of income is going to impact key decisions about company operations, then perhaps it is important enough to include in the Income section of a P&L. Conversely, if the income is inconsequential, unrelated to the primary business, passed through to a vendor, or if the income could in any way skew the results of a key management report (such as by artificially inflating sales), then it should not be a part of the top line revenue. Here are some more examples of money that we might not classify as income.

- Prepayments, deposits, or "escrow" payments for work to be performed in the future, particularly if those payments are refundable
- Reimbursement for pass-through expenses such as travel expenses or shipping costs, unless such costs are marked up
- Refundable security deposits that guarantee the safe return of equipment or real estate
- Customer-paid fees for permits, which might be needed by a contractor to start work
- Gifts, lottery winnings, or found money
- Windfall payments that result from lawsuits, particularly if they are not related to work done for a customer
- Interest earned on deposits in the bank
- Tax refunds

While we don't want to classify these things as income, they certainly must show up in our books somewhere. Let's look at where else they might go.

IF NOT TOP LINE, WHERE?

There are four alternatives for recognizing revenue that does not meet our criteria for top line income: (1) it can be included in Income anyway, but clearly separated into its own category; (2) it can reduce expenses; (3) it can be listed at the bottom of the P&L in a section all its own, appropriately called "Other Income and Expense"; or (4) it can be captured by the balance sheet—a topic that we will address in detail later. For now, let's focus on just the first three ways to list income on the P&L.

Separate Income Categories

Since Kim does not make $36,063 directly from the sale of a car, lumping all that income together into one category called "Auto Sales" would be misleading. He may, however, decide that some of the other income is closely enough related to his core business to warrant careful tracking.

In this case, Kim could put some of the income into a separate category and continue to include it in the Income section of the P&L. Loan origination fees (i.e., commissions on loans to car buyers) might be one item that Kim could keep in the Income section, but put into a separate category. Loans are not Kim's primary reason to be in business. The income, however, is very closely related to selling cars, and he will certainly benefit from reporting how much income comes from the loans he closes. Table 2.3 shows this item properly recorded.

Table 2.3. Kim's Cars Corrected P&L

Kim's Cars	
Profit & Loss	
January	
Income	
4000 - Car Sales	20,000
4010 - Loan Origination Fee	1,000
Total Income	21,000
Cost of Goods Sold	
5100 - Car	10,000
5200 - Manufacturers Rebate	−5,000
Total Cost of Goods Sold	5,000
Gross Profit	16,000
Expense	
6110 - Fees, Registration, Title, & Tag	2,500
6130 - Payroll	1,500
6150 - Rent	1,000
6160 - Sales Tax	1,000
6170 - Utilities	750
Total Expense	6,750
Operating Income	9,250
Other Income/Expense	
Other Income	
7100 - Loan Interest Collected	353
7210 - Buyer-Paid Registration Fees	2,500
7220 - Buyer-Paid Sales Tax	1,000
Total Other Income	3,853
Net Other Income & Expense	5,397
Net Income	14,647

Expenses Category

Another place to put money received (such as manufacturer rebates) would be in the Expense or Cost of Goods sections. Typically, these sections would include only *costs*, but there may be times when we receive money directly related to a cost. A reimbursement, rebate, or refund, for example, directly offsets the cost of a specific expense. To categorize this correctly, we could record it as a negative expense in the same account as the cost, or we could create a separate expense account just for the rebates. By categorizing the original expense and the rebate separately in this way, it becomes simple to create reports that show *both* the total cost of an item and the amount of discounts as they change over time. We will explore expenses further in Chapter 3. Table 2.3 shows the rebate money Kim receives recorded in a way that offsets the cost of goods sold.

Note that the practice of putting money received into an expense account will produce a "negative" expense. That's going to look funny to most folks, because it is not a common practice. If circumstances warrant it, however, a negative expense might be exactly what you want to show. A manufacturer's rebate is one case in which showing a negative expense is more common and can help us see what the real "net" cost of our expenses are.

What else might qualify as money received that shows up in the Expense or Cost of Goods sections of the P&L? Refunds, discounts, and purchase incentives (particularly if the amount is inconsequential, such as a loyalty card credit) are best categorized as an expense—with amounts put in the *same* category as the items that generated them.

Other Income

Keep in mind that some income is simply not related in any way to the company's business. In this case, pushing it all the way to the bottom of the P&L is really the best move.

Every P&L should have a section called Other Income or, better yet, Other Income and Expense. It can contain all sorts of nonoperational items including interest income and one-time windfalls, such as a payment resulting from a lawsuit. Other Income and Expense is a perfect place to put both income and expense items that are uncontrollable or simply unrelated to the operations. Table 2.3 shows how Kim records interest collected as an "other income," which helps show that Kim is not really in the business of collecting loan interest.

BREAK IT DOWN, THEN WRITE IT DOWN

The criteria we've outlined above shows what does *not* belong in the Income section of the P&L. What's left?

Hopefully, there remain some categories that we do want to show as income. "Sales" can be a good catchall, but it is most helpful to break "Sales" into smaller categories. Why? Because we often make decisions about business activities based on how important they are to our top line.

Let's consider Chris. When Chris opened her first "Canine Services Studio," she provided the typical pet services including dog training, boarding, and grooming. In addition to these, she now sells some really unique services, such as using trained dogs to chase flocks of Canadian geese off commercial property. On top of all of that, she also offers her clients a line of all-natural dog food by the case.

Chris would not dream of lumping all her income into one account called "sales." In fact, each of the items we mentioned above has its own line in the Income section of her P&L. She watches how these line items change from month to month and the percentage of total income that each activity generates. She knows that *how* she generates sales is as important as *how much* she sells.

Why It Matters

Chasing geese is highly profitable, but Chris has to do this work herself—along with all of her highly trained dogs, of course. Since the number of hours she can spend chasing geese is limited, so is the amount of money she can make doing that. Finally, time spent chasing geese is time away from her retail shop, where customers may be waiting to buy other services.

Chris has made a decision to limit (and eventually eliminate) the geese abatement services from her business. In fact, she gets quite worried when she sells too much of those services because it jeopardizes her opportunities to build a stronger, longer-lasting business with other customers.

Instead of driving around town on an actual goose chase, she prioritizes the income she can make from training. She knows her training drives loyal customers who also buy grooming and boarding services. Chris can hire professional trainers and groomers as her business grows, but using dogs to chase geese is more difficult. So she watches both numbers like a hawk—the geese-chasing revenue so it does not get too high, the training revenue so it does not drop too low.

We can learn a good lesson from Chris. Every business owner should identify the categories that make up sales, and track various *kinds* of income that will shape the business now and into the future.

SUMMARY

- ☑ It is up to us to decide which items go into which section of the P&L.
- ☑ The content of the P&L should closely match the actual operations of our business and its unique business model.
- ☑ All income must be stated on the P&L somewhere, but business owners have choices.
- ☑ The Income section should include revenue that meets four basic criteria: Control, Customers, Transaction, and Timing.
- ☑ Any revenue that does not meet these criteria can be placed in its own category, offset expenses, or be moved to the Other Income section.
- ☑ Where you put the income will impact what you see in financial reports, which can influence key business decisions—so always consider the reporting and decision-making cycle when designing the P&L.

3

Expenses and Profits

Let's review the four sections of our P&L: Income; Cost of Sales; Expenses; and Other Income and Expenses. We saw in Chapter 2 how to identify and categorize income. The next step is to record expenses.

Even a simple business can have a huge number of categories of expenses. Consider paying salaries to employees, for example. For this one task, we might have to keep track of not just wages, but state taxes, federal taxes, state unemployment fees, federal unemployment insurance, health insurance, workers compensation insurance, pretax deductions for a 401(k), posttax deductions, garnishments, bonuses, overtime, expense reimbursement, and more. Whew!

Happily, expense categories are only a problem if they get out of hand. Tax reporting issues aside, we are generally free to arrange our expenses just as we are our income.

Like income, expenses should be categorized in ways that are meaningful to the business. Grouping expenses in ways that roughly mirror the operations is usually best, since it can help us make decisions about the operations. In this chapter we will examine this further. We will also look at how the two expense sections on the P&L are different and how we can decide which expenses go into which section. This turns out to be a pretty important decision, so we'll look closely at what we mean by "Cost of Sales" and "Expenses."

START WITH A BLANK SLATE

There are a limitless number of things on which we can spend our money. To impose a sense of order and control, a business owner must quickly come to terms with the idea of putting these innumerable things into a much smaller number of buckets. On financial statements, those buckets are called *categories*.

If we stare only at a pile of receipts or even a mile-long list of individual expenses, we are not going to understand how our business operates or how to align our expenses with our business goals. Sorting expenses into meaningful categories is the only way to make sense out of the chaos and to manage them adequately. Just as we separated income into categories, expenses likewise should be categorized. The key, of course, is to make the list of categories as short as possible while keeping them truly meaningful.

Deciding which categories are needed is the first step. Assigning those categories to the proper section on the P&L is the second step. As we saw with income, expenses can also legitimately go into any of the P&L sections: Income, Cost of Sales, Expenses, or Other Income and Expenses. There are some good rules of thumb that will help us first create a list of categories and then assign them to the best P&L section.

BUILD THE BIG CATEGORIES

Not all expenses are created equal. On a day-to-day or month-to-month basis, most expenses are pretty dull. Many expenses (like, say, an electricity bill) vary only a bit from month to month. Likewise, there's not a lot you can do to impact the power bill. Even if you were able cut it by half, you might not save enough to justify the effort.

These humdrum bills need to disappear into the background so we can get a clearer picture of more meaningful expenses like, perhaps, payroll or travel costs. It is good practice to create categories into which you can drop many of the less important expenses.

Let's start with the simple stuff. Water, electricity, phone and Internet access are pretty common—and not very interesting—expenses. Unless you are running a car wash or a Laundromat, watching the water bill is probably not high on your priority list. In order to tuck these bills away, it is common to lump them all into one category called "Utilities."

What else can we group together? Office supplies, postage, and printing are three big areas of spending that are often lumped together as "Office Supplies." Categories like this can be expanded to include any items that essentially serve the same function, whether the items themselves are truly similar or not. So whether your office runs on toner and paper or iPads and apps, consider putting these expenses together under a broad category like Office Supplies. Table 3.1 lists

Table 3.1. Common Expense Categories

Category Name	What It Contains
Utilities	Electricity, water, sewer, trash, telephone, cell phone, Internet access, cable TV
Occupancy	Rent, common area maintenance, property tax, special assessments, cleaning, HVAC repairs and maintenance, other building maintenance, landscaping, safety inspections, etc.
Information Technology	Technical support, Internet access (if not in Utilities), PC repair, printer ink, subscriptions to cloud services, PCs, software and networking expenses (anything not capitalized)
Travel, Meals, and Entertainment	Airfare, hotels, car rental, mileage reimbursement, parking, and tolls; plus meals and any expense related to entertaining a customer, whether during travel or at home
Employee Development	Training, off-site meeting expense, performance rewards, all-employee meals, company parties, team-building events
Office Supplies	Paper, pens, staples, coffee, bottled water, toilet paper, paper towels, cleaning supplies, stamps, etc.
Legal and Professional Fees	Lawyers, consultants, and accountants (including tax preparation costs)

some of the common groups of expenses. Try some of these headings to get you started.

> Note that for tax reasons, some expenses must be tracked separately. For example, meals and entertainment should be separated from other travel expenses because some meals and entertainment expenses are not fully tax deductible. Use a subcategory under "Travel, Meals, & Entertainment" for this purpose, and ask your CPA which expenses to capture in that sub-account.

Building big categories can be really useful, but don't go overboard. Making one big category called "Office Expenses" is tempting, but if that category contains everything from rent to printer ink to administrative assistant services, you've gone too far. The purpose of categorization is to be specific without being overly detailed.

When watching every purchase is *not* important (or spending cannot be controlled), big categories can simplify a P&L, which in turn helps you focus on those expenses that are more controllable and more important. Don't let the purchase of paper clips distract you from managing larger, more controllable expenses such as wages or bank fees.

KEEP IT SIMPLE

Today's accounting software packages are quite sophisticated, but a good P&L should be simple and easy to read. Creating too many expense accounts—or too many layers of accounts—is the first step toward complexity and confusion. It's up to us to keep our expense categories clear, concise, and compact.

Despite the amazing capabilities of software such as QuickBooks and Peachtree Accounting, it is helpful to keep your expense categories to just two levels: accounts and sub-accounts. For example, "Meals" might be a sub-account under "Travel, Meals, and Entertainment." But going further and creating a third level of accounts called "Meals with Customers" or "Meals while Traveling" adds an unnecessary level of complexity and very little additional benefit.

Remember, if one particular kind of expense is really that important, then it should have its own top-level category. Burying things in multiple levels of detail just makes a lot more work for the bookkeeper and adds opportunity for mistakes and inaccuracies.

VARIABLE OR FIXED

In order to assign an expense to the proper section of the P&L, we have to decide whether an expense is created as a *direct result* of making a sale. Often this is a simple matter: when we sell lemonade, we have to buy lemons. Sometimes it's a bit trickier: do we count the wages of the boy at the lemonade stand? How about the cost of those glasses we accidently break while serving lemonade? If we incur an expense as a *direct result of making a sale*, we call it a "variable" expense and record it in the P&L under the header "Cost of Sales."

If we have to pay an expense *even if we don't sell anything*, then the expense is considered "fixed" and should be recorded under the more general "Expenses" section on the P&L. These fixed expenses include rent and utilities, which are also part of a category called *overhead* expenses. Overhead is just one type of fixed expense, but people often use the word overhead incorrectly to mean *all* fixed expenses. Since we are most interested in whether a cost is variable or fixed, let's avoid using the term overhead.

> The section of a P&L that contains expenses related directly to sales is called either "Cost of Goods Sold" or "Cost of Sales." Note that if a business is product-centric, like manufacturing or retail, we more often use the term "Cost of Goods Sold." These are equivalent terms, however, and you can use whichever makes more sense to you. Within this book, we will use the slightly broader term, "Cost of Sales."

Raw materials used to create a product are *always* variable. Rent, utilities, and salaries are examples of *fixed* expenses that most businesses have. When an expense has both fixed and variable components (like utilities shared between an office and a small factory), it's usually best to consider it a fixed cost.

Variable expenses vary with the number or value of the sales we make. To sell another glass of lemonade, we need more lemons, more sugar, more water, and another cup. The cost of those inputs should always be captured in the Cost of Sales section.

Remember Kim the car dealer? Kim's Cost of Sales certainly includes the cost of the cars he sells. Chris, the dog groomer, includes the cost of shampoo in her Cost of Sales.

OPERATIONAL OR EXTRAORDINARY?

In order to get great reporting about expenses, the expense categories (and what goes into them) need to stay the same from month to month and from year to year. It wouldn't make sense to categorize the water bill under "Water" in January and then put it in "Utilities" in February.

We can, however, differentiate between expenses that are normal and expected from those that are extraordinary or unexpected. The water bill is a normal, expected expense that we'd list under (fixed) Expenses. If a water pipe bursts and floods the office, however, we might have a particularly high water bill along with repair and plumbing costs. Those extraordinary expenses are not only unexpected, but have nothing to do with the day-to-day operation of our business.

Other examples of extraordinary expenses (or gains) are:

- The purchase or sale of a business or business unit
- Legal settlements or financial awards from a lawsuit
- Selling or getting rid of a large asset
- A one-time change in the value of inventory (such as obsolescence or unusual spoilage)
- An expense resulting from any change in the way the business does accounting

In cases of extraordinary or unexpected (and nonrecurring) expenses, the P&L can tell the story of what happened by breaking expenses into new or different categories. Money spent to recover from a flood or natural disaster could rightly be listed in its own category. So could a large legal penalty or settlement against the company, or a write-off for inventory destroyed in a fire. Those kinds of expenses could rightly be grouped at the bottom of our P&L under "Other Income and Expenses." By setting them apart from the normal operating expenses, we can continue to compare our regular expenses month to month.

WHEN EXPENSES ARE INCOME

There are times when, after considering all of the above rules for expenses, we simply cannot find a good home for an expense item. No categories seem to fit.

Don't panic. Perhaps the expense is not an expense at all, but a reduction of income. When we issue our customers a refund, accept a coupon, or take back a returned item, those expenses are more properly categorized as a reduction of income. Typically, these *negative* income items are listed separately in the Income section, as in Table 3.2.

Deciding when to include an expense in the Income section is straightforward: If the customer initiated the expense as part of a sale transaction, then there is good reason to record the expense as a negative income amount. Notice that refunds and returns are transactions initiated by a customer (reducing income from that customer).

By contrast, a cost initiated by the business is more likely an expense. For example, if Kim the car dealer gives away a new iPad to each customer who buys a car, the cost of the iPad is a promotional or marketing expense, and not a reduction of income. Table 3.3 shows how Kim might record this.

Table 3.2. Income Section of P&L

Rockford Computer Sales & Service Profit & Loss January	
Income	
4000 - Sale of Hard Goods	1,575
4010 - Sale of Soft Goods	1,682
4020 - Service Revenue	1,500
4030 - Returns, Exchange, & Refunds	−200
4040 - Discount & Coupons	−125
Total Income	4,432

WHY BOTHER?

It's tempting to say that all expenses are the same, and that whatever we've spent in our business simply reduces our total profit. That's true, of course. So why is it important to assign our costs to the correct section of the P&L?

How we organize our costs changes how we view our business and how we manage the business for maximum profits. There is a difference, for example, between a business that has a lot of *variable* costs recorded in the Cost of Sales section, and one for which the majority of expenses are *fixed*, appearing in the Expense section. Managing those two businesses requires two very different perspectives and two different strategies. Assigning expenses to the appropriate place on the P&L turns out to be pretty important.

When we get our expenses into the right category, and our categories into the right section of the P&L, the rest of the P&L starts to come together. Each section subtotal starts to tell us a story, and the resulting profit lines—what we called running totals in Chapter 1—emerge as a guide to managing the business.

SPEAKING OF PROFIT

As we have discussed, the subtotal for each section in the P&L rolls up into a running total. The sum of all the sales and discount accounts gives us Total Income. Total Income less the subtotal of all Cost of

Table 3.3. Kim's Cars Marketing Expenses

Kim's Cars Profit & Loss April	
Income	
4000 - Car Sales	20,000
4010 - Loan Origination Fee	1,000
Total Income	21,000
Cost of Sales	
5100 - Car	18,000
5200 - Manufacturers Rebate	−5,000
Total Cost of Goods Sold	13,000
Gross Profit	8,000
Expense	
6110 - Fees, Registration, Title, & Tag	2,500
6120 - Marketing/Promotional	1,200
6130 - Payroll Expense	1,250
6150 - Rent	1,000
6160 - Sales Tax	1,000
6170 - Utilities	750
Total Expense	7,700
Operating Income	300
Other Income/Expense	
Other Income	
7100 - Interest Collected from Loans	353
7210 - Buyer-Paid Registration Fees	2,500
7220 - Buyer-Paid Sales Tax	1,000
Total Other Expenses	3,853
Net Income	4,153

Sales gives us Gross Profit. Gross Profit less the subtotal of the Expenses section gives us Operating Profit. And finally, Operating Profit less the subtotal of all Other Income and Expenses gives us Net Profit. Table 3.4 provides a quick review of this.

Table 3.4. P&L Showing Three Profit Lines

Rock Solid Manufacturing Profit & Loss January 2014	
Income	
4000 - Sales to Distributors	35,256
→ Total Income	35,256
Cost of Goods Sold	
5000 - Cost of Goods	20,935
Total Cost of Goods Sold	20,935
→ Gross Profit	14,321
Expense	
6110 - Advertising & Promotion	398
6120 - Bank Charges	159
6130 - Payroll Expenses	2,325
6140 - Rent and Utilities	1,492
Total Expense	4,374
→ Operating Profit	9,947
Other Income/Expense	
Other Income	
7100 - Gain on Sale of Asset	5,926
Total Other Income	5,926
Other Expense	
8100 - Amortization Expense	628
8300 - Depreciation	396
Total Other Expense	1,024
Net Other Income	4,902
→ Net Profit	14,849

Notice that the word "profit" appears several times. Unless we specify Gross Profit, Operating Profit, or Net Profit, a discussion of profitability can get quite confusing.

Gross Profit

Gross profit, the difference between what our customers pay and what it costs us to make the sales, is the first place on the P&L to use the word "profit." Having a positive gross profit is a mandatory first step toward running a "profitable" business, but by itself, gross profit is not enough. Companies with high gross profits include service businesses (doctors, lawyers, accountants) and software businesses. It costs very little for Microsoft to deliver one more copy of Windows, for example, which keeps their gross profit quite large.

Operating Profit

Operating profit is simply what's left of gross profit after we deduct all our operating expense (from the Expense section). Operating profit is a better measure of whether the business can meet all its financial obligations. Any business can have a high (or low) operating profit.

Net Profit

Net Profit is truly the "bottom line." Because net profit is after (below) the section called Other Income and Expenses, all regular *and irregular* costs have been accounted for. One word of caution: Some financial statements will show net profit before taxes, while others will show taxes as an expense. When taxes are not included within the standard P&L, there is often one more line added to the bottom showing taxes and thus, "Net Profit after Tax."

It is always important to be specific when talking about profits—both for clear communication and for setting management strategy.

COMMON-SIZING PROFITS

We simply cannot have a good understanding of "profit" without referring to a specific kind of profit—a specific line on the P&L. To make a discussion of profits even more clear, we often quote profits as a percentage, rather than simply as a dollar amount. Percentages are helpful because dollar amounts are relative. It is a far different thing for Google to post a profit of $1 billion than for a local website developer to make such a claim, and yet we may still want a way to compare these two businesses. Using percentages gets around this problem.

When we talk profit percentages, we are measuring profit as a percentage of sales. Quite simply, any number can be divided by total sales to create a percentage. Table 3.5 shows the simple formula we used to calculate the percentage profit at Rocky's Pizzeria.

The same process can be used to highlight any number on a P&L. To start, measuring the total cost of goods, the total expenses and the various profit lines is often helpful. Table 3.6 demonstrates how we show various percentages on the P&L.

Table 3.5. Profit as a Percentage of Sales

Rocky's Pizzeria Profit & Loss January		
Ordinary Income/Expenses		
Income	Dollars ($)	Percent (%)
4000 - Food	9,500	
4010 - Wine	1,479	
4030 - Beer	2,536	
4040 - Soft Beverages	930	
→ Total Income	14,445	100.00%
Cost of Goods Sold		
5000 - Food	3,300	
5010 - Wine	535	
5030 - Beer	759	
5040 - Soft Beverages	33	
5050 - Labor	2,962	
Total Cost of Goods Sold	7,589	
→ Gross Profit	6,856	47.46%

NOTE: $6,856 profit / $14,445 income = 0.4746 = 47.46%

Table 3.6. P&L Showing Key Percentages

	Rock Solid Manufacturing	
	Profit & Loss	
	February	
	Dollars ($)	Percent (%)
Income		
4000 - Product Sales	35,256	100.00%
Total Income	35,256	
Cost of Goods Sold		
5000 - Cost of Goods	21,154	
Total Cost of Goods Sold	21,154	60.00%
Gross Profit	14,102	40.00%
Expense		
6110 - Advertising & Promotion	398	
6120 - Bank Charges	159	
6130 - Payroll Expenses	2,325	
6140 - Utilities	492	
Total Expense	3,374	9.57%
Operating Income	10,728	30.43%

Speaking of profits as a percentage of income is a great way to compare two businesses or the results between two time periods for the same business. The dollar profits of Google are surely different from those of the local web development company. *But their percentage profit might be very similar.* The owner of the web development company might even want to use Google's profit percentages as a target for her own business.

Further, if we want to compare our profits from June with those from November, it is useful to strip away any natural variability in sales from spring to fall, and any natural growth between the two periods. So rather than comparing, say, $25,000 gross profit in June to $65,000 gross profit in November, it might be more useful to compare the profits as a percentage of sales. Table 3.7 shows how we do this for our cost of sales and gross profit. Calculating percentages helps us "common-size" two different periods from the same company. Note that we could

Table 3.7. Comparing Two Months Using Percentages

Rock Solid Manufacturing
Comparative P&L
June & November

	June 2014		November 2014	
Income	Dollars ($)	Percent (%)	Dollars ($)	Percent (%)
4000 - Sales - Manufactured Goods	42,727	100%	111,100	100%
Total Income	42,727	100%	111,100	100%
Cost of Goods Sold				
5100 - Cost of Goods	5,100	12%	12,600	11%
5200 - Direct Labor (Payroll)	6,425	15%	17,300	16%
5300 - Overhead Labor Cost Assigned	3,210	8%	8,350	8%
5400 - Equipment, Fuel & Fees	2,999	7%	7,865	7%
Total Cost of Goods Sold	17,734	42%	46,115	42%
Gross Profit	25,000	59%	65,000	59%

also be comparing two different companies; so long as we "common size" the P&L using percentages, the actual numbers don't matter so much.

WHAT IS COMMON?

A common-sized view of profits is a great way to track our performance over time or to compare our performance to other companies in the same industry. In either case, it matters little what the actual sales of the company (or companies) are, since common-sizing brings the results to a common scale.

Common-sizing becomes even more powerful when we apply it to the whole P&L. In fact, every line item in a P&L can be common-sized—expressed as a percentage of total income. Table 3.8 shows a fully common-sized P&L. Notice how each line of income and expense has both a dollar amount and a percentage.

Table 3.8. Simple Common-Sized P&L

<table>
<tr><td colspan="3" align="center">Rocky's Pizzeria
Profit & Loss
January</td></tr>
<tr><td>Ordinary Income/Expenses</td><td></td><td></td></tr>
<tr><td>Income</td><td>Dollars ($)</td><td>Percent (%)</td></tr>
<tr><td>4000 - Food</td><td>9,500</td><td>66%</td></tr>
<tr><td>4010 - Wine</td><td>1,479</td><td>10%</td></tr>
<tr><td>4030 - Beer</td><td>2,536</td><td>18%</td></tr>
<tr><td>4040 - Soft Beverages</td><td>778</td><td>5%</td></tr>
<tr><td>Total Income</td><td>14,293</td><td>100%</td></tr>
<tr><td>Cost of Goods Sold</td><td></td><td></td></tr>
<tr><td>5000 - Food</td><td>3,300</td><td>23%</td></tr>
<tr><td>5010 - Wine</td><td>535</td><td>4%</td></tr>
<tr><td>5030 - Beer</td><td>759</td><td>5%</td></tr>
<tr><td>5040 - Soft Beverages</td><td>433</td><td>3%</td></tr>
<tr><td>5050 - Labor</td><td>2,962</td><td>21%</td></tr>
<tr><td>Total Cost of Goods Sold</td><td>7,989</td><td>56%</td></tr>
<tr><td>Gross Profit</td><td>6,304</td><td>44%</td></tr>
<tr><td>Expenses</td><td></td><td></td></tr>
<tr><td>6030 - Bank Charges</td><td>235</td><td>2%</td></tr>
<tr><td>6040 - Insurance Expense</td><td>125</td><td>1%</td></tr>
<tr><td>6050 - Laundry & Cleaning</td><td>300</td><td>2%</td></tr>
<tr><td>6060 - Rent</td><td>1,425</td><td>10%</td></tr>
<tr><td>6070 - Repair & Maintenance</td><td>75</td><td>1%</td></tr>
<tr><td>6200 - Payroll Expenses</td><td>970</td><td>7%</td></tr>
<tr><td>6310 - Utilities</td><td>427</td><td>3%</td></tr>
<tr><td>6320 - Waste Removal</td><td>125</td><td>1%</td></tr>
<tr><td>Total Expenses</td><td>3,682</td><td>26%</td></tr>
<tr><td>Operating Profit</td><td>2,622</td><td>18%</td></tr>
<tr><td>Other Income & Expense</td><td></td><td></td></tr>
<tr><td>Other Expense</td><td></td><td></td></tr>
<tr><td>8300 - Depreciation</td><td>463</td><td></td></tr>
</table>

(*continued*)

Table 3.8. (Continued)

	Rocky's Pizzeria Profit & Loss January	
Total Other Expense	463	
Total Other Income & Expenses	–463	–3%
Net Income	2,159	15%

With a fully common-sized P&L, we can have a meaningful discussion of each expense (or income) line. Has our cost of sales increased or decreased? Are we paying too much for phone service? How much are we spending on salaries in the accounting department? Each of those questions can be answered by comparing two or more common-sized P&Ls to each other.

Consider Pat, who owns a landscaping business. Naturally, Pat is busiest during the spring, but she has some regular customers who pay her every month for services. Pat needs to keep a handle on her cost of sales even as her income fluctuates through the seasons. Sales are up during the spring weather in May but decline rapidly as the weather gets cooler in October.

When sales are down, her cost of sales is also down. But are the costs moving *relative* to sales, or should she be cutting back on some expenses during the slow times? Only a percentage measurement can say for sure. If costs are falling less than sales, Pat could end up with a dangerously high cost of sales (and thus, a dangerously low gross profit). Take a look at Table 3.9. During which period did her landscape company post better gross profits? The answer depends, of course, on whether we are asking about total *dollar* profits or *percentages*. In some ways her company is arguably better off in the second period, when dollar profits have fallen but percentages have increased.

PUTTING IT ALL TOGETHER

Once we have thoughtfully assigned expenses into the correct categories and sections of the P&L, the first building block of good financial statements is complete. Common-sizing a P&L by dividing each line by the total sales makes it easy to compare and contrast a company's results with other similar companies or between two periods for the same company. A carefully constructed P&L tells an important story about the health and function of a business.

There are times, however, when a P&L does not tell the *right* story or the *whole* story. In the next chapter, we'll begin to pull apart our carefully constructed P&L in order to understand how to make it say even more.

Table 3.9. Comparative Common-Sized P&L

Rocky Point Landscaping Company
Comparative Profit & Loss
May & October

Ordinary Income/Expenses	May		October	
Income	Dollars ($)	Percent (%)	Dollars ($)	Percent (%)
4000 - Consulting	7,565	14%	9,500	37%
4010 - Landscaping	30,798	57%	5,500	22%
4020 - Lawn Maintenance	15,243	28%	10,372	41%
Total Income	53,606	100%	25,372	100%
Cost of Goods Sold				
5000 - Cost of Goods Sold	13,073	24%	9,800	39%
5010 - Labor	25,680	48%	3,500	14%
5020 - Equipment & Fuel	336	1%	125	0%
Total Cost of Goods Sold	39,089	73%	13,425	53%
Gross Profit	14,517	27%	11,947	47%
Expenses				
6030 - Bank Charges	336	1%	325	1%
6040 - Dues & Subscriptions	125	0%	250	1%
6050 - Equipment & Tools	300	1%	800	3%
6200 - Payroll	2,800	5%	950	4%
6200 - Rent	1,000	2%	1,000	4%
6310 - Uniforms	427	1%	100	0%
6320 - Utilities	400	1%	275	1%
Total Expenses	5,388	10%	3,700	15%
Operating Profit	9,129	17%	8,247	33%

SUMMARY

☑ It is up to the business owner to decide which expenses go into which categories and which sections of the P&L.

☑ All expenses must be stated on the P&L somewhere, but business owners have choices.

☑ Expense categories should be kept as simple as possible. Big categories are helpful, as long as the expenses inside them are closely related. This makes reporting easier to understand.

☑ Some expenses, including refunds and discounts, should be listed as categories within the Income section of a P&L.

☑ Variable expenses are generally placed in the Cost of Sales section. Fixed expenses are generally placed in the Expense section. Extraordinary or one-time expenses often fall to the Other Income and Expense section.

☑ How we organize expenses impacts our measures of profit, and thus deepens our understanding of how (and how well) our business operates.

☑ Using percentages to "common-size" the P&L is a powerful way to track expenses over time or to compare the performance of two businesses.

4

Making a P&L Work for You

Clearly and thoughtfully categorizing income and expenses will result in a P&L that tells us a lot about our company. The P&Ls we created in Chapter 3 are straightforward and easy to read. Life is messy, however, and a simple, "standard" P&L is often not enough. When our business becomes complex, a standard P&L may feel like it is constricting or constraining our ability to understand and manage the business.

There are, in fact, important measures of profitability that a simple P&L can miss. If a small business owner were to sell her business, for example, the buyer might ask what her total *personal* benefit is from owning the business. That measure of profitability might include owner salaries, payroll benefits, car payments, owner draws, and other personal expenses borne by the company.

Unfortunately, "total personal benefit of ownership" (more properly called "owners discretionary cash flow") is not a line item on any standard P&L. This calculation and other important measures of profitability require us to pull apart our carefully crafted P&L and then to reconstruct it in a way that answers specific questions or provides specific management insight. This process of disassembling and reassembling a P&L is called "recasting."

RECASTING FOR SPECIAL SITUATIONS

Selling a business is certainly a special situation—something that does not happen often and is not particularly related to managing the business day to day. Not surprisingly, it calls for a different approach to calculating profits and does not fit nicely on a standard P&L. It is a simple matter to recast a P&L to calculate what we need.

Similarly, borrowing money from a bank, raising venture capital, and other intensive looks at financial performance will inevitably require a different perspective on profits that we can only get by recasting a P&L. Indeed, even day-to-day management can call for unique reconstructions of the P&L. Each business owner or manager may identify problems or opportunities by recasting a P&L to suit his or her particular viewpoint or objective. The P&L is a flexible and adaptable tool that can be recast—taken apart and put back together—in a number of ways until we find the right perspective we need to make informed management decisions.

Different situations will call for different calculations. Here are some of the most common measures of profitability that require us to recast our P&L.

EBITDA

Bankers will almost always ask for your EBITDA—which stands for Earnings Before Interest, Tax, Depreciation and Amortization. Why? Bankers like to see how much money a business could be making if it paid no interest, tax, depreciation, or amortization because it is another way (like common-sizing) of comparing companies to each other. Often, however, our standard P&L has those four items in the Expense section, so calculating EBITDA means doing a quick recast.

EBIT

Like EBITDA, the simpler EBIT (Earnings Before Interest and Tax) measures operational profit as if the company had no debt and paid no taxes. It makes a good metric to compare two companies that have different amounts of debt or are in different tax structures. Unlike EBITDA, however, EBIT shows profitability after depreciation and amortization expenses, which will reflect the company's investment in assets. (For more on assets and depreciation, see Chapter 5, "Balance Sheet Basics.")

EBITDA (and to a lesser extent EBIT) are widely used in almost every industry. In fact, most private companies can be meaningfully compared to each other simply by EBIT or EBITDA results. These numbers give us an instant gauge of the size of a company by stripping out all the other detail. How much money a company makes on an EBITDA basis is a fair (although not perfect) way of judging its size, economic value, and health.

Note that EBIT, which captures the cost of depreciation and amortization, is the better choice when we want to compare two companies that have different asset strategies. For example, we'd look at EBIT for two manufacturers that make a similar product but have purchased different equipment. Perhaps one has rented equipment that the other owns. Or perhaps one upgraded to new equipment recently while the other uses very old equipment. We would want to show the profits of each company including the cost of the relative equipment (assets). EBIT can help us compare these results in the face of such different business strategies, while EBITDA might skew the apparent profits by hiding the cost of the new assets.

Discretionary Cash to Owner (DCO)

In a small private company, discretionary cash to owner is a measure that tries to capture the true and complete financial benefit to the company owner. Unlike employees, who collect a specific wage each hour or month, owners have the ability to use various business expenses to their own benefit—such as driving a company car or buying company-funded health insurance. They also receive profits, have advantageous tax treatment, and enjoy investment opportunities. Recasting a P&L to find the total DCO is an attempt to calculate all of that benefit.

Note that you will never see DCO on a financial statement from a public company. When there are more than just a few owners, the company tends to control costs more tightly so that it never pays for an owner's personal expenses. In a small company, it is almost inevitable that the company will pay for something that could be called "discretionary."

Modified Gross Margin

Managing a dynamic business can require focusing on particular aspects of income and expenses, which aren't otherwise obvious in a P&L. By recasting our P&L, we can manipulate both income and expense to emphasize any aspect of our business. Is it important to include the administrative staff's overtime hours in your cost of sales? Would it be interesting to see gross margin for only certain accounts? Recasting the P&L allows business operators to play "what if" by moving income and expenses in helpful ways.

ADD BACK WHAT YOU WANT

The simplest (and most objective) recast starts with a complete P&L and then "adds back" certain expenses to the bottom line. Adding expenses back means increasing the net profit of the business. This is the method we use for EBITDA, EBIT, and DCO. Table 4.1 shows a standard P&L that has been adjusted with a series of add-backs.

Table 4.1. EBIT and EBITDA

<table>
<tr><td colspan="2" align="center">Rock Solid Manufacturing
Profit & Loss
March</td></tr>
<tr><td>Income</td><td></td></tr>
<tr><td>4000 - Product Sales</td><td>35,256</td></tr>
<tr><td>Total Income</td><td>35,256</td></tr>
<tr><td>Cost of Goods Sold</td><td></td></tr>
<tr><td>5100 - Cost of Materials</td><td>5,982</td></tr>
<tr><td>5200 - Direct Labor</td><td>7,568</td></tr>
<tr><td>5400 - Shop Consumables</td><td>3,521</td></tr>
<tr><td>Total Cost of Goods Sold</td><td>17,071</td></tr>
<tr><td>Gross Profit</td><td>18,185</td></tr>
<tr><td>Expense</td><td></td></tr>
<tr><td>6100 - Advertising & Promotion</td><td>398</td></tr>
<tr><td>6200 - Automobiles</td><td>795</td></tr>
<tr><td>6500 - Tools & Equipment (Not Rentals)</td><td>599</td></tr>
<tr><td>6600 - Office Rent & Utilities</td><td>195</td></tr>
<tr><td>6650 - Legal, Professional, & Consulting</td><td>300</td></tr>
<tr><td>6700 - Non-Mfg Payroll Expenses</td><td>2,325</td></tr>
<tr><td>6900 - Interest Expense</td><td>2,057</td></tr>
<tr><td>Total Expense</td><td>6,669</td></tr>
<tr><td>Operating Profit</td><td>11,516</td></tr>
<tr><td>Other Expense</td><td></td></tr>
<tr><td>8100 - Depreciation & Amortization Expense</td><td>628</td></tr>
<tr><td>8200 - Income Tax</td><td>275</td></tr>
<tr><td>Total Other Expenses</td><td>903</td></tr>
<tr><td>→ Net Profit</td><td>10,613</td></tr>
<tr><td>Add Back Selected Expenses</td><td></td></tr>
<tr><td>8200 - Income Tax</td><td>275</td></tr>
<tr><td>6900 - Interest Expense</td><td>2,057</td></tr>
<tr><td>→ EBIT</td><td>12,945</td></tr>
<tr><td>8100 - Depreciation & Amortization Expense</td><td>628</td></tr>
<tr><td>→ EBITDA</td><td>13,573</td></tr>
</table>

Recasting should not be confused with reporting. We can "report" on any aspect of the business without looking at the business as a whole. A true recast, however, attempts to show the whole business in a new way—perhaps by adjusting for new circumstances or new accounting rules.

The process of recasting a P&L through add-backs allows us to see both the original and the modified calculations. The original net profit is the key to understanding the actual business and how it is run today. The modified numbers, like EBIT, show what *could* happen if certain expenses were eliminated.

In some cases, recasting eliminates *noncash expenses*, like depreciation and amortization. Recasting to reduce or eliminate noncash expenses is one way to approximate cash flow. Noncash expenses and cash flow are addressed in Chapter 9, "Cash Flow Statement Basics."

EBIT IN THE REAL WORLD

To understand add-backs a bit better, take the example of Jeff, who is selling his printing business, and Susan, who is buying it.

Over the years, Jeff has built a big print shop. He has invested in large offset printing presses, expensive digital presses, and even heavy-duty equipment to move heavy rolls of paper around the print room floor. Although his business has a good gross margin, Jeff has had to borrow heavily from the bank to afford this new equipment. Those debts cause him to pay thousands of dollars each month in interest expense. As a result, his net profit numbers are low and sometimes his business runs at a loss.

Susan, on the other hand, is ready and able to pay cash for Jeff's business. She has enough savings to purchase the business, pay off all the loans, and keep the business running while she makes the transition to running the business as the owner.

Susan would certainly want to recast Jeff's P&L to see how the business will run without the expense of interest payments to the bank. She can accomplish this by adding back interest payments and taxes (since taxes will change when profit changes), which gives her EBIT. Jeff's EBIT is likely to be very close to Susan's net profit number after she purchases the company.

RECASTING COSTS TO MODIFY GROSS MARGIN

Susan's new printing business provides another great example of recasting a P&L to show a modified Gross Margin number. During the busiest season, the print shop staff often takes on additional duties. Administrative assistants stay late to process orders; print operators deliver finished jobs in their personal trucks. Additionally, Susan rents out a storage unit to keep additional paper rolls at the ready.

Normally, administrative overtime wages, mileage reimbursement and facilities rent would all be in the Expenses section of the P&L. These costs are generally regarded as overhead—fixed expenses that occur every month whether Susan sells any printing or not. But in her busy time, Susan decides that these costs are more closely related to the additional revenue and are therefore more properly listed in the Cost of Sales section.

Susan knows she has to keep a close handle on these expenses. The busy times of year can make or break a company. So when the dust has settled, she recasts her P&L to move these costs *above* the gross margin line to the Cost of Sales section.

To show both her normal and extraordinary expenses separately, Susan could even calculate her standard gross margin without the added costs, and then a new modified gross margin that includes the costs. Table 4.2 shows what this might look like. Notice that the gross margin calculation is followed by an additional line called "Extraordinary Variable Costs," and the sum is what Susan chose to call her "Seasonally Adjusted Gross Profit."

GETTING MORE VARIABLES

Just as Susan needed to capture additional variable expenses during her busy season, she may want to adopt something similar for year-round expense management. Consider that a print shop has some easily identifiable raw materials: paper and ink make up the majority of Susan's hard product cost. Of course, she also has shop labor to run the presses and salespeople to sell the jobs. Even if her variable expenses were just those four things, she might well want to track them separately.

Table 4.2. Susan's Print Shop

<table>
<tr><td colspan="2" align="center">**Susan's Print Shop**
Profit & Loss
January</td></tr>
<tr><td>**Income**</td><td></td></tr>
<tr><td>4000 - Printing Services</td><td>45,258</td></tr>
<tr><td>Total Income</td><td>45,258</td></tr>
<tr><td>**Cost of Goods Sold**</td><td></td></tr>
<tr><td>5100 - Paper and Ink</td><td>5,982</td></tr>
<tr><td>5200 - Direct Labor (Payroll)</td><td>7,568</td></tr>
<tr><td>5300 - Equipment (Rented)</td><td>3,864</td></tr>
<tr><td>Total Cost of Goods Sold</td><td>17,414</td></tr>
<tr><td>Gross Profit</td><td>27,844</td></tr>
<tr><td>5400 - Extraordinary Variable Costs</td><td>3,254</td></tr>
<tr><td>⟶ Seasonally Adjusted Gross Profit</td><td>24,590</td></tr>
<tr><td>**Expense**</td><td></td></tr>
<tr><td>6100 - Advertising & Promotion</td><td>398</td></tr>
<tr><td>6200 - Automobiles</td><td>795</td></tr>
<tr><td>6400 - Dues and Subscriptions</td><td>65</td></tr>
<tr><td>6450 - Employee Services</td><td>283</td></tr>
<tr><td>6500 - Tools & Equipment (Not Rentals)</td><td>599</td></tr>
<tr><td>6550 - Postage and Delivery</td><td>57</td></tr>
<tr><td>6650 - Legal, Professional, & Consulting</td><td>300</td></tr>
<tr><td>6700 - Payroll Expenses</td><td>2,325</td></tr>
<tr><td>6800 - Tax, Business</td><td>1,500</td></tr>
<tr><td>6850 - Travel & Entertainment</td><td>425</td></tr>
<tr><td>6950 - Utilities</td><td>492</td></tr>
<tr><td>Total Expense</td><td>7,239</td></tr>
<tr><td>Net Income</td><td>17,351</td></tr>
</table>

She might do this by recasting her P&L to show both a Cost of Goods (COG) and a Cost of Sales (COS). Although these terms are generally used to mean the same thing, we can clearly use COG to denote the cost of raw materials like paper and ink, while COS would include the additional expenses of labor and sales commissions. In this case,

Table 4.3. COGS and COS from Susan's Print Shop

Susan's Print Shop Profit & Loss February	
Income	
4000 - Printing Services	45,258
Total Income	45,258
Cost of Goods Sold	
5200 - Ink	5,982
5300 - Paper	3,864
Total Cost of Goods Sold	9,846
Cost of Sales	
5400 - Shop Labor	7,658
5500 - Sales Commission	5,275
Total Cost of Sales	12,933
Gross Profit	22,479
Expense	
6100 - Advertising & Promotion	398
6200 - Automobiles	795
6450 - Employee Services	283
6500 - Tools & Equipment (Not Rentals)	599
6550 - Postage and Delivery	57
6650 - Legal, Professional, & Consulting	300
6700 - Payroll Expenses	2,325
6800 - Tax, Business	1,500
6850 - Travel & Entertainment	425
6900 - Uniforms	2,057
6950 - Utilities	492
Total Expense	9,231
Net Income	13,248

COS would also be a great place for Susan to put her seasonal expenses (overtime, rent, and mileage reimbursement) that we examined above. This modified P&L could become a useful tool for her to use each month to keep an eye on the gross margin of the product itself and the total expense of creating and selling a job. Table 4.3 shows what this might look like.

Table 4.4. Recast Net Income and DCO

Rock Solid Manufacturing Recast Net Income Last Year	
Net Profit after Tax (from P&L)	18,380
Add-Backs for EBITDA	
8300 - Interest Expense	6325
8400 - Taxes, Income	23000
8200 - Depreciation	8900
8100 - Amortization Expense	6280
Total Add Backs	44,505
EBITDA	62,885
Add Back Discretionary Cash to Owner (DCO)	
6210 - Lexus Lease Payments (Owner's Auto)	5,230
6400 - Country Club Dues (for Owner)	4,800
6520 - Health Insurance (Owner)	15,500
6720 - Owner Salary	120,000
6740 - Matching 401(k) Owner	25,000
6850 - Travel & Entertainment (Owner's Portion)	14,600
6970 - Home Office Expenses (Owner)	2,400
DCO - Total Discretionary Cash to Owner	187,530
Recast Net Profit	250,415

DISCRETIONARY CASH TO OWNERS

Much has already been said about DCO—discretionary cash to owners—but let's take one more detailed look.

If we venture out to buy a small business (or sell one we already have), DCO will be one of the first figures we will encounter. Every business broker and investment banker will calculate the DCO for any private business he represents, because DCO helps to determine the asking price. (All other things being equal, a business generating $1 million in cash each year is worth more than one generating $100,000 in cash.)

Table 4.4 shows how DCO is typically calculated. Note that this is a standard "add-back" process. The buyer wants to see the company's actual financial statements, but also the recast numbers. Knowing the actual financial results will help paint the bigger picture of the company's health, while the DCO calculation can identify expenses that are truly discretionary—and thus could be cut or modified as needed.

Notice how large a difference this makes. The recast statement in Table 4.4 shows that the Net Profit was reported as just $18,300 last year. (This could have been from a standard P&L or from the tax returns.) By the time we add back all the noncash expenses and the "discretionary" expenses that benefit the owner, the company shows a "Recast Net Profit" of more than $250,000.

What does this really say? If a new owner were willing to finance the company with cash (eliminating interest payments on loans), she could expect the company to return approximately $250,000 of cash per year. Likewise, this recast statement can help even the current owner answer that nagging question, "Where is all my profit?"

SUMMARY

- ☑ A standard P&L is just the start. Business owners and managers should create their own methods of showing income and expense in ways that help them manage the business.
- ☑ Bankers, investors, and others outside the business will want to calculate some common measures of profitability, like EBIT and EBITDA.
- ☑ Restating a P&L for purposes of calculating different profit measures is commonly called recasting the P&L.
- ☑ Recasting is often done with add-backs—expenses that are added back to increase measures of net profit.

☑ It is good practice to show each line of add-backs at the bottom of a traditional P&L so readers get the complete picture.

☑ Business brokers and buyers often use a kind of recast P&L that shows Discretionary Cash to Owner.

☑ Managers can manipulate income and expenses to recast a P&L in almost any way that they find useful.

☑ One common recast method is to reorganize all variable expenses into Cost of Goods and, separately, Cost of Sales.

Part 2

THE BALANCE SHEET

5

Balance Sheet Basics

Just as the P&L tells the story of how a business makes money, the balance sheet tells the story of how the company manages its money. Has the company racked up a lot of debt? Has it taken money from—or paid money to—investors? Does the company have any money in the bank? Those are questions answered only by the balance sheet.

In short, a balance sheet answers the question "How much do we have?" while the P&L answers the question "How did we get it?" Or, said another way, the balance sheet says "where we are" while the P&L shows "how we got here."

This definition highlights one important difference between a P&L and a balance sheet: The P&L describes events that happened *over a period of time*, but a balance sheet describes only what exists *at a particular instant*. Because of this, the balance sheet is often called a *snapshot* of the company's financial health: it depicts conditions at a single moment, and it does not show how things have changed over time.

In this chapter we'll look at creating and reading the balance sheet.

WHAT ACTUALLY BALANCES

Historically, a balance sheet was created by drawing a line down the center of a piece of paper. On one side was a list of what a company owned, called assets. On the other side was the list of what the company owed, either to lenders (liabilities) or owners (equity).

A company always starts with nothing—the balance sheet is the "original" financial statement and can exist even before any income or expense has happened. At the very beginning, of course, a company has no money of its own—no intrinsic value simply because it exists—so a business must get its economic value from either lenders or investors.

The balance sheet records these amounts; every business naturally creates a balance sheet at the instant it forms. Whether we write it down or not, the balance sheet exists, and *the amounts are always in natural balance.*

In short, the amount of money a company has (or spends) must equal, or balance with, the amount of money it has received—not just from profits, but from borrowing and investment. So, on our historical balance sheet, the left side of the page always balanced with the right side. Today, the concept of balance remains, even though we may not write a balance sheet in the historical two-column format we see in Table 5.1. Notice how the tally at the bottom of each side of the page matches the other.

Today's balance sheets often consist of just long tallies of accounts. The concept of balance still applies, of course, but the numbers are arranged differently. Finding the balance may not be quite as obvious. Table 5.2 shows the same information formatted a bit differently. This single-column format is typical of a modern balance sheet like we

Table 5.1. Historical Format Balance Sheet

Rocky's Pizzeria Balance Sheet As of December 31			
ASSETS		LIABILITIES & EQUITY	
Current Assets		Current Liabilities	
Business Checking	25,000	Accounts Payable	20,000
Business Savings	15,000	Credit Cards	22,000
Accounts Receivable	7500	Total Current Liabilities	42,000
Total Current Assets	47,500		
		Long-Term Liabilities	
Property & Equipment		Building Mortgage	15,500
Building	35,000	Total Long-Term Liabilities	15,500
Machinery	25,000		
Inventory	15,000	Shareholders Equity	
Less Accumulated Depreciation	–20,000	Opening Equity	35,000
Total Property & Equipment	55,000	Net Income	10,000
		Total Shareholders Equity	45,000
TOTAL ASSETS	102,500	TOTAL LIABILITIES & EQUITY	102,500

Table 5.2. Simple Modern Balance Sheet

Rocky's Pizzeria **Balance Sheet** **As of December 31**	
ASSETS	
Current Assets	
Business Checking	25,000
Business Savings	15,000
Accounts Receivable	7500
Total Current Assets	47,500
Property & Equipment	
Building	35,000
Machinery	25,000
Inventory	15,000
Less Accumulated Depreciation	−20,000
Total Property & Equipment	55,000
TOTAL ASSETS	102,500
LIABILITIES	
Current Liabilities	
Accounts Payable	20,000
Credit Cards	22,000
Total Current Liabilities	42,000
Long-Term Liabilities	
Building Mortgage	15,500
Total Long-Term Liabilities	15,500
EQUITY	
Shareholders Equity	
Opening Equity	35,000
Net Income	10,000
Total Shareholders Equity	45,000
TOTAL LIABILITIES & EQUITY	102,500

might generate from accounting software. Before we dive into how to read a balance sheet, let's just define the basics.

SETTING UP THE BALANCE SHEET

Just as there were sections to the P&L statement (Income, Cost of Sales, Expense, and Other Income and Expense), there are sections within a balance sheet. The three balance sheet sections are called Assets, Liabilities, and Equity.

Similarly, just as each section of the P&L had several accounts, so do the sections of the balance sheet. In the same way that "Materials" might be an P&L account under "Cost of Sales," we will list accounts for all the things we own and owe under the sections of the balance sheet. Knowing where to put each account is key, so let's define each section very carefully.

Assets

Asset accounts are where we record the value of things the company owns. Think "car": If the company buys an automobile, the car itself is the asset. Assets can be *physical*, *financial*, or *intangible*.

Here are some examples of assets:

- *Physical*: A car, building, desk or computer
- *Financial*: Money in the bank or money owed to us
- *Intangible*: A patent or trademark

Anything that has an intrinsic value and is owned by the company can be counted as an asset.

Keep in mind that things *owed to* the business are also assets. If a customer owes us money, we treat that the same as if we already had the money. Thus, our outstanding invoices to our customers—called *accounts receivable*—are assets. So are payroll advances (loans to employees) and refundable payments (such as security deposits or prepayments) that we may have made to our vendors. Each of these amounts is still owned or controlled by our business and is, therefore, an asset on our balance sheet.

Liabilities

Liability accounts record the value of what we owe to other companies or other people. If we borrow money from the bank to buy a car, the car is an asset. But the *loan* owed to the bank is a liability. Liabilities can be actual (a loan, money owed to a vendor, unpaid credit card balances) or projected (the future cost of bad debt, providing repairs under warranty, or any other cost we believe is certain). Note that liabilities are described in positive numbers, even though their value to the business can be thought of as negative. That is, if we owe the bank $200, that appears on the balance sheet as a $200 liability (and not -$200).

> Note: On the P&L and balance sheet, the natural sign of every account and each transaction is positive (+). Thus, both income and expenses are expressed in positive numbers, as are both assets and liabilities. When we encounter a negative amount in any account, it immediately tells us that the amount is the opposite of what we would expect: a negative expense amount (like a rebate we receive from a manufacturer) or a negative income amount (like a refund we give to our customer).

Equity

Equity accounts are where we record value contributed by, or accumulated on behalf of, shareholders. When a business starts, this may simply be the dollars actually contributed by the founders. As a business grows, however, the equity section likewise may have various accounts recording the value of profits left in the business (retained earnings), profits from the current period (net income), and amounts paid to the shareholders (distributions). We will explore equity in greater depth in subsequent chapters.

> The balance sheet accounts and the accounts from the P&L together create what is called the *chart of accounts*. Every account in which a business tracks value (dollars!) will appear either on the balance sheet or the P&L. The chart of accounts is simply the master list of all the accounts that we use to organize our money. Bank accounts appear on the chart of accounts, as do accounts that track income, expenses, assets, liabilities, and equity.

Tying It Together

In the day-to-day course of business, we often complete transactions that will impact either the assets we own or the liabilities we owe. Something as simple as writing a check or purchasing printer ink with a credit card will have an impact on the balance sheet. As we move through this book, we'll see more and more how the financial statements are tied together, how they complement each other, and how transactions flow between the statements in order to paint a more complete picture of the business.

STARTING FROM SCRATCH

As we've said, all businesses have a balance sheet, whether we write it down or not. At the beginning of a new business, the balance sheet is very simple. Reviewing a start-up balance sheet is a great way to see how key transactions are recorded and can eventually create a more complex document, such as the one we saw previously. Let's take a walk through the first few transactions on a brand new balance sheet.

Recently, Jo and Marc started a new business to build websites for musicians called "RockStar Websites." They each had skills, ideas, and a bit of money. By creating a business together, they hoped to create something much bigger than themselves.

Of course, the new business would have expenses. To start, each partner contributed $1,000 to a common bank account. With that single transaction, a new balance sheet was born. Table 5.3 shows Marc and Jo's balance sheet on day one of their business. Notice that it shows only $2,000 contributed as equity and $2,000 deposited into a checking account.

Table 5.3. A Start-Up Balance Sheet

RockStar Websites Balance Sheet As of January 1	
ASSETS	
Current Assets	
Checking/Savings	
1010 - Business Checking	2,000
Total Checking/Savings	2,000
TOTAL ASSETS	2,000
LIABILITIES & EQUITY	
Equity	
3000 - Owners Equity	2,000
TOTAL EQUITY	2,000
TOTAL LIABILITIES & EQUITY	2,000

Remember when we said the balance sheet shows us how much we have? The business created by Marc and Jo now has $2,000. They have no customers or sales, no expenses, and no profit—nothing that would even go on a P&L. At this point, they have only a balance sheet. The sheet balances because their savings (an asset) balances with the contribution (equity) they made. In other words, Assets = Liabilities + Equity. Of course, in this case, liabilities are zero. Jo and Marc made only one transaction (depositing their initial capital), and the balance sheet is the only record of this transaction.

Now imagine that Marc and Jo borrow another $500 from a friend and deposit that money into the business checking account. They still have not made any sales or profits, but the balance sheet needs to reflect the addition of the loan amount, which we record as shown in Table 5.4.

Now that they have some capital in the bank, Marc and Jo decide to get busy. They use $1,000 to purchase an important piece of software. Since the software is expensive, they agree to call it an asset (also called

Table 5.4. Balance Sheet with Loan Liability

RockStar Websites Balance Sheet January 15	
ASSETS	
Current Assets	
Checking/Savings	
1010 - Business Checking	2,500
Total Checking/Savings	2,500
TOTAL ASSETS	2,500
LIABILITIES & EQUITY	
Liabilities	
Current Liabilities	
2100 - Loan from John Doe	500
Total Current Liabilities	500
TOTAL LIABILITIES	500
Equity	
3000 - Owner Equity	2,000
TOTAL EQUITY	2,000
TOTAL LIABILITIES & EQUITY	2,500

Table 5.5. The First Asset Purchase

RockStar Websites Balance Sheet As of January 15	
ASSETS	
Current Assets	
1010 - Business Checking	1,500
Total Current Assets	1,500
Fixed Assets	
1510 - Software	1,000
Total Fixed Assets	1,000
TOTAL ASSETS	2,500
LIABILITIES & EQUITY	
Liabilities	
2100 - Loan from John Doe	500
Total Current Liabilities	500
TOTAL LIABILITIES	500
Equity	
3000 - Owner Equity	2,000
TOTAL EQUITY	2,000
TOTAL LIABILITIES & EQUITY	2,500

"capitalizing the expense"), and the balance sheet reflects that in Table 5.5.

Note that Marc and Jo *still* do not have a P&L. They have only shifted money around on the balance sheet—from value in the bank to the value invested in the software. They still have no customers or sales, no expenses, and no profits. When the company eventually has sales or expenses, those transactions will have an impact on the company's balance sheet. We'll examine that more in the next chapter.

SUMMARY

☑ A balance sheet is the first financial statement that exists when a business is created. It does not rely on any purchase or sale transactions.

☑ The balance sheet has three sections: Assets, Liabilities, and Equity. Assets are what the company owns. Liabilities and Equity are what the business owes.

☑ Liabilities are promises to pay. Equity is the value that is owed to the stockholders, or founders, of the business.

☑ A balance sheet is naturally in balance. If a balance sheet is ever out of balance, it indicates an error in recording a transaction.

☑ To be in balance, what the company owns should equal what it owes. That is, Assets = Liabilities + Equity.

☑ A company starts with nothing—no value of its own—so everything that it owns (assets) comes either from the business owner (equity), or from borrowing (liabilities).

☑ The balance sheet can capture and record the transfer of value between asset, liability, and equity accounts without creating any change to the P&L.

6

How a P&L and a Balance Sheet Work Together

We've seen the P&L describe how money comes into and out of the business to generate profit: income is naturally offset by expenses, and the result is either a profit or loss. We said that the P&L describes "how" we make money. Because it shows money coming and going over a period of time, we can think of the P&L as a "movie" of the money flowing through the business.

We also said that a balance sheet describes "how much" we have at any one point in time. Because a balance sheet does not describe money coming and going (but only what exists at a specific moment in time), accountants sometimes say it is a "snapshot."

Those are useful analogies, but the relationship between a P&L and the balance sheet is deeper than the relationship between a movie and a single frame or snapshot. The two documents interact in such a way that neither can tell the whole story without the other. Each contains only half of the complete picture. Let's look at how the two documents work together, complement each other, overlap, and sometimes can even appear contradictory.

WORKING TOGETHER

The balance sheet we made for Marc and Jo's website business in Chapter 5 had assets, liabilities, and equity, all before Marc and Jo had even found their first customer, or made their first website. Clearly, of the two documents, the balance sheet comes first—just as the first frame of a film can exist before there is a complete movie. Table 5.3 (in the previous chapter) shows Marc and Jo's RockStar

Websites balance sheet after their first day in business together. If they did nothing else, this balance sheet would never change.

The website company is not going to sit still, however. Marc and Jo are out selling and building websites, buying software, hiring employees, and making a profit (or a loss). As their money moves around, the scene changes quite dramatically, and the balance sheet will reflect that.

Let's take it one step at a time and examine what happens to the balance sheet when the P&L shows revenue and expenses, which generate either a profit or a loss.

The P&L Shows a Profit

Good news: RockStar Websites sold a $4,000 job, paid some expenses, and made a profit. Even better, the customer paid cash, so Marc and Jo were able to pay a few small expenses in cash, too. Only a few days have passed, but already the P&L in Table 6.1 shows a tidy profit of $2,500, which our business owners promptly put in the bank.

If we take a snapshot of the business at this point, that $2,500 would certainly appear in the picture. It is, in short, something the business owns. Recall our definition of assets. The profit of the business—now

Table 6.1. RockStar Websites' First Sale

RockStar Websites Profit & Loss January	
Income	
4000 - Sales & Services	4,000
Total Income	4,000
Cost of Sales	
5100 - Web Design Labor	1,000
Total Cost of Sales	1,000
Gross Profit	3,000
Expense	
6100 - Advertising & Promotion	200
6550 - Postage and Delivery	57
6950 - Utilities	243
Total Expense	500
Net Ordinary Income	2,500

deposited into the bank—is a balance sheet financial asset we have mentioned: cash in the bank.

Having identified this as an asset, and listed it on the left side (or top) of our balance sheet, we now have a problem. The balance sheet is out of balance. How do we make the balance sheet balance? Remember: Assets = Liabilities + Equity. In other words, that same $2,500 must also be either a liability or equity.

In the case of the $500 loan, we knew that the asset (cash in the bank) was borrowed from a friend and thus was matched to a liability (debt). In the case of a profit, however, it may seem that this value came from nowhere. Instead of asking where it came from directly, we can ask where the profit would go if the business closed up shop today. A business is only an intermediary that holds things that rightly belong to others. For each thing it owns, a business must also owe equal value to someone else: either lenders (liabilities) or owners (equity).

In the case of profits, there is certainly no lender who gave Marc and Jo those dollars. The value was created by their website business, and who owns the business? The shareholders do. That means that although the business *created* the profit, the value now *belongs* to Marc and Jo in proportion to their ownership. After just a short time in business, Marc and Jo's equity in the business is growing fast. Table 6.2 shows the balance sheet on the same date as the P&L.

Back to our question: If the business closed today, where would that profit go? Based on this balance sheet, RockStar Websites could repay its debt of $500, and the remaining $4,000 would belong to Marc and Jo. With one sale, they doubled their investment.

The P&L Shows Revenue

It should be clear that a cash profit is recorded on the balance sheet as owner's equity. But there's a deeper interaction between the P&L and the balance sheet here. What if the company made the sale, but the customer has not yet paid? Or the customer paid, but the money has not yet been deposited into the bank? Is it still an asset?

Most assuredly, money that is *owed to the business* is treated in the same way as *money in the bank*. But our balance sheet so far doesn't seem to have a place for money that is not in the bank. We will have to create new accounts to hold that value.

Remember the $4,000 sale that RockStar Websites made on our P&L in Table 6.1? We previously assumed that Marc deposited the full

Table 6.2. Balance Sheet after Profitable Sale

Rock Star Websites
Balance Sheet
As of January 17

ASSETS	
Current Assets	
1010 - Business Checking	4,000
Total Current Assets	4,000
Fixed Assets	
1510 - Software	1,000
Total 1500 - Fixed Assets	1,000
TOTAL ASSETS	5,000
LIABILITIES & EQUITY	
Liabilities	
2100 - Loan from John Doe	500
Total Current Liabilities	500
TOTAL LIABILITIES	500
Equity	
3000 - Owner Equity	2,000
3010 - Net Income	2,500
TOTAL EQUITY	4,500
TOTAL LIABILITIES & EQUITY	5,000

amount in the bank (Table 6.2). What would happen if, instead, the customer had given Marc a check for $1,200 and wanted to pay the rest next month? What if Marc got busy with other things and never made it to the bank?

Even though the full $4,000 value is not in a *bank* account, it still *must* have a home in a balance sheet account. For money received but not deposited, we create an account called "Undeposited Funds." We'll put the $1,200 in that account until Marc gets to the bank. For money owed to us by customers, we create an account called "Accounts Receivable." The additional $2,800 due from the customer goes in Accounts Receivable until the customer actually pays. Table 6.3 shows how this might look. Note that the bank account is showing

Table 6.3. Recording Noncash Sales

Rock Star Websites	
Balance Sheet	
As of January 17	

ASSETS	
Current Assets	
1100 - Business Checking Account	0
1100 - Accounts Receivable	2,800
1300 - Undeposited Funds	1,200
Total Current Assets	4,000
Fixed Assets	
1510 - Software	1,000
Total Fixed Assets	1,000
TOTAL ASSETS	5,000
LIABILITIES & EQUITY	
Liabilities	
Current Liabilities	
2100 - Loan from John Doe	500
Total Current Liabilities	500
TOTAL LIABILITIES	500
Equity	
3000 - Owner Equity	2,000
3010 - Net Income	2,500
TOTAL EQUITY	4,500
TOTAL LIABILITIES & EQUITY	5,000

a $0 balance because Marc paid the expenses associated with making the first sale.

In this way, the P&L and balance sheet work together to tell us the whole story. The P&L shows a sale and even a profit, but the balance sheet tells us whether the customer has paid for that sale and exactly where the money is. Is it in the bank, a desk drawer, or still waiting to be received? The balance sheet will tell us.

In case all this sounds like too much complexity, remember that modern accounting software does all of this for us, including setting up a balance sheet account for undeposited funds.

Accounts receivable (AR) is an important concept in accrual accounting. Having an AR account balance says that we have earned money even though we have not received payment. Conversely, if a company only sells for cash, such as a restaurant or retail shop, it will not have an AR account.

The P&L Shows Expenses

Just as sales *increase* our assets and our profits, expenses move the needle in the opposite direction. An expense paid reduces the cash we have in the bank (reducing the asset) and likewise decreases our profit (reducing the equity). Presto! The balance sheet stays in balance.

Maybe, however, we haven't actually paid for the expense yet. How do we record an expense without a payment? If we still *owe* money to someone (whether a vendor or a lender), it is always a liability. When Marc and Jo borrowed $500 from their friend, we saw how they recorded that cash loan as a *liability*; an unpaid vendor bill is much the same. An unpaid vendor bill is just a loan from a vendor, and so we create a liability account to keep track of it. In this case, we use a special liability account called "Accounts Payable."

For simplicity, all unpaid vendor bills go into the same "Accounts Receivable" account. This convention helps us avoid making hundreds of small "loan" liability accounts.

Back to our heroes, Marc and Jo, who have just incurred an expense but did not yet pay for it. If we record only the liability for the expense on the balance sheet, then we are again left with an imbalance. Once added to the right side of our balance sheet as a liability, this expense has to be offset against either an asset or a reduction in equity. (Remember, there are only three choices on a balance sheet.) In this example, the P&L shows an expense, which reduces profit. And as we know, profit is always recorded in the equity section. Since the expense reduces the P&L profit, it also reduces the balance sheet account called Net Profit, which puts our balance sheet back into balance.

Let's say this another way. A *paid* expense of $100 reduces cash in the bank (asset) and reduces profit (equity); an unpaid expense of $100 increases what we owe our vendors (liability) and reduces profit (equity) by the same amount. By the rules of accrual accounting, even though we have not *paid* for the expense, the *promise to pay* has reduced our profits.

Tip: Asset or Expense? When a business purchases something, the purchase can be recorded as a simple expense (a meal or a box of paper) or as an asset (a car or office building). It is ultimately up to the business owner to decide which is which, but a purchased asset is generally something with a high value that will last several months or years. Assets are listed on the balance sheet. Expenses are listed on the P&L.

The P&L Shows a Loss

A loss on the P&L is the same as an expense without offsetting revenue. So we've now come full circle. When we had a profit, our shareholders benefited. In the same way, business losses go to shareholders, too. Just as profits increased the owner's equity, a loss reduces their equity.

Since the loss must be balanced by a reduction of assets or an increase in liabilities, the next question is, "How did we pay for the loss?" There are only two possible answers: We borrowed from somebody (an increase of liabilities), or we used something we owned (a reduction in an asset). In this case, taking cash out of the bank is a reduction of an asset. If savings were not enough, we might have sold or traded something else of value—a car, a computer, or a patent—to pay for the loss. In any case, each of these actions results in a reduction in the value of the assets on the balance sheet.

COMPLEMENTING AND OVERLAPPING

As we've said, neither the balance sheet nor the P&L contain all the details, yet together they start to paint a complete picture. Let's look at a couple more examples in which the two statements complement each other.

Credit Cards

The P&L clearly shows *when* and *where* a business is spending money. *How* we spend that money is a question best answered by the balance sheet. As we happily go about our business buying things, the payment for those items must either be cash (reducing our bank balance, which is an asset) or credit, increasing our debt (which is a liability). In particular, when we use credit cards to pay for expenses, the *expense* shows up on the P&L—but to see the *payment*, we have to look at the balance sheet.

On the balance sheet, a credit card is a liability account. We have promised to pay the credit card company something, and we use a liability account to track how much we owe. A credit card is a debt, so when a purchase is made with a credit card, the transaction looks like this:

Purchase
- Increases expenses, which decreases profit on the P&L
- Decreased profit reduces equity on the balance sheet
- Increases credit card liability on the balance sheet

But we are not done yet. Now we must pay the credit card company back what we owe, and that takes real money. So the payment—when we actually use cash to pay the credit card debt—creates another transaction that is only seen on the balance sheet.

Payment
- Decreases cash in the bank, an asset on the balance sheet
- Decreases the credit card balance, a liability on the balance sheet

Note that profit does not change in this second transaction because we have already incurred the expense in the first transaction. Note also that the payment transaction does not appear on the P&L. And since the balance sheet does not show the movement of money (only where it landed), we would have to look at two balance sheets—one before and one after—in order to see the changes in the bank balance and the credit card balance.

Installment Loans

Big purchases sometimes require big loans. Cars, a computer network, or maybe an office building are examples of things for which we might take out a bank loan or mortgage. Payments on those loans is another area in which the P&L and the Balance Sheet work together to tell the whole story. To understand this more fully, let's look at the difference between renting and buying an office.

Buying a Building/Booking an Asset Transaction

Remember Pat, our landscape business owner from Chapter 3? For years, Pat paid $2,000 each month in rent at a small (and somewhat unflattering) location. Recently, however, Pat found a nice warehouse and office building surrounded by more than an acre of land. It was a foreclosure sale, and Pat could not resist the opportunity to grow Rocky Point Landscaping at this great location. Financially, Pat was thinking primarily that the mortgage payment was about the same as the current rent, and so month to month, the profits would be about the same.

Pat's business decision was spot-on. The move provided the space and flexibility the company needed to serve more customers more efficiently. Financially, however, Pat's calculation was incomplete. The move did change the business—both the balance sheet and the P&L now looked very different. Let's look first at the balance sheet. Table 6.4 shows the balance sheet before and after the purchase. Notice that Pat took on not only a great new asset (the building), but also a large liability (the mortgage). Why are the values different? The difference between the mortgage and the value of the property is Pat's down payment: Notice how the bank account balance changed when Pat wrote the check for that down payment. Together, the new mortgage and the change in the bank account add up to the value of the land. So once again, our balance sheet remains in natural balance.

Pat's P&L also changed in ways that she did not anticipate. Operating profit actually increased dramatically after the purchase because the P&L treats rent very differently from a mortgage payment. Table 6.5 shows the before and after for the P&L. Notice that there is no rent expense, which makes the business appear much more profitable.

Together, these illustrations show the entire transaction and its impact on the business from both a P&L and a balance sheet perspective. There are three important things to take notice of in these illustrations:

1. There is no *expense* on the P&L showing the cost of the property, only a new balance sheet asset account called "Building"

2. The operating profit is larger because there is no expense for rent in the new P&L
3. There are two new costs associated with ownership: depreciation and interest expenses

Table 6.4. Before and After Balance Sheet

"BEFORE"	
Rocky Point Landscaping Company	
Balance Sheet	
May 31	

ASSETS	
Current Assets	
Business Checking	75,000
Customer Invoices	15,000
1120 - Inventory Asset	5,000
Total Current Assets	95,000
Fixed Assets	
Computer Equipment	5,000
Equipment	25,000
Total Fixed Assets	30,000
TOTAL ASSETS	125,000
LIABILITIES & EQUITY	
Liabilities	
Current Liabilities	
2000 - Accounts Payable	25,000
Total Current Liabilities	25,000
Total Liabilities	25,000
Equity	
32000 - Retained Earnings	50,000
Net Income	50,000
Total Equity	100,000
TOTAL LIABILITIES & EQUITY	125,000

(*continued*)

Table 6.4. (Continued)

"AFTER"
Rocky Point Landscaping Company
Balance Sheet
May 31

ASSETS

  Current Assets

    Business Checking   50,000

    Customer Invoices   15,000

    1120 - Inventory Asset   5,000

  Total Current Assets   70,000

  Fixed Assets

    Building   75,000

    Computer Equipment   5,000

    Equipment   25,000

  Total Fixed Assets   105,000

TOTAL ASSETS   175,000

LIABILITIES & EQUITY

  Liabilities

    Current Liabilities

      2000 - Accounts Payable   25,000

    Total Current Liabilities   25,000

    Long Term Liabilities

      2200 - American Bank - Building   50,000

    Total Long Term Liabilities   50,000

  Total Liabilities   75,000

  Equity

    32000 - Retained Earnings   50,000

    Net Income   50,000

  Total Equity   100,000

TOTAL LIABILITIES & EQUITY   175,000

These fundamental changes are common when a business replaces a monthly expense, like rent, with an owned asset. Whether the rental expense was for a building, a car, or a piece of equipment, the effect would be the same. Let's look at why and how these three things happen.

- *Where is the cost of the building?* There is no "expense" for the new building. Why? Buying a building is clearly not something Pat does each month. It's a major purchase that will last many years, so it would not make sense to call it an expense. Instead, we have properly

Table 6.5. Before and After P&L

<table>
<tr><td colspan="2" align="center">"BEFORE"
Rocky Point Landscaping Company
Profit & Loss
Month of May (PAYING RENT)</td></tr>
<tr><td>Ordinary Income/Expenses</td><td></td></tr>
<tr><td>**Income**</td><td></td></tr>
<tr><td>4000 - Consulting</td><td>7,565</td></tr>
<tr><td>4010 - Landscaping</td><td>10,798</td></tr>
<tr><td>4020 - Lawn Maintenance</td><td>15,243</td></tr>
<tr><td>Total Income</td><td>33,606</td></tr>
<tr><td>**Cost of Goods Sold**</td><td></td></tr>
<tr><td>5000 - Cost of Goods Sold</td><td>13,073</td></tr>
<tr><td>5010 - Labor</td><td>5,680</td></tr>
<tr><td>Total Cost of Goods Sold</td><td>18,753</td></tr>
<tr><td>Gross Profit</td><td>14,853</td></tr>
<tr><td>**Expenses**</td><td></td></tr>
<tr><td>6030 - Advertising & Marketing</td><td>3,250</td></tr>
<tr><td>6040 - Insurance</td><td>300</td></tr>
<tr><td>6200 - Payroll Expenses</td><td>8,500</td></tr>
<tr><td>⟶ 6200 - Rent</td><td>2,000</td></tr>
<tr><td>6320 - Utilities</td><td>275</td></tr>
<tr><td>Total Expenses</td><td>14,325</td></tr>
<tr><td>Operating Profit</td><td>528</td></tr>
</table>

(continued)

Table 6.5. (Continued)

"AFTER"	
Rocky Point Landscaping Company	
Profit & Loss	
Month of May (PAYING MORTGAGE & DEPRECIATION INSTEAD)	
Ordinary Income/Expenses	
Income	
4000 - Consulting	7,565
4010 - Landscaping	10,798
4020 - Lawn Maintenance	15,243
Total Income	33,606
Cost of Goods Sold	
5000 - Cost of Goods Sold	13,073
5010 - Labor	5,680
Total Cost of Goods Sold	18,753
Gross Profit	14,853
Expenses	
6030 - Advertising & Marketing	3,250
6040 - Insurance	300
6200 - Payroll Expenses	8,500
6320 - Utilities	275
Total Expenses	12,325
Operating Profit	2,528
Other Income/Expense	
Other Expense	
⟶ 8100 - Depreciation Expense (Building)	500
⟶ 8300 - Interest Expense (Mortgage)	396
Total Other Expense	896
Net Income	1,632

recorded it as an asset on the balance sheet. The money we paid for the building is not "spent"; it is simply *transferred between asset accounts*. The company still owns the building, so that value remains on the balance sheet.

- *Where is the cost of rent?* There is no expense for rent. Because the business now owns the building, Pat no longer pays rent. This has the potential to really change her profits, so we have to find something else to take its place.
- *What are depreciation and interest expenses?* Because Pat bought a building (an asset) that will last for many years, we want to spread the cost out over the "useful life" of the asset. Spreading an asset's cost across time is called depreciating an asset, and this is how we account for one large purchase that will last a long time. Also, because Pat borrowed from the bank to make the purchase, she now owes interest to the bank each month.

In a sense, we can say that depreciation and interest expenses have replaced the expense of rent. Whether the depreciation expense is a good substitute for rent is a different matter. Depreciation *rates* are set by accounting rules and tax laws, so Pat's monthly depreciation expense may be either more or less than an equivalent rent.

Pat knows, however, that she must make monthly mortgage payments to the bank, so she may wish to compare those payments to her prior rent. So where are they in our financial statements? Mortgage payments are a combination of interest expense (which we can see on the P&L) and a *transfer* of money from our bank account to the principal of the loan (which happens on the balance sheet). To understand Pat's business, we now need to see both the P&L and the balance sheet. Together they tell us that Pat is not paying rent, but instead paying off a mortgage.

Hint: Recast it! Many business owners find it easier to manage their business when they can see the actual amount paid for a mortgage or car loan (instead of the depreciation and interest expenses). One way to do this is to *recast* a P&L (explained in Chapter 4) by categorizing loan payments as a monthly expense. This eliminates depreciation and interest and puts the full amount of payments on each month's P&L where we can see them and manage them. Keep in mind that this is a recast *for management purposes only*, and in order to keep our balance sheet in order (and pay taxes accurately), we still must record loan repayments properly at the end of each period or year.

CONTRADICTIONS

One of the most interesting situations in business is when the P&L and the balance sheet appear to contradict each other. Table 6.6 shows "Rocky Start Web Auctions"—a business that is losing money on its P&L and yet has an amazing balance sheet. It is certainly possible that these financial statements describe the same company on the same day. In fact, Rocky Start Web Auctions looks like a lot of early-stage companies that are well funded at the beginning but are struggling to turn a profit during their first years. Many web-based businesses started this way, including Amazon and Facebook, both of which lost money for several years after startup.

Table 6.6. Well-Funded Losses

Rocky Start Web Auctions Profit & Loss JAN - JULY	
Ordinary Income/Expenses	
Income	
4000 - Auction Income	25,000
4010 - Membership Dues	10,798
Total Income	35,798
Cost of Goods Sold	
5000 - Cost of Goods Sold	13,073
5020 - Server & Bandwidth	10,866
Total Cost of Goods Sold	24,932
Gross Profit	10,866
Expenses	
6030 - Advertising	13,500
6040 - Credit Card Fees	1,074
6050 - Payroll	27,400
6310 - Office Rent & Utilities	950
6320 - Supplies & Postage	2,750
Total Expenses	45,674
Net Profit	−34,808

(*continued*)

Table 6.6. (Continued)

Rocky Start Web Auctions	
Balance Sheet	
As of JULY 31	

ASSETS	
Current Assets	
Business Checking	275,000
Accounts Receivable	15,000
Inventory	115,000
Total Current Assets	405,000
Fixed Assets	
Servers and Network	50,000
Software Development	1,250,000
Total Fixed Assets	1,300,000
TOTAL ASSETS	1,705,000
LIABILITIES & EQUITY	
Liabilities	
Accounts Payable	112,500
Total Liabilities	112,500
Equity	
32000 - Retained Earnings	1,627,308
Net Income	(34,808)
Total Equity	1,592,500
TOTAL LIABILITIES & EQUITY	1,705,000

Because this illustration shows a year-to-date P&L, the profit on the P&L matches the profit line in the equity section of the balance sheet. This may not always be the case: a monthly P&L will show profit from a single month, while the balance sheet (a snapshot) shows the entire year-to-date profit.

The key to reading these two financial statements together is to understand both what we are looking at *and the time frame that gives it context.* Since a P&L always shows transactions over a period of time, it is easy to imagine a P&L for one disastrous month during or after an amazing year in which the company amassed great wealth. In that case, the balance sheet, showing the bank balance and the *accumulated* profits for the year, may look quite different from the P&L of this one lousy month. Likewise, a poorly managed company may show a great deal of profit during one period, but the balance sheet may tell the more complete story of excessive borrowing, losses from prior periods, and continuing contributions from the owners to cover losses or poor cash flow.

Both financial statements—and a bit of patience—are needed to tell the complete story. In the next chapter, we'll see how a business owner can use this interplay between the P&L and the balance sheet to tell a more accurate story of the whole business and how he might use these same strategies to manipulate and hide certain facts.

SUMMARY

- ☑ The P&L and the balance sheet work together to paint a more complete picture of the business.
- ☑ The P&L tells us how much we spent and when we spent it, but the balance sheet tells us whether we used cash or credit to pay for things.
- ☑ Because they measure different things, a company can show a healthy P&L but a weak balance sheet—or vice versa.
- ☑ Each transaction on the P&L will have some impact on the balance sheet, but some transactions that show up on the balance sheet do not create any changes in the P&L.
- ☑ Purchasing an asset does not show up as an expense transaction on the P&L.
- ☑ The cost of purchasing an asset is spread out over multiple months or years using the idea of depreciation, which is an expense category on the P&L.

7

Games People Play by Manipulating the Balance Sheet and P&L

We've talked a lot about how flexible financial statements can be and how each business owner can decide on rules and categories for both income and expenses. This makes financial statements powerful analytical tools that can also be dangerously deceptive.

Over the ages, various groups and governments have put accounting rules in place to minimize deceptive practices. What we now call GAAP—Generally Accepted Accounting Principles—are one set of rules that tries to standardize reporting. Even GAAP, however, leaves many things open to interpretation and manipulation.

The rules rightly allow for some interpretation. It is vitally important, for example, that a landscape company can classify a car as a long-term asset, but a car dealer classifies a car as inventory. If rules were too strict, financial statements would become less useful and, frankly, less accurate. Moving from interpretation to manipulation, however, is something else entirely. Flexible rules are a double-edged sword that business owners, accountants, and regulators have learned to treat with great care and respect.

In this chapter we will take a look at some of the legitimate *and not-so-legitimate* ways that accounting rules can be bent, or broken.

LEGITIMATE CHANGES TO FINANCIAL STATEMENTS

We've made a lot of choices on our P&L and balance sheet so far. Some were straightforward, like purchasing a building (an asset) instead of paying rent (an expense). Some decisions were less clear-cut, such as classifying rebates as income rather than a reduction of expenses. When the rules allow flexibility, our decisions should be shaped by clear management objectives: we want to measure and manage one aspect of the business, so we record transactions a certain way.

What if, as business owners, we simply want to make the financial statements look more favorable? One business owner may wish to show more profit in order to position the company for sale, while another business owner hopes to minimize profit for tax reasons. It may seem like walking a thin line, but there are plenty of situations in which purposeful manipulation of the financial reporting can actually produce "better-looking"—and even more meaningful—financial statements without ever straying into a legal or ethical problem.

Let's take a look at some situations when we have legitimate choices that significantly change our financial statements.

CAPITALIZING EXPENSES

The most common way to increase a company's apparent profitability is to shift expenses off of the P&L and onto the balance sheet. When a business makes a large purchase, the purchase could be "capitalized," meaning we create an asset rather than an expense. As we have seen, an asset is depreciated, so the expense that shows up on the P&L is quite small compared to the initial purchase price (although, of course, depreciation lasts many periods, whereas a purchase expense occurs once).

There are times when capitalizing an expense is not only correct but also called for. Some costs, like leasehold improvements (building new walls in a rented office, for example), are correctly classified as an asset. Other times, the rules are not so clear. A large new phone system is clearly an asset, but is the cost to train the staff an expense or an asset? What if the contract with the phone company lumps it all together? Should we expense the *value* of training, even if the invoice from the vendor says the training is free when we buy the phone system?

The decision to capitalize expenses works both ways. Shifting items to the balance sheet increases profits and boosts the assets we have listed on the balance sheet. Conversely, choosing to record the purchase as an expense rather than an asset reduces profits (which could lower taxes in the short run) and puts the entire expense into one period (which could increase profits in later periods). Capitalizing or expensing an item truly becomes a strategic decision that impacts profits, taxes, and other areas of business.

TIME SHIFTING INCOME AND EXPENSES

The nature of accounting is to wrap up all the transactions in a single month or year and call that period "closed," or finished. Business, however, can't be so neatly containerized. Sales and spending continue past the end of a month or year, so there is always a temptation to fudge the dates on some transactions and force them into prior or later periods.

There are some good reasons to do this, including simply correcting quirks in the calendar. A power bill for example, is a monthly expense. If we do not receive the February power bill until March 1, that's no reason to skip the expense in February. Clearly, the February P&L should contain an expense for power, so entering the expense in February is a reasonable and legitimate use of this technique.

For internal reporting—that is, when financial statements are prepared for management and not used for tax or other external purposes—time shifting can be an important way to smooth out revenue and expenses on periodic reports. It can be difficult to manage a business when several large invoices land arbitrarily in one month, so assigning part or all of the expense to another month may help make sense of what is actually going on in the business.

CHANGING REPORTING PERIODS

One month or year can show a loss, while the next shows an extreme profit. That's the nature of business. In order to generate reports that show more consistency, managers may elect not to report on a strict *calendar* year and instead look at a more representative period, such as the *last 12 months* (also called LTM, or TTM—trailing 12 months). This is a respected way to characterize financial results, for example, in a fast-growing company, or toward the end of one period when the last period's data would be out of date.

Some businesses have such variability in their monthly results that they skip monthly reports altogether and look only at quarterly results. This makes it difficult to make real-time decisions, but if the reporting is more accurate on a quarterly basis, it could be a good move.

REVENUE RECOGNITION

Businesses with multi-month delivery cycles and big invoice values are expected to spread income out as it is earned, rather than showing it all in the month when an invoice was created. GAAP has some rules about this, which are too complex for this book. Suffice it to say that spreading revenue across multiple periods is often not only a good idea but also a legal requirement.

INVENTORY VALUATION

Inventory is one area where small changes in recording can have large impacts on the financial statements. Old inventory can be "written down"—meaning it is devalued or discounted—simply because it is old. The thought is that last year's models left in inventory are not worth as much as this year's. Writing down inventory is an accepted way to take an expense in the current period and adjust the cost of goods for future sales.

INVENTORY EXPENSE RECOGNITION

When a company buys or creates inventory that has a rapidly changing price (gasoline, for example), we can create or destroy profits simply by deciding how to recognize the cost of the inventory we are holding. Should we value it at the price we paid for the oldest inventory still on hand? Or the price we paid most recently for the newest pieces? Or at the price we will pay to replace it next week?

There are generally accepted rules for guiding this decision, and it is important to remain consistent. Changing the method at any point can have a substantial impact on profitability, since it will shift the cost of goods and/or change the value at which the inventory is recorded.

VALUING GOODWILL

There are many things in a business that have no real market value— or at least, no value that is easy to discern objectively. When one company buys another, for example, the price naturally includes the value of how well customers know and like the brand. This is generally called "goodwill," and proper accounting calls for that to have an assigned value. Exactly how the value is assigned is somewhat subjective—perhaps even arbitrary—but it will have a large impact on financial statements.

Whether we want to assign intangibles a larger value or a smaller value depends on the financial goals of the business. As with capitalizing assets (above), how you value goodwill (an asset) will impact both the P&L and the balance sheet.

OTHER INTANGIBLES (PATENTS/COPYRIGHTS/ADVERTISING)

When a company patents a new technology or files for a copyright on a new design, it can list these things among its assets on the balance sheet and capitalize some of the expenses. Even certain expenses associated with direct advertising (such as infomercials) can become balance sheet assets. Although tax laws speak very specifically to these issues, there are times when managers or business owners must estimate the value of these intangibles for purposes other than tax calculations. Adjusting these values to match market conditions (among other realities) can be an important method for accurately depicting the company's health through its financial statements. This is a tricky area, however, and a good opportunity to speak to a CPA about the specifics of the situation.

CROSSING ETHICAL AND LEGAL LINES

As we've seen, there are plenty of legitimate reasons for changing the way we record things on our books. With all that flexibility, it should not be shocking that some people choose to cross the line: bending the rules so far as to misrepresent the facts or hide important facts. The headlines are full of such transgressions: from the Enron debacle of the 1990s to the Wall Street meltdown of 2008. There seems to be no end to how "creative" managers can be when creating financial statements. It is a constant battle between the rule writers and the rule breakers.

For the rest of us, complying with the rules (specifically GAAP in the United States) is easy enough and provides enough flexibility to push and mold our financial statements into useful reports. In fact, it is far better to regard GAAP as a guide to creating useful and practical reports than to try to wiggle out of its strictures.

Let's be clear, however. When a particular change does not comply with GAAP, that does not necessarily make it unethical or illegal. We have already discussed situations, such as the purchase or sale of a private company, when non-GAAP reporting may be desirable. Even large public companies have been known to dismiss GAAP guidelines if they have a strong case for doing so. In its 2009 annual report, Dr Pepper Snapple Group wrote the following:

The Company reports its financial results in accordance with accounting principles generally accepted in the United States of America ("U.S. GAAP"). However, management believes that certain non-GAAP measures that reflect the way management evaluates the business may provide investors with additional information regarding the company's results, trends and ongoing performance on a comparable basis. (Dr Pepper Snapple Group, Inc., 2009 Annual Report, page 13, accessed at http://investor.drpeppersnapplegroup.com/annuals.cfm)

The point is that GAAP compliance is not the end-all measure of whether a financial statement is presented fairly and accurately. What is more important is the intent of the person preparing the statement, compliance with tax laws, and the disclosure of enough detail to allow a person reading the statements to understand how and why the results are being reported.

Please note that this book is not about tax or legal compliance and should not be relied upon for that purpose. It is always best to consult with a knowledgeable CPA or tax attorney before using financial statements for tax, regulatory, or any other outside use. In the meantime, remember that *financial reports are meant to inform us and help us make better decisions.* Financial statements that are knowingly false, that twist reality beyond recognition, or that are based on wants instead of facts will not provide useful management information. No good can come out of "creative accounting" that is deceptive or fictitious.

When financial statements are fair and accurate, the owners of the business are rewarded with a clear picture of the value of their ownership. In the next chapter we'll look deeper into the third section of the balance sheet that expresses shareholder value: equity.

SUMMARY

- ☑ Generally accepted accounting principles (GAAP) leave a lot of flexibility for managers to manipulate financial reports.
- ☑ It is not illegal or unethical to mold financial reports to match the specific circumstances of the business.
- ☑ Financial managers can spread out income or expenses to smooth financial results across reporting periods.
- ☑ Reports can be prepared to show any meaningful period of time—a month, quarter, or year—regardless of how that corresponds to the calendar.
- ☑ How a business treats inventory values can significantly impact cost of sales, and thus profits, from period to period.

☑ Businesses can assign various values to intangible property, including goodwill, patents, and trademarks, all of which can change the company's financial results.

☑ Financial reports provide important management information, so they should reflect the information that managers need to know in a format that makes sense—even if it is not GAAP-compliant.

☑ Financial reports used for tax or legal purposes must be somewhat more stringently prepared, and business owners should consult with a CPA or attorney about the specifics of their situations.

8

Equity and Capitalization

In prior chapters we have discussed how the income statement works together with the balance sheet. The interplay between income and expenses on one, with assets and liabilities on the other, creates two perspectives on the same transactions. This gives us a fuller understanding of how the business is working. Recall that we also said the balance sheet is the "original" document of a business. A balance sheet is created at the moment a business comes into being. There may be no income and no expense, perhaps not even any liabilities. But there is one thing that every balance sheet has: equity.

IT TAKES MONEY TO MAKE MONEY

My grandfather was fond of saying, "It takes money to make money." Although I do not know if he understood balance sheet accounting, I think he'd appreciate the deeper meaning of what he said. The fundamental truth in that cliché can help us understand the concept of equity. In short, equity is the money that starts a business. It is what exists before the business makes its first sale. Likewise, equity is the value, or money, that lingers when the rest of the business has ceased to exist. Equity represents "what the business is worth," and in turn, equity is the account on the balance sheet that represents the value of ownership of the business. In fact, some types of companies give each individual owner a separate equity account on the balance sheet that shows the portion of the business value owned by that person.

Every business has an owner, or owners. Even if the owners are themselves other businesses, somewhere down the line there are real people who said, "I want to start a business," and by that very act became owners and equity holders in the organization they created.

The instant a business forms, the owner has an account all her own on the balance sheet and that account represents and keeps track of what she owns.

Business or Company? From a financial point of view, there is no difference between a "business" and a "company." An individual who paints houses may say that he has a painting *business*. That same individual could, however, register with his state government to be recognized as a *company*. The only difference is the paperwork. The act of forming a company is called "incorporating." Whether we are incorporated or not, however, the financial statements are exactly the same.

STOCK

It is likely that each of us already has ownership in several companies. Equity is bought and sold every day in the form of company stock. The New York Stock Exchange, the NASDAQ, the London AIM, and hundreds of other markets exist where ordinary individuals can buy and sell the equity (stock) of companies all around the world. One share of Google stock (which would currently cost about $900) represents a tiny fraction of ownership of Google, but it is ownership nonetheless.

A stock certificate is very real. In some sense, however, equity is imaginary. Most small companies—and certainly all businesses that are not legally incorporated—do not have stock certificates. A printed certificate is not necessary to the concept of equity. An owner is an owner, and the equity account on the balance sheet may be the only proof of what that ownership is worth.

Pop Quiz: If a business owns equity (stock) in another business, where does that value show up? Answer: the value of the equity is an asset to the business that owns it.

Take Jesse, who is a talented engineer and machinist. When Jesse left his job to become an entrepreneur, he formed a company to mill aircraft parts out of steel. Even though Jesse took the additional legal step to

Table 8.1. Start-Up Balance Sheet

The Machine Shop Balance Sheet As of January 31	
ASSETS	
Current Assets	
1010 - Business Checking	0
1020 - Savings Acct.	0
1300 - Cash on Hand	1
Total Current Assets	1
TOTAL ASSETS	1
LIABILITIES & EQUITY	
Liabilities	
2010 - Visa Credit Card	0
TOTAL LIABILITIES	0
Equity	
3000 - Stockholder Equity (100 shares)	1
TOTAL EQUITY	1
TOTAL LIABILITIES & EQUITY	1

incorporate (that is, to register his company with the state), he did not bother to print stock certificates. Nonetheless, he assigned himself ownership of The Machine Shop, Inc., and the company's balance sheet reflects his ownership. Even though no paper stock certificates exist, we still call Jesse an owner, or a stockholder. Table 8.1 shows the first balance sheet from The Machine Shop on the day it was formed. Jesse's equity is reflected in the "Stockholder's Equity" account.

Our Company, We Decide

Notice that Jesse decided that his company would have 100 shares of stock, and that each would be worth just one penny ($0.01). In essence, Jesse decided that the business, in the first instant it was created, was worth exactly $1.

Tip: When registering a company, some states levy fees that are based on the value of the authorized shares of stock. Defining or declaring stock to be worth a great deal of money could impact fees and/or taxes. For an example, see the Fee Schedule from the Secretary of State of Nevada in the Appendix.

As the founder of the company, that decision is entirely up to Jesse. There is no right or wrong decision; no right or wrong quantity of "stock"; no right or wrong value to assign to each share on that first day. The only thing that *might* impact our decision about this issue would be the number of partners (other owners) creating the business —or the number we might have in the future. The number of shares should be easily divisible between the owners now and in the future.

Do the Math: If a company is formed with three equal owners, setting up 100 initial shares would not allow a truly equal split. Instead, 300 shares (or 3,000 or three million) might be a better choice, so that each owner can claim an exact, equal number of shares.

If our company is a legal entity, it is not necessary to *use* all of the shares immediately. In other words, the shares declared at the beginning of the company do not need to be claimed by any particular owner. Instead, the company can hold back some shares for future owners. As long as there is at least one share owned by one owner, the company has a viable ownership structure and can show a stockholder's equity account on the balance sheet. In fact, many new business owners decide to create a much larger number of shares than is actually needed, just to provide flexibility for future ownership negotiations.

Note: Shares that are declared (when a company is legally formed, or incorporated) but not issued to an owner are called "treasury stock." There is no limit to the amount of treasury stock that a company can hold.

CAPITALIZATION

When a company is formed, it generally needs money to spend. (Even the process of becoming incorporated costs something.) It generally is up to the owners (i.e., stockholders) to inject the first few dollars into the business. This process, known as *capitalization*, is the same whenever we invest money into our business. (Note that I said "when we invest money." It is also possible to lend money to a business we own, but let's talk about investment for now.) In this case, we are either purchasing additional stock or increasing the value of stock we already own.

Pop Quiz: Does equity capitalization (an investment by an owner) create a transaction on the P&L statement? Answer: Although equity investments do not show up on the P&L, they do show up on the balance sheet and, as we'll see later in this book, on the cash flow statement.

Let's revisit Jesse at The Machine Shop. After incorporating, Jesse's first expense was to purchase a large machine tool called a CNC Router. This very cool—and quite expensive—tool can turn a block of steel into a finely carved airplane part in just a few minutes' time. The machine cost Jesse $40,000, and the manufacturer was asking for 25 percent, or $10,000, in advance.

The last time we checked in, Jesse's balance sheet and bank accounts were looking a little skinny. Obviously, his brand new business does not have cash in the bank for these expenses, so Jesse had to dig into his personal savings. His first step was to write a check to the company. By capitalizing the company in this way, he increased his equity in the business and gave the business the cash it needed to start making purchases. Table 8.2 shows how Jesse recorded this transaction on his balance sheet.

Table 8.2. Initial Capital Contributions

<table>
<tr><td colspan="2" align="center">The Machine Shop
Balance Sheet
February 1</td></tr>
<tr><td>ASSETS</td><td></td></tr>
<tr><td>Current Assets</td><td></td></tr>
<tr><td>1010 - Business Checking</td><td>10,000</td></tr>
<tr><td>1020 - Savings Acct.</td><td>0</td></tr>
<tr><td>Total Current Assets</td><td>10,000</td></tr>
<tr><td>TOTAL ASSETS</td><td>10,000</td></tr>
<tr><td>LIABILITIES & EQUITY</td><td></td></tr>
<tr><td>Liabilities</td><td></td></tr>
<tr><td>2010 - Visa</td><td>0</td></tr>
<tr><td>TOTAL LIABILITIES</td><td>0</td></tr>
<tr><td>Equity</td><td></td></tr>
<tr><td>3000 - Stockholder Equity</td><td>10,000</td></tr>
<tr><td>TOTAL EQUITY</td><td>10,000</td></tr>
<tr><td>TOTAL LIABILITIES & EQUITY</td><td>10,000</td></tr>
</table>

WORKSHEET

Let's track Jesse's investment from his personal bank account through the business as he purchases his first machines.

- *Step 1*: Jesse invests $10,000 into The Machine Shop by writing a check from his personal account to the business account. The balance sheet in Table 8.3 shows the result. Jesse's money increased his equity and also shows up as an asset—cash in the bank.
- *Step 2*: Jesse writes a check to the manufacturer as a deposit on the CNC Router. The router is a big machine, so he correctly decides to capitalize the expense. That way, the $10,000 remains on the balance sheet as an asset, but now it is called a deposit. He doesn't own the machine yet, so he can't list the machine on the balance sheet. This transaction decreased the cash in the bank and created a new asset in the same amount. Table 8.3 shows the deposit.
- *Step 3*: Jesse takes possession of the machine, but when he does, he has to sign an agreement to pay the balance due over the next

Table 8.3. Recording a Prepayment or Deposit

<table>
<tr><td colspan="2" align="center">**The Machine Shop**
Balance Sheet
January 31</td></tr>
<tr><td>**ASSETS**</td><td></td></tr>
<tr><td>Current Assets</td><td></td></tr>
<tr><td>1010 - Business Checking</td><td>0</td></tr>
<tr><td>1020 - Savings Acct.</td><td>0</td></tr>
<tr><td>Total Checking/Savings</td><td>0</td></tr>
<tr><td>Other Current Assets</td><td></td></tr>
<tr><td>1400 - Deposit</td><td>10,000</td></tr>
<tr><td>Total Other Current Assets</td><td>10,000</td></tr>
<tr><td>Total Current Assets</td><td>10,000</td></tr>
<tr><td>TOTAL ASSETS</td><td>10,000</td></tr>
<tr><td>**LIABILITIES & EQUITY**</td><td></td></tr>
<tr><td>Liabilities</td><td></td></tr>
<tr><td>2010 - Visa Credit Card</td><td>0</td></tr>
<tr><td>TOTAL LIABILITIES</td><td>0</td></tr>
<tr><td>Equity</td><td></td></tr>
<tr><td>3000 - Stockholder Equity</td><td>10,000</td></tr>
<tr><td>TOTAL EQUITY</td><td>10,000</td></tr>
<tr><td>TOTAL LIABILITIES & EQUITY</td><td>10,000</td></tr>
</table>

12 months. Since he has paid only $10,000, he still owes the manufacturer $30,000. This is a liability, and since he has signed a payment plan, we'll show this as a loan. Also, since this is a one-year loan, we will call this a "Current Liability." Loans longer than one year are generally called "Long-Term Liabilities." Table 8.4 shows the balance sheet for The Machine Shop after the CNC router has been delivered. As we see, this transaction created an asset equal to the entire cost of the machine ($40,000). To make the transaction complete (and balanced), we eliminated the Deposit account ($10,000) and created a liability for the loan amount ($30,000). Notice that Jesse's equity did not change.

Table 8.4. Buying an Asset

The Machine Shop
Balance Sheet
As of February 15

ASSETS	
Current Assets	
1010 - Business Checking	0
1020 - Savings Acct.	0
Total Checking/Savings	0
Other Current Assets	
1400 - Deposits	0
Total Other Current Assets	0
Total Current Assets	0
Fixed Assets	
1510 - CNC Router	40,000
Total Fixed Assets	40,000
TOTAL ASSETS	40,000
LIABILITIES & EQUITY	
Liabilities	
2500 - Loan CNC Router	30,000
Total Current Liabilities	30,000
TOTAL LIABILITIES	30,000
Equity	
3000 - Stockholder Equity	10,000
TOTAL EQUITY	10,000
TOTAL LIABILITIES & EQUITY	40,000

> Tip: Never pay business expenses using a personal check or credit card, and never pay personal expenses using a business check or credit card. Instead, put personal money into a business as equity, and take money out of the business as either a "Return of Equity" or as payroll. Keeping the two quite separate will protect you in case of an audit or any other business liability. It can also protect the business in case of a personal liability.

BUILDING EQUITY

We've seen how an owner puts equity into a business: writing a check and depositing it into a company account is easy. Over time, however, a business owner wants the value of her ownership to increase, which means that she hopes to accumulate equity. How does this happen?

All equity comes from one of only two sources: owner's contributions, or profits. "Net Profit" is a familiar term used on the P&L, and the same account shows up again on the balance sheet in the equity section. Remember that "Net Profit" is reset to zero ($0) at the beginning of each period; this means that the Net Profit line on both the P&L and the balance sheet reflect the profits for the current period only. After an annual period ends, or "closes," we transfer the prior year's Net Profit value to the balance sheet account called "Retained Earnings," which allows us to zero-out Net Profits. In this way, last year's profit does not disappear, but is simply transferred to the balance sheet.

Just as Net Profits can have either a positive value (profit) or negative value (loss), the Retained Earnings account also tracks the *accumulated* profit or loss of the business *to date*. That is, Retained Earnings holds the total accumulated profit or loss of the business since the business started. The only exception is the current period results (for example, year-to-date net profits), which are still reported in the Net Profit account.

NOTE: Net profit, as reported on the P&L, is also shown on the balance sheet, in the Net Profit account for the current period and in the Retained Earnings account for prior periods. Total Equity is the combination of these accounts and all other equity transactions over the life of the company.

WHERE DOES PROFIT GO?

So long as the company makes a profit, the owner's equity will increase as profits accumulate in the Retained Earnings account. Notice that we call this account *Retained* Earnings. As the name implies, these are profits that are held in the business. Since all profits eventually land in Retained Earnings, it is possible for the owner's equity (Total Equity) to grow larger each year. There are, however, at least three ways that profits come out of the equity account:

1. *Losses*: A loss in any period will reduce Total Equity.
2. *Return of Capital*: An owner may simply withdraw any amount that has been previously contributed.
3. *Dividends*: A business can reward its investors by distributing profits to the business owners. Any payment of profits to owners is called a dividend. Since "dividend" is a word that has a specific tax meaning, private businesses often use the term "owner's draw" to refer to any distribution of profits back to the owners.

There are always reasons why a business might post a loss, return capital to owners, or pay dividends to stockholders. In a healthy, profitable business, however, Total Equity ought to grow over time. Why? Because a business needs a certain amount of equity to continue operating.

Having equity does not mean that we simply allow earnings to accumulate in one big pile of cash. In fact, the opposite is usually true. Highly profitable companies know that profits must be reinvested into new capabilities, new markets, and new competitive advantages—anything that helps the business continue to grow and thrive.

Healthy businesses do not simply spend all their profits, however. Because equity represents the core value of the business (remember, equity is the difference between what we own and what we owe), equity makes it easier to borrow money, weather downturns, and attract other investors. The great balancing act of business is keeping enough equity for use in the future while also maximizing growth and opportunities today.

START AND FINISH

Equity accounts serve both ends of the financial life of a business: They capture the initial contributions of the people who start a business, and they capture the final disposition of net profits that result from operating the business. The Equity section is the gateway for cash flowing between the business entity and the company owners. Taken by itself, the Equity section shows us a complete history of the company's lifetime profitability and gives us an interesting look at how the owners have managed those profits (to their own benefit or detriment!). A detailed look at the Equity section of the balance sheet can answer any question about the company's ownership, what it took to get the business started, and what the final result has been for those people who remained owners.

Having looked at assets, liabilities and equity, we've now covered the entire balance sheet—the second of the three fundamental financial statements. In Part 3, we'll look more closely at how we track the sources and uses of cash using the cash flow statement.

SUMMARY

☑ It takes money to make money; when starting a company, an owner's financial contributions are tracked in the Equity section of the balance sheet.

☑ Owners can put money into a business as equity. They can also withdraw equity from the company.

☑ Equity increases through the natural accumulation of profits. Current period profits are shown in the Equity section in the Net Profit account.

☑ At the end of each annual period, the balance of the Net Profit account is reset to zero, and the profit (or loss) is moved to the Retained Earnings account.

☑ Losses, withdrawals, and dividends can all decrease Total Equity.

☑ The Equity section of the balance sheet tells the financial story of the owners' role in the company—when they have had to contribute money into the business and when they have received money from the business.

☑ The Equity section is the gateway for all outside money that is invested into the business by owners, and distributed from the company to the owners.

Part 3

THE CASH FLOW STATEMENT

9

Cash Flow Statement Basics

Every entrepreneur I have ever met has, in one way or another, asked me the same question: "If I'm making all this profit, where is it?" It's a classic dilemma: our accrual-based P&L shows that we are operating a robust business that drops thousands of dollars to the bottom line—but the bank account always seems to be empty.

There's no single answer to the question, "Where's all my money going?" but there is one way to find out: create a cash flow statement.

WHAT IS A CASH FLOW STATEMENT?

Let's start with what a cash flow statement is *not*. It is *not* a means of judging profitability (that's the P&L), and it is *not* going to tell you what you own or owe (that's the balance sheet). Further, it is not a statement that we can manipulate or change the way we changed the P&L in the last chapter.

So what's left? Plenty. A cash flow statement shows where the money went during a period of time. That's not to say that it shows what the money was spent on (again, that's found on the P&L); rather, it shows how money *moved around*. Remember how we said the balance sheet is a "snapshot" of your finances? One way to imagine the cash flow statement is as a *comparison* between two balance sheets (and thus, a description of how money flowed between the balance sheet accounts during the period between the two snapshots). This is a slight oversimplification, but it is an important concept to grasp as we look more deeply at cash flow statements.

Table 9.1. P&L for Rocky Road Ice Cream Factory

Rocky Road Ice Cream Factory Profit & Loss January	
Income	
4000 - Sales	33,250
Total Income	33,250
Cost of Goods Sold	
5100 - Cost of Goods (Ice Cream)	10,600
5200 - Direct Labor (Payroll)	6,000
5400 - Disposables, Paper, Cups, etc.	2,500
Total Cost of Goods Sold	19,100
Gross Profit	14,150
Expense	
6100 - Advertising & Promotion	2,250
6300 - Bank Charges	159
6450 - Repairs and Maintenance	1,283
6550 - Depreciation	389
6700 - Payroll Expenses	1,750
6900 - Uniforms	1,300
6950 - Rent & Utilities	2,750
Total Expense	9,881
Net Profit	4,269

The cash flow statement, for example, shows how much money you paid toward a bank loan—which would show up as a change in the bank loan balance between one balance sheet and the next.

Take the example of Kelly, who purchased an ice cream shop called the Rocky Road Ice Cream Factory. The business seemed to be doing quite well, and so the old owners set a very high price on the business. Kelly took out a large loan to buy the business. Table 9.1 shows Kelly's P&L, which confirms that the company continues to operate at a profit.

The Rocky Road P&L shows that the company made $4,269 in profit in January. Unfortunately, the bank account was quickly drying up. By the end of the second month, Kelly had a hard time making payroll and paying vendors for ingredients.

Table 9.2. Simple Statement of Cash Flows

Rocky Road Ice Cream Factory Statement of Cash Flow (Indirect Method, January 1–31)	
Operating Activities	
Net Income (EBIT)	4,269
Add Back Non-Cash Expenses	
6550 - Depreciation	389
6700 - Amortization	0
EBITDA	5,158
Change in Receivables	500
Change in Payables	0
Operating Cash Flow	5,658
Change Due to Financing	
Debt Payments	(9,500)
Net Cash Increase (Decrease) for Period	(4,342)

Table 9.2 shows why cash became tight so quickly: although Rocky Road generated $5,158 in cash during January, the payments to the acquisition loan totaled $9,500, leaving Kelly with $4,342 less cash than at the beginning of the month. Quite simply, Kelly used all the business's cash—and more—just to pay back the acquisition loan. A cash flow statement and some simple math showed us that Kelly would have to dramatically increase the sales at the ice cream shop just to cover the loan payments.

Reading a cash flow statement like this one from Rocky Road is not difficult. The key is to tell the story from top to bottom. When the numbers on the statement are positive, we call that a "source of cash," and when the numbers are negative, we call that a "use of cash." In this case, the cash flow statement in Table 9.2 tells the following story:

1. Operations generated $4,269 in profit.
2. Because depreciation is a noncash expense, we can add that back in as a source of $389 cash.
3. Accounts receivable decreased during the month, when some old customers paid their bills; this was a source of $500 cash.
4. But then we used cash to pay the loan back with $9,500.

5. So by the end of the month, we used $4,342 more than our sources provided.

By using the phrases "source of cash" and "use of cash," reading the cash flow statement becomes more straightforward—and the story of Rocky Road Ice Cream Factory becomes crystal clear.

Kelly's story had a sad ending, but it provides a good lesson for us all: of the three financial statements, the cash flow statement is the single most important when judging the ultimate viability of any business. The old adage is true—"cash is king"—and the cash flow statement tells us precisely whether the king is going to live or die.

COVERING ALL THE ANGLES

Cash has many uses that cannot be seen on a single P&L or balance sheet. In addition to simply paying current bills, cash can be used to do many things: repay debt, send dividends to shareholders, buy back stock from shareholders, invest in property or equipment, purchase inventory, or pay for expenses from a different period. A cash flow statement shows whether, and to what extent, the business did all of these things with its cash.

There's a positive side to this equation, too: a cash flow statement also shows where the cash comes from. Not all cash comes from current sales or profits. Besides the cash a business generates from current operations, it can also harvest cash from sales made in previous months, by taking out new loans, receiving new investments from shareholders, or by selling assets.

The complexity of cash flow in a business is, in fact, hidden by the more straightforward P&L and balance sheet. So while those two documents are essential to understanding the foundation and operation of the business, a cash flow statement provides a bridge between them and an important way to measure the one thing every business needs: cash.

Finally, remember that a statement of cash flows is built upon the transactions recorded in the other financial statements. There can be no statement of cash flows without both a P&L and a balance sheet. If we are assembling a cash flow statement by hand, it is mandatory to build a complete P&L and balance sheet first, as we shall see.

TWO STANDARD FORMATS

There is no universally accepted way to format a cash flow statement. There is, however, agreement that cash comes from, or is used by, three basic business activities: operations, investing and financing. Operations is the normal course of taking payments from customers and paying expenses to vendors. Investing is the cash used to purchase assets—or generated when assets are sold. Financing is money borrowed from or repaid to lenders. These three areas are generally used as the three sections of a cash flow statement.

Over the years, two very different ways of explaining cash flow have emerged. They differ primarily in the operations section. The first, called the *direct method*, says that cash is the result of selling and spending, and uses cash-based income and expense numbers to figure the cash from operations. The second method, called the *indirect method*, is distinctive because it starts with the accrued net profit, which comes straight from the (accrual based) P&L. To this, we must then add back things that did not use cash (depreciation and amortization) and calculate the change in cash from the balance sheet accounts, AR and AP.

Both methods produce the same final result (through slightly different calculations). The differences between the two methods is largely theoretical, and a business owner should use whichever he finds to be easier.

Let's look at each of these methods more carefully.

The Direct Method

The direct method starts with the cash collected from sales. This is typically a direct measurement of cash sales, although it can be calculated from accrual statements.

The direct method continues by subtracting cash used to pay expenses, purchase inventory, and for other expenses. What results is cash collected or used in day-to-day operations. Table 9.3 shows a direct method statement of cash flows.

Note that the direct method is the format most often used for small businesses and easily generated by popular accounting software packages, including QuickBooks. Entrepreneurs should focus on this approach.

Table 9.3. The Direct Method Cash Flow Statement

Rock Solid Company Statement of Cash Flow (Direct Method, January 1–31)	
OPERATING ACTIVITIES	
Cash Sales (Sales + Change in AR)	15,000
Cash Expense (Expense + Change in AP)	–5,000
Net Cash Provided by Operating Activities	10,000
INVESTING ACTIVITIES	
Computer Purchase (Change in Asset)	–2,000
Net Cash Provided by Investing Activities	–2,000
FINANCING ACTIVITIES	
Credit Card (Paid Down)	–3,000
Loan Amount Received from Bank	1,000
Shareholder Distributions	–5,000
Net cash provided by Financing Activities	–7,000
Net cash increase for period	1,000

Despite the widespread use of the direct method in small businesses, larger companies more often use the indirect method, particularly when reporting their financial results to investors. Let's take a quick look at the indirect method.

> We can easily read a cash flow statement if we pay special attention to the sign (+/-) of the amounts listed. A positive number is a "source of cash," and a negative number is a "use of cash." To aid with learning, we can talk ourselves through one of the illustrations by reading it aloud: "Loan payments were a use of cash … reducing our AR was a source of cash …" Doing this can then tell a story that answers the age old question, "Where's all my money?"

The Indirect Method

If the direct method can be called "top down," the indirect method for creating a statement of cash flows is certainly the opposite: a "bottom-up" approach. This method starts with the bottom line on

Table 9.4. The Indirect Method Cash Flow Statement

<table>
<thead>
<tr><th colspan="2">Rock Solid Company
Statement of Cash Flow
(Indirect Method, February 1–28)</th></tr>
</thead>
<tbody>
<tr><td>**OPERATING ACTIVITIES**</td><td></td></tr>
<tr><td>Net Profit (Accrual) from P&L</td><td>1,750</td></tr>
<tr><td>*Adjustments to Reconcile Net Profit to Cash from Operations*</td><td></td></tr>
<tr><td>Depreciation and Amortization (Noncash Items)</td><td>250</td></tr>
<tr><td>Decrease in Accounts Receivable (Cash Received from Customers)</td><td>7,500</td></tr>
<tr><td>Increase in Accounts Payable (Additional Credit from Vendors)</td><td>10,500</td></tr>
<tr><td>Net Cash from Operating Activities</td><td>20,000</td></tr>
<tr><td>**INVESTING ACTIVITIES**</td><td></td></tr>
<tr><td>Purchase of Computer (Fixed Assets)</td><td>−2,000</td></tr>
<tr><td>Purchase of New Vehicle (Fixed Asset)</td><td>−26,000</td></tr>
<tr><td>Net Cash from Investing Activities</td><td>−28,000</td></tr>
<tr><td>**FINANCING ACTIVITIES**</td><td></td></tr>
<tr><td>Cash Distribution to Owner/Shareholder</td><td>−10,000</td></tr>
<tr><td>Take Out New Loan for New Vehicle Purchased</td><td>26,000</td></tr>
<tr><td>Payments Made on Old Credit Card Debt</td><td>−1,000</td></tr>
<tr><td>Net Cash from Financing Activities</td><td>15,000</td></tr>
<tr><td>Total Net Cash Change during Period</td><td>7,000</td></tr>
</tbody>
</table>

our (accrual) P&L and works backwards, adding back in all the items that did not require cash or that otherwise misrepresented cash.

The first items added back are the non-cash items, including depreciation and amortization. Next, we calculate how much of the net profit was not transacted in cash by finding the change in accounts receivable and accounts payable during the period. Taking the difference between a beginning balance and ending balance of AR, for example (by comparing two balance sheets) results in an accurate adjustment to sales, *converting accrued sales into cash collections.*

Whereas the direct method seeks to add up a list of operational transactions that actually use cash, the indirect method looks for non-cash items in order to add them back to an accrual total. Table 9.4 shows a statement of cash flows calculated using the indirect method.

Although they differ somewhat in how they arrive at cash from operations, the two methods look quite similar in the investment and finance sections. In both cases, we calculate cash used or created by comparing two balance sheets—one from the beginning of the period and one from the end of the period. This concept is fundamental to understanding the cash flow statement.

ONE BOTTOM LINE

Notice that the end result of both methods is "Change in Cash." This figure really pulls it all together for the entrepreneur. "Change in Cash" is one number that is ultimately important and easy to verify.

When a business owner can see how the change in her bank account balance equals the "Change in Cash" line on a cash flow statement, then we have finally answered her question, "Where's all my money?"

If the Change in Cash line is positive, we have more cash at the end of the period than at the beginning. A positive change in cash means we have accumulated cash. Likewise, if the change is negative, we have used, or depleted, our cash.

An Amount but Not a Balance

Note that our statement of cash flows does *not* show an actual bank account balance. Rather, the Change in Cash line represents an amount of money that was saved or spent, not the remaining balance.

Tie It All Back to the Bank Statement

It is not difficult, of course, to reconcile the cash flow statement with the bank statement (and some accounting systems produce statements that do this). We can do this ourselves by comparing the bank statement balance on the date the cash flow statement began with the bank balance on the date the report ends. Adding this simple bank reconciliation to the end of a statement of cash flows is an excellent way to double check the math and to show how a statement of cash flows applies to, and meshes with, our other business metrics. The simple formula is:

Beginning Balance + Change in Cash = Ending Balance

Keep in mind that the Change in Cash is a total of all cash accounts. If we have more than one cash account, the beginning and ending balances

Table 9.5. Cash Flow Statement and Balance Reconciliation

A Rock Solid Company Statement of Cash Flow (Indirect Method, March 1–31)	
OPERATING ACTIVITIES	
Net Income (Accrual)	7,500
Adjustments to Reconcile Net Income	
to Net Cash Provided by Operations:	
1100 - Accounts Receivable (change)	7,500
2000 - Accounts Payable (change)	3,280
Net Cash Provided by Operating Activities	18,280
INVESTING ACTIVITIES	
1510 - Computer/Printer	–679
Net Cash Provided by Investing Activities	–679
FINANCING ACTIVITIES	
3300 - Shareholder Distributions	–20,057
Net Cash Provided by Financing Activities	–20,057
Net Cash Increase for Period	–2,456
Cash at Beginning of Period	13,257
Less Change in Cash for Period	–2,456
Cash at End of Period	10,801

are the sum (total) of all those accounts. Add together all checking accounts, savings accounts, and even petty cash to get to the total number.

Some small business accounting software does something similar by placing the beginning and ending balance of all cash accounts at the end of the report (see Table 9.5). It is still up to us to tie this back to the individual account balances.

> *The Same but Different*: Although both the direct and indirect cash flow calculation methods result in the amount of change in cash during a period, it is not uncommon for them to have slightly different details, particularly among publicly reporting companies. These differences are caused primarily by small differences in reporting requirements between international accounting standards. Most small business owners should be quite content to use the direct method alone.

INTERPRETING THE CASH FLOW STATEMENT

Compared to the other financial statements we have reviewed, the cash flow statement is pretty cut and dried. Although it reflects the choices we made in our P&L, there are no decisions to be made when calculating cash flow. The math is the math, and there are no choices to make or rules to bend—nothing we can do to influence how the numbers stack up.

That does not mean that it lacks usefulness. In fact, the cash flow statement is full of juicy guidance for us as we manage our business.

Where to Look

As we have noted, most common cash flow statements are broken into three sections. Conveniently, "Cash Flow from Operations" (CFO) is the top section. If we want to know whether a company has a reasonable business model—that is, if it is able to generate cash on a day-to-day basis—we need look no further. But this first section does not tell the whole story.

> *Note*: For the remainder of this book, we will refer only to cash flow statements created by the "direct method." It is the method best suited for small business and is the most common format found in small business accounting software.

The second section, "Cash Flow from Investment" (CFI), shows us whether the company is investing in new equipment and other assets. It would not be unusual for a small business to have no transactions in this section. If this section is actually generating cash, however, it may be a sign that the managers have been forced to sell off assets to offset losses.

The third section is where things get really interesting. Is the business borrowing heavily from a bank, credit card company, or its investors? "Cash Flow from Financing" (CFF) reveals whether the business is getting deeper into debt or working its way out. Large amounts of cash flowing into or out of a loan account should raise an eyebrow, and a quick look at the balance sheet will confirm how much debt a business has.

The total change in cash is merely the sum of these three sections. Each section may contribute cash or use cash, but their simple sum tells the whole story:

$$\text{Total Change in Cash} = \text{CFO} + \text{CFI} + \text{CFF}$$

With these three sections in mind, let's look at the specific results we might see on a cash flow statement and what it means. In particular, we should emphasize the results from operations, since that sets the stage for understanding the other sections and the cash flow statement as a whole. Determining whether the cash flow from operations is a positive or negative value is the first step to a clearer understanding of what is really going on inside the company and how it can be improved.

Positive Cash Flow from Operations

Every business owner dreams of strong, positive cash flow from operations. It can certainly be one indicator of a strong business model, good management, tight financial controls, and a healthy market.

On a cash flow statement, however, positive cash flow can also signal the start of bad times. Why? Refer to the top lines: "Sales" and "Change in Accounts Receivable." When we see sales decline, the business will be spending less money on cost of sales expenses—and catching up on its AR. That means old customers are paying cash for old invoices, but the business is not reinvesting the money into new sales. Cash is actually accumulating in the business. Look for a large net positive change in AR as one indicator that sales are slowing down.

If positive cash flow is driven by AR collections, it could signal that revenue is declining and the business is slowing down. In fact, if the revenue decline is caused by an overall stagnation in the market, positive cash flow can tell us even more.

A great manager will find ways to squeeze more and more cash out of a mature market: He'll cut out investment in assets (or even begin selling assets), trim every unnecessary expense, and then simply ride the remaining revenue until the end. This is such a well-used strategy that it has a name—Boston Consulting Group coined the phrase "Cash Cow" to describe companies in mature markets that require little investment but continue to throw off cash.

Negative Cash Flow from Operations

In the long term, negative cash flow is a problem for any company. When the cash is gone, the game is over. If a cash flow statement shows that cash flow from operations (CFO) is negative, the company could be looking at a real problem. This is particularly true when operational losses are not offset by additional cash from investment or financing. When both CFO and total change in cash are negative, the company is burning through reserves and has not found a bank or investor to help stem the tide.

There is a situation, however, that we have not considered. A negative CFO—and even a negative total change in cash—does not necessarily spell doom. In fact, there are plenty of examples of fast-growing businesses that have negative cash flow over long periods of time.

Rapid growth consumes cash faster than almost anything else, which is the primary reason we see venture capital (VC) companies and private equity groups (PEGs) investing millions into new technology start-ups. Growth is expensive. The faster the growth is, the more expensive it becomes. Growing companies are spending on their cost of sales as well as increasing their overhead by hiring more staff and renting bigger offices. In short, they need more of everything as they buy their way up the sales curve.

The result of all this spending is naturally a negative CFO (and likely also a negative cash flow from investing as the company purchases more assets like computers and equipment). So, for some, a negative cash flow from operations indicates an investment strategy rather than a poorly managed company. The clue to this will be *positive* cash flow from *financing*, where we'll see that shareholders (or lenders) are contributing significant dollars to fund the operating losses over the long term. In this sense, a rapid growth company looks very similar to a company in a rapid decline. The key difference, of course, is whether sales are going up (growth), or down (decline).

DRAWING CONCLUSIONS

Cash is so important, and so much can be gleaned from the cash flow statement. It is surprising how seldom this foundational statement is used. Looking at just the basic information available—whether the cash flow is positive or negative from each section of the cash flow statement—we can make a good guess about the status of a business. Table 9.6 shows some of the assumptions we can draw based only on the cash flow statement, and how we might test these assumptions.

Table 9.6. Statement of Cash Flow Assumptions

Source	Sign	Confirming Evidence
Cash Flow from Operations	Positive (+)	Cash received from Sales/Income, current or past (accounts receivable), other cash received from customers (such as deposits and prepayments)
	Negative (-)	Cash paid for Operating Expense, either current or past (accounts payable), spending on prepayments and deposits
Cash Flow from Investing	Positive (+)	Sale of equipment, property, or other assets
	Negative (-)	Purchase of equipment, property, or other assets
Cash Flow from Financing	Positive (+)	Cash received from Shareholder (Sale of Stock) or Bank (loan)
	Negative (-)	Cash paid to Shareholder (Dividends), repurchase of stock, or repayment of loan

PREDICTING CASH FLOW

Predicting the cash flow for a business is vital. Entrepreneurs need to be acutely aware of how much cash is available, how long it will last, and what factors are accumulating or depleting the cash.

As we've seen, the fastest-growing companies can be the biggest consumers of cash, while declining companies can actually throw off more cash even as they fall apart. Knowing what to expect as conditions change can help us manage our most critical asset (cash) in any situation. Table 9.7 can be a helpful guide as we run our operations day to day. This shows how changes in some simple operating results impact cash flow.

Let's look at a simple example from Marc and Jo's company, RockStar Websites. Summers are always a slow time for RockStar Websites, and this causes an annual cash crunch. This year, Marc is planning a big promotion in June to solve the problem before it starts. He's running ads on Google and Facebook that will cost him about $500 cash, but he figures that just two new customers will pay for that and more. If he gets those two new customers, is cash likely to be better off or worse? What if he gets five new customers, or 10?

Table 9.7. Predicting Cash Flow

P&L	Increase	Decrease
Accrued Sales	Use of Cash	Source of Cash
Gross Margin %	Source of Cash	Use of Cash
Operating Expense %	Use of Cash	Source of Cash
Net Profit Margin %	Source of Cash	Use of Cash
Balance Sheet	**Increase**	**Decrease**
Assets		
Accounts Receivable	Use of Cash	Source of Cash
Buying Equipment or Assets	Use of Cash	N/A
Value of Inventory	Use of Cash	Source of Cash
Liabilities		
Accounts Payable	Source of Cash	Use of Cash
Loans	Source of Cash	Use of Cash
Credit Card Balances	Source of Cash	Use of Cash

The key to planning cash flow at RockStar Websites is to understand that most of Marc and Jo's customers pay half or more of the price when the job is finished. To get a job done, however, RockStar Websites has to pay for designers, coders, photographers, and hosting—on top of their normal overhead expenses. Employees and subcontractors like to be paid in cash. So does the landlord and the power company. As a result, any delay in the website project—or any delay in the final payment from the customer—will cause RockStar Websites to be out of pocket a great deal for each project. If Marc's timing is off, or the promotion is *too successful,* RockStar Websites' cash flow problem could get much worse before it gets any better.

Lesson learned: If we expect new customers to pull us out of a cash flow crunch, first look at the cost of sales and plan the timing of payments. If we are making more sales but allowing them to accrue (giving our customers credit), the illustration correctly indicates that we are using cash and can expect our cash flow to get worse. Sales, of course, is a number we find on the P&L.

Look again at Table 9.6, focusing on the balance sheet accounts and how they impact cash flow. If we are increasing our *accrued* sales (e.g., sales that are not paid for with cash), those sales dollars are accumulating in the account called Accounts Receivable (AR). As we would expect, the illustration also shows that as AR increases, it "uses" cash and makes our cash flow position worse.

If that does not seem intuitive, consider this: Accounts receivable represents cash that we should have, but do not. Think of it as a reservoir of cash—a stopping point in our business cycle where cash can pause (or get stuck) before it finally flows back into our bank account.

This concept of a cash cycle is one key to understanding cash flow on a whole new level. In the next chapter, we will look at all the reservoirs of cash in the cash cycle.

SUMMARY

☑ The cash flow statement is the third and final financial statement. It provides important information not found on either the P&L or the balance sheet.

☑ A cash flow statement answers the question, "Where did all my money go?" It shows exactly how cash was made and spent during the report period.

☑ There are two ways to make a cash flow statement: the direct method and the indirect method. The direct method is more appropriate for small businesses and appears as a standard report in QuickBooks.

☑ The calculations in a cash flow statement rely on information from the P&L and the balance sheet. Unlike those other statements, however, there are no choices to make when preparing a cash flow statement.

☑ A cash flow statement has three parts: Operations, Investing, and Finance. Each part tells us something different about how the company makes and spends cash.

☑ Cash flow statements help us interpret the strengths and weaknesses of a business.

☑ By understanding how our actions and accounts roll up into the cash flow statement, we can begin to predict—and manage—our cash on a day-to-day basis.

10

The Cash Cycle

Every business, no matter how small or how large, does two basic things: it buys something, and it sells something.

- Kim's car dealership buys cars. It sells cars.
- Chris' Canine Services Studio buys dog food and shampoo, plus it buys time from its employees. It sells pet training, grooming, and boarding.
- Kelly's Rocky Road Ice Cream Factory buys milk, sugar, eggs, toppings, and hourly labor. It sells ice cream.
- Jo's RockStar Websites buys photographs, hard disk space, and specialized services from coders. It sells finished websites and maintenance contracts.

Notice that without buying something, a business will have nothing to sell. And the more it sells, the more it has to buy. It's a cycle really—an endless circle of consuming inputs and creating outputs. And along the way, the business is churning through dollars—dollars going out the door to pay vendors, and dollars coming back in as customers pay the business.

It is probably no surprise that there is a name for this circle of spending and receiving. We call this the *cash conversion cycle*, or just *cash cycle*, and measuring this cash cycle is important to our understanding of overall cash flow. Naturally, that means that the cash cycle is also an important management concept—something that, once understood, can be managed and changed to help us improve our business performance.

Whereas a cash flow statement measures *how much* cash we spend, the cash cycle tracks *how long it takes* to spend it and get it back. In other words, how many days does our business require to convert $1 of cash expense into $1 of cash sales? Let's look at the cycle more closely.

THE STOPS ON THE CASH CYCLE

We already know that we buy inputs and sell outputs. Each of these steps is counted in the cash cycle—and there's one more: we keep some inventory on hand.

We've described these three points in the cycle in terms of "things"—inputs, outputs, and inventory—but we are actually concerned with the cash value represented by these items and how long the cash stays at each point before moving on. So we'll draw the cash cycle showing each step as we buy and pay for materials, hold inventory, and finally sell our goods and receive payment. See Figure 10.1.

Figure 10.1. The Cash Conversion Cycle

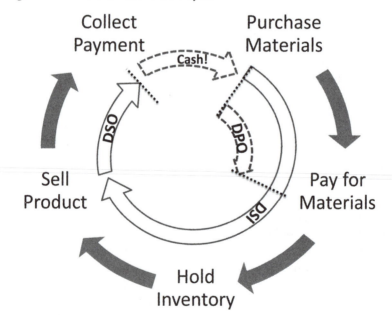

Source: Adapted from Eugene F. Brigham and Joel F. Houston, *Fundamentals of Financial Management*, 8th ed. (New York: Thompson, 1998), p. 658.

> Note that in this illustration of the cash cycle, we describe "buying materials" and "holding inventory." These are simply terms that represent what a business requires to produce goods or services. We can substitute any term that more accurately describes the labor and materials found in our cost of sales—parts, ingredients, hours, designs, etc.

CALCULATING THE CASH CYCLE

Ultimately, we want to calculate the number of days that a dollar spends traversing from vendor to inventory to customer and back again. To calculate the total days in this cycle, we measure the time between each point. It would be nearly impossible to go to a calendar and try to count the days between every step for every customer, so we have developed some simple math that does the work for us.

Each calculation starts with a balance sheet value (A/P, A/R, Inventory) and divides by a number from the P&L (COS or SALES), so it is important to use a balance sheet from the last day of the same period covered by the P&L. Table 10.1 shows a balance sheet and P&L from Rocky Point Landscaping. We can use just these two statements to calculate the company's cash cycle. For simplicity, we've used an annual P&L for this exercise. Notice that the balance sheet is from the last day of the annual P&L period.

Table 10.1. Rocky Point Landscaping Financial Statements

Rocky Point Landscaping Profit & Loss Year Ending December 31	
Ordinary Income/Expenses	
Income	
4010 - Landscaping	159,576
4020 - Lawn Maintenance	182,916
Total Income	342,492
Cost of Sales	
5000 - Cost of Goods Sold	156,876

(*continued*)

Table 10.1. (Continued)

Rocky Point Landscaping
Profit & Loss
Year Ending December 31

5010 - Labor	68,160
5020 - Equipment, Fuel, and Fees	4,032
Total Cost of Sales	229,068
Gross Profit	113,424
Expenses	
6030 - Bank Charges	1,500
6040 - Dues & Subscriptions	1,000
6050 - Equipment & Tools - Non Rental	25,000
6200 - Payroll Expenses	102,000
6310 - Uniforms	1,200
6320 - Utilities	8,000
Total Expenses	138,700
Net Ordinary Income	90,368
Other Income/Expense	
Other Expense	
8100 - Depreciation Expense	7200
8300 - Interest Expense	4800
Total Other Expense	12,000
Net Income	78,368

Rocky Point Landscaping
Balance Sheet
As of December 31

ASSETS	
Current Assets	
Business Checking	75,000
Accounts Receivable	15,000
Inventory	5,000
Total Current Assets	95,000
Fixed Assets	

(*continued*)

Table 10.1. (Continued)

Rocky Point Landscaping Balance Sheet As of December 31	
Landscape Equipment	5,000
Trucks & Vehicles	25,000
Total Fixed Assets	30,000
TOTAL ASSETS	125,000
LIABILITIES & EQUITY	
Liabilities	
Accounts Payable	29,000
Total Liabilities	29,000
Equity	
Retained Earnings	17,632
Net Income	78,368
Total Equity	96,000
TOTAL LIABILITIES & EQUITY	125,000

Days Payable Outstanding

Starting at the top of the cycle, we want to know the date we bought (or received) the inputs and the date we paid for them. With most accounting software, the best we can do is to measure the days between the date of the bill from our vendor and the date of our payment to the vendor. We could do this for each and every payment, but there's a simpler way.

Instead of worrying about any *one* bill or payment, we calculate the *days payable outstanding* (DPO), which is an average of how long we take between *all* our bills and payments.

> Note: Since the cash cycle calculates the time between a purchase and a payment, we must be sure to enter vendor *bills* into our accounting system as we receive them. If we fail to enter the bills, the balance sheet will show an incorrect balance for accounts payable (AP)—or none at all—and the cash cycle calculation will not work. With that in mind, entering bills more accurately can improve the cash cycle—at least by making it more accurate and meaningful.

Like all cash cycle calculations, days payable outstanding is figured as a fraction of a year multiplied by 360 days. The equation and the results for Rocky Point Landscaping are here:

$$DPO = \frac{Accounts\ Payable}{Annual\ Cost\ of\ Sales} \times 360\ days$$

$$DPO = \frac{\$\ 10,000}{\$156,876} \times 360 = 23\ days$$

This tells us right away that Rocky Point is paying their bills in an average of 23 days. That's not bad—they clearly have established some credit with their vendors. As you'll see, a bigger DPO number is generally better. The bigger this number is, the longer we take to pay bills and thus, the longer our cash is *available*. The other two calculations in this cycle show how long our cash is *unavailable*.

Days Sales of Inventory (DSI)

Working our way around the circle, we now see the period between buying materials and making a sale, or Days Sales of Inventory (DSI). Depending on your industry, this could be called a number of things, but the key concept is that we are holding inventory. The first inner circle in Figure 10.1 is called the Inventory Conversion Period, the time required to buy, hold, and sell the inventory. We calculate DSI in much the same way we did DPO. Pull the total value of inventory on hand (from the balance sheet), then divide by the total cost of all inventory sold during the year. For simplicity, most textbooks will use the Cost of Goods Sold to represent the annual value of inventory sold. Here is the Days Sales of Inventory calculation, and the result for Rocky Point.

$$DSI = \frac{Inventory\ on\ Hand}{Annual\ Cost\ of\ Goods\ Sold} \times 360\ days$$

$$DSI = \frac{\$\ 5,000}{\$156,876} \times 360 = 11\ days$$

This calculation shows that Rocky Point has enough inventory on hand to last about 11 days of average sales. It would help to hold less inventory (and therefore more cash), but in some situations it is necessary to have enough inventory to get through a complete delivery cycle. If Rocky Point can receive inventory weekly or more often, then 11 days of inventory may be more than is needed.

Note that the Inventory Conversion Period overlaps the Payables Deferral Period (which we calculated as DPO). This is simply how the math works—the value of inventory is calculated on the day it is purchased (the bill is entered), not on the day it was paid for. Anchoring both payables and inventory to the same bill date allows us to subtract one from the other, as we will see in a moment.

Days Sales Outstanding (DSO)

The final stop on our cycle is the sale process. Our accounting records (or software) allows us to measure our sales and our payments. From these two numbers we can tell how many days our invoices go unpaid. Remember, when a customer buys something without paying, he effectively has our cash and it is not yet available for us to use. The formula below shows how we calculate days sales outstanding (DSO).

$$DSO = \frac{Accounts\ Receivable}{Annual\ Sales} \times 360\ days$$

$$DSO = \frac{\$\ 15,000}{\$342,492} \times 360 = 16\ days$$

Like all the calculations we are doing here, DSO is an average for the specific period of the reports we're using. It does not show how quickly or slowly any one client pays his bill, but instead calculating the average number of days of credit we extend to all our clients. After all, if we are giving them credit, they are not paying us cash! DSO tells us how long it takes to convert a sale (an invoice) into cash (a payment).

In the case of Rocky Point, our customers are taking just 16 days to pay our bills. That's pretty good, but we can probably do better. We could ask for more money in advance, start accepting credit cards, or just give fewer customers credit. An all-cash business, like a restaurant, has zero DSO. We want to move this number as low as possible.

Adding It All Up

Finally, we have traversed the entire circle, and our cash is back in the bank, ready to once again be sent to a vendor and start the cycle all over again.

Did you notice that DSI and DSO represents days that we *do not* have cash, while DPO represents days that we *do* have cash? When we add up all the periods around the circle, we will *subtract* the DPO, while we *add* DSI and DSO. Here is the final calculation.

$$Cash\ Conversion\ Cycle = DSO + DSI - DPO$$
$$Rocky\ Point's\ Cycle = 16 + 11 - 23 = 4\ days$$

The cash cycle answers one fundamental question: "How many days does it take one dollar to cycle through my business?" For Rocky Point, we now know that it takes an average of just four days to get one dollar all the way through the business.

Even though we have drawn the cash cycle as a circle, note that the number of days we calculated is the number of days between when we pay a vendor with cash and when our customers pay us with cash. We are not so concerned with how long we hold onto our cash—after all, that is the goal! Rather, we are interested in how long our cash is outstanding and not available to the business.

Take a moment now to collect the information needed to calculate your own cash cycle. From a current (12-month) P&L, and a current balance sheet, fill in the values in the worksheet provided in Table 10.2.

Table 10.2. My Cash Cycle

My Cash Conversion Cycle	
1 Year Profit & Loss Statement	
a. Total Sales	$_____
b. Total Cost of Sales	$_____
Year End Balance Sheet	
c. Accounts Payable	$_____
d. Accounts Receivable	$_____
e. Inventory	$_____

(*continued*)

Table 10.2. (Continued)

My Cash Conversion Cycle	
Calculate Your Own Cash Cycle Values	
DSO = (d/a)*360	_____Days
DSI = (e/b)*360	_____Days
DPO = (c/b)*360	_____Days
Cash Cycle Days	
DSO + DSI − DPO =	_____Days

> *Note*: In this book we assume that a year has 360 days for most calculations. This helps keep our calculations simple and consistent, since 360 breaks down nicely into 12 months of 30 days each. Others will use 365 days per year, since it is more accurate. Either convention is fine—as long as we use it consistently. There's no reason to worry about leap years.

INTERPRETING THE CASH CYCLE

Now we have a number of days. What does it mean if our cash cycle is, say, 90 days? A 90-day cycle means that our business is missing the cash that could be generated in three months (90 days) of sales. Remember, the cash cycle measures the time required to get cash from our customers, so if our average monthly sales is $100,000, then approximately $300,000 of our cash is tied up waiting for customers to pay. If we allow the cash cycle to creep up to four months (120 days), we will be missing the benefit of another $100,000 of cash. Conversely, if we can get the cash cycle down to 60 days, we will free up $100,000 of cash.

To calculate exactly how much cash is tied up in a business, we can think of the days in the cycle as a fraction of the year, and thus the value is a fraction of our yearly sales. This is, essentially, the reverse of the equations we used to find the number of days. With this step we are converting days back into dollars. Try the math for yourself. Take the number of days in your cycle, divide by 360, and multiply by your annual sales. This will tell you how much cash your business has tied up in the sales processes.

$$Cash\ Tied\ Up = \frac{Cash\ Cycle\ Days}{360} \times Annual\ Sales\ Dollars$$

Using the results of your cash conversion cycle, above, calculate how much cash is tied up in your business.

The more days in a cash cycle, the more cash is needed to keep the business running smoothly. So, as you can see, a shorter cash cycle is always better. Can you imagine a business with zero days of cash conversion? What about a negative cash conversion cycle? It is possible; however, it is uncommon. There are several things we can do to manage our business toward a lower—and perhaps even a negative—cash cycle.

MANAGING THE CASH CYCLE

Nobody wants to run out of cash. Frankly, nobody wants to invest more cash into a business than is needed. The point of a business should be to *generate* cash, not to *use* it. To minimize the use of cash in our businesses, we need to carefully watch the cash cycle and manage our operations to keep the cycle under tight control. Let's work our way around the circle again and see how to minimize the cash encumbered by our business.

Pay Slowly

Our cycle starts with purchasing materials and labor. Since we don't start counting our cash cycle days until we make a payment for these inputs, the longer we can wait to pay for them, the better. Big companies are infamous for paying slowly. The bigger they get, the slower they seem to pay. This is how they manage their own cash cycles. It is harder for a small business to stretch out payments, but doing so is the first important step to decreasing the cash cycle.

Tip: Convince vendors to wait longer for their payment by offering to send more business their way. Better customers get better terms. A minimum purchase contract might be enough to entice them to allow an extra 30 days to pay. In exchange for better terms, offer to give them a credit application, a written purchase order, and a credit card for automatic or past due payments.

Let's not forget that the cash cycle takes into account all cost of sales, including labor. This means that moving from a once-a-week payroll cycle to a once-a-month payroll cycle will have a direct impact on the cash cycle (for labor associated with cost of sales, anyway).

Note: Not all accounting systems (or accountants) capture the daily value of labor, so it may not be possible to see the cash cycle change based on payroll policy changes. Nonetheless, paying less frequently is the same as paying more slowly and will free up an incremental amount of cash.

Decrease Inventory

Holding a large amount of inventory for a long period of time is a terrible way to use cash for most businesses. As a rule, inventory loses value over time (except, perhaps, fine wine or rare artifacts). So not only do we have a lot of cash tied up in inventory, but we also lose a bit of that cash each day. It would be much better to buy inventory only as we need it and keep on hand only enough to serve customers while the next batch is being made or delivered. Of course, that kind of highly efficient inventory management was popularized in the 1990s by Japanese car manufacturers and called JIT—Just In Time inventory management—or "Lean Production," as James Womack called it in his groundbreaking 1990 book *The Machine That Changed the World: The Story of Lean Production* (reprint, New York: Free Press, 2007).

Keeping inventory lean and mean is, of course, a challenge that requires us to plan inventory levels accurately: A clothing retailer, for example, must order enough stock each week or month (sometimes even before a season starts) to accommodate an unknown number of customers. If, however, they could order goods each day, and have them delivered the next day, the retailer could drastically reduce the amount of stock on hand.

Tip: Check out Appendix 1 for a case study on Dell Computer. Dell has mastered their cash cycle time, and now uses cash from customers *and* cash from their vendors.

Now imagine a retailer that can order goods *after* a customer has decided what to buy. If this were possible (and the customer could wait), the retailer could hold *no* inventory.

Collect Quickly from Customers

Although we want to pay our vendors slowly, we certainly want our customers to pay quickly. The faster *they* pay, the shorter our cash cycle time becomes. Collections can be a huge headache for companies—customers take their time paying, or don't pay at all. Even when they do pay, checks and wire transfers can go awry, credit cards can be declined, and payments get lost in the mail. Most companies I've seen that have cash problems have collection problems.

An improvement to collections is also the best opportunity we have for turning our cash cycle around. Moving customers from slow-pay to prepay can be an arduous task, but will have immediate, positive impact on the cash cycle and on the business in general.

> *Tip*: Offer customers a small discount for faster payment. A 2% discount for cash in advance is a win-win for both parties. They pay less for your products or services and you save the expense of collections and the risk of bad debt. If the customer does not have a good credit history, make prepayment mandatory. You may lose their business, but at least you won't lose your shirt!

Remember Chris, who owns the Canine Services Studio? Her business is booming, and she's been able to open up a second location. That took a lot of cash: a deposit on the lease, the cost of upgrades to the space, a new sign, etc. Where did that cash come from? In this case, it came from customers who paid—not just early, but in advance. Chris's unique business model creates a negative cash cycle, which helps her afford fast growth.

When a customer comes into Chris's Canine Services Studio, she doesn't ask them to sign up for *one* training session; she sells them on an entire *package* of training sessions. Usually, that's about three months' worth of work.

Here's the kicker: Chris takes payment in advance and has a strict no-refunds policy. So before Chris has incurred a single penny of expense, she has collected hundreds—in some cases thousands—of dollars of cash. As a result, Chris has no A/R and no bad debt. Her bank account is stuffed full of customers' money, so when she needs to put a deposit down on a new store location, she literally uses her customers' money to do it.

The Canine Services Studio has an ideal collections policy: customers prepay, so the business never has cash tied up in the cost of sales. Not every business can do that, of course. Restaurants and retail stores get pretty close. When customers pay cash for a meal or a purchase, the days sales outstanding (DSO) is naturally zero. The proliferation of credit cards has pushed this out just a bit, however. Most banks now deposit credit card funds within one to three days, so even retailers and restaurants typically have a positive DSO. This makes Chris's accomplishment (and Dell's, as you can see in Appendix 1) that much more amazing.

SUMMARY

- ☑ The cash cycle, or cash conversion cycle, tells us how a company uses its cash to fund inventory and accounts receivable.
- ☑ The cash cycle is expressed in a number of days. In dollar terms, this is equivalent to days of sales.
- ☑ Converting cash cycle days back into a dollar value demonstrates the value of cash that is tied up (encumbered) by the inventory and accounts receivable.
- ☑ Managers should seek to minimize the cash conversion cycle time by paying vendors more slowly, minimizing the value of inventory held, and collecting from customers more quickly.

Part 4

RATIOS AND ANALYSIS

11

Answering Questions Using Trends and Ratios

Accountants have long been labeled as backward-looking bean counters. I've even been known to complain about accountants and accounting reports, because using the results of last year to plan next year's business is a bit like driving a car forward while looking only in the rearview mirror.

It's true, of course, that the data in our accounting records is historical by definition. Even the best accounting software can track only results—sales that have already happened, expenses that we have already incurred. As entrepreneurs, conversely, we are compelled to look forward, leaving the past behind. There is a natural disconnect.

As Winston Churchill said, however, "Those who fail to learn from history are doomed to repeat it." It is vitally important that we take guidance from the past. So while we cannot drive forward looking only in the rearview mirror, every entrepreneur must, on a regular basis, look backward to learn from the historical record of her business. The three financial statements—P&L, balance sheet, and cash flow—form the foundation of this record. On this foundation we can begin to build more and more customized measures of our performance, growth, profitability, and efficiency. Eventually, looking at the historical information will, as Churchill observed, help us plan a better, brighter, and perhaps more profitable future.

To grow more and more profitable, we must be able to make better and better decisions. Decisions like how much inventory to purchase, or whether to borrow more money, will shape our future. Making better decisions, however, in turn relies on finding the answer to questions. If our decision is how much inventory to buy, then it would certainly be helpful to know things like "Are our sales growing?" To decide whether to take on a bank loan might require asking a more difficult question: "Will we be able to pay this back next year?"

Answering some questions is simple: Calculating whether sales are moving up (or down) from one month to the next only requires a quick comparison of the sales recorded on the P&L statements from each of the two months. The answer will show us the *trend*. Other questions, like those about repaying debt, may require a much deeper analysis of business performance—and this means looking at the relationship, or *ratios*, between multiple accounts on multiple financial statements. Let's look at both trends and ratios and how they work together.

TRENDS VERSUS RATIOS

In addition to the basic financial results shown on a financial statement, accountants and business owners use trends and ratios as two primary tools to evaluate a company's performance.

Trends

Trends show us the movement of a single value over time. Spotting the trends can reveal important information that we need to manage our business. We look for trends to answer questions such as these:

- Are we paying more for rent this year than we did last year?
- How fast are sales growing from year to year?
- Was the spring quarter more profitable than summer?

Comparing the same account across any two or more periods (weeks, months, quarters, or years) can provide a quick and straightforward way to see a trend. We might express the result in an absolute (sales are up $3,000 this month), or as a percentage (sales are up 6% this month). Either way, an astute manager can use trend data to spot market opportunities, quash out-of-control expenses, and evaluate organizational changes. Finding a trend is as simple as subtracting the results of one month from another:

February Sales – January Sales = $X

Tracking key data over multiple months, however, makes trend data even more useful. Knowing that sales are lower in February than

January is interesting, but knowing that sales fell during each of the last 18 months in a row is really important. Trends—and long-lasting trends in particular—should never be taken lightly.

Ratios

Trends only take us so far, however, before they run out of steam. Comparing just a single account across time cannot answer more complex questions such as:

- How many salespeople do we need to hit our sales goal?
- Are we growing as fast as we can?
- Do we need to borrow money?
- How much can we borrow, and can we afford to repay it?

To answer these (and many more) questions, we turn to calculating ratios. In mathematics, a ratio is defined as the result of dividing one number into another. In finance, the same is true: financial ratios simply *divide the value of one account by the value of another account.* (Sometimes the values used in a ratio are the sum of several similar accounts, or an operating result, rather than just the value of one account.) For example, one common ratio, called the Current Ratio, is found by dividing two account values from the balance sheet, like this:

$$Current\ Ratio = \frac{Total\ Current\ Assets}{Total\ Current\ Liabilities}$$

We will discuss this ratio later. For now, it is important only to understand that we can take the values from various accounts or sums on our financial statements (in this case, two balance sheet subtotals: Total Current Assets and Total Current Liabilities) and use them to tell us something completely new and unique (in this case, whether we could quickly pay off all our debts if the need arose).

Using Both Trends and Ratios

Finally, the most powerful financial analysis comes from tracking the *trend of a ratio*. When we examine how a ratio changes over time, we learn more about a business than is possible with either ratios or trends alone. In fact, many ratios are useful only when we know whether they are trending up or down. Let's take one example. The Current Ratio shown above is one way a banker measures a company's ability to repay debt. As we can see from the formula, the Current Ratio shows how much short-term debt we have compared to our short-term assets (like cash in the bank). Having more cash than debt is a good position to be in, but it is hard to say whether we should have twice as much or five times as much. Should our current ratio equal 1 or 5? The desired or target value for this ratio is different for each company (and varies greatly from industry to industry). Therefore, in order to know whether *today's* Current Ratio is good or bad depends on where it has been historically, and where we want it to be in the future. Is it improving or declining? Is it likely to continue to improve or decline? Showing the ratio moving over time—in other words, knowing *the trend of the ratio*—is a valuable analysis tool and tells us much more than any single ratio at any single point in time.

In the next sections, we will use both ratios and trends to evaluate financial statements. For the first part of our look at ratios, we will use data contained on either the balance sheet or the P&L (and often both). The calculations are straightforward, so use your own financial statements—or those of the sample companies we've discussed—to follow along and see what these ratios can tell you about a business.

SIMPLE RATIOS: COMMON-SIZING THE P&L

Recall that in Part 1 of this book we looked at how to "common-size" a P&L statement. We said that in some cases it is more useful to look at percentages instead of dollars—for example, calculating the percentage of net profit helps us to compare one business to another, or one month to the next. When we calculate percentages within a P&L (to create a common-sized P&L), what we are really doing is figuring a bunch of simple ratios, or fractions. A common-sized P&L shows all the results as a percentage of sales. We calculate those percentages by dividing each item into total sales.

$$Net\ Profit\ Percentage = \frac{Net\ Profit}{Total\ Sales} \times 100\%$$

On a fully common-sized P&L, each line is compared to the total sales in this way. These ratios are always expressed as a percentage. This makes a P&L easier to read, but it also seems more natural. Saying "our gross profit margin is 50%" is more natural or intuitive than stating that gross profit is "0.5 times sales."

As we've said, a fully common-sized P&L has *every line* converted to a percentage of sales. This is so common that accounting software will often do these calculations as part of generating a P&L. The result can be a confusing page full of ratios. For a quick analysis of a business, however, we are unlikely to care what percentage of sales are spent on the phone bill, car insurance, or office supplies. Instead, it is more helpful to examine the key lines on the P&L and their common-sized ratios. Here are some of the most common:

$$Percentage\ Cost\ of\ Goods = \frac{Cost\ of\ Sales}{Total\ Net\ Sales} \times 100\%$$

$$Gross\ Margin = \frac{Gross\ Profit}{Total\ Net\ Sales} \times 100\%$$

$$Operating\ Profit\ Margin = \frac{EBITDA}{Total\ Net\ Sales} \times 100\%$$

$$Net\ Profit\ Margin = \frac{Net\ Profit}{Total\ Net\ Sales} \times 100\%$$

Note that we use the words "margin" and "percentage" interchangeably. This is a convenience rather than a rule—saying "Net Profit Percentage" is fine if that suits you. Let's be clear, however, that when we mean dollar amounts, we use the base term, such as "net profit." When we mean the ratio of one amount compared to total net sales, we will say "margin" or "percentage." Since all the ratios on a common-sized P&L are calculated the same way, we know that they all represent a percentage of total net sales. We will use the results of these basic "common-sizing" ratios in many other calculations, so it is important to understand them thoroughly.

Since calculating a ratio is as simple as dividing two numbers, it may seem that there are an endless number of possible ratios. While some combinations will not be meaningful, it is certainly true that analysts and scholars have created hundreds of useful ratios that are both meaningful and easy to calculate. (And, with a simple spreadsheet, they can be updated on a daily or weekly basis.)

Don't panic—no entrepreneur needs to be bogged down examining 100 different ratios each month or week. In fact, the only reason to use any ratio is to answer key questions about our business.

QUESTIONS ANSWERED BY A COMMON-SIZED P&L

We've already seen some of the questions that ratios can answer, such as, "How profitable is the business?" In this section, we will pose some more important questions and explore the ratios that help us answer those questions. Not all of them will apply to every business, and you will certainly find some more useful than others. Let's see how we'd answer these common questions:

How Much Do We Spend on Marketing?

We've already seen how a common-sized P&L provides a ratio for each and every expense item (and all the income items, too). Measuring key expense categories, like marketing, can help us find opportunities for both cost savings *and spending increases*. The common-sized P&L tells us that the ratio of marketing expense to sales is:

$$Marketing\ Expense\ Ratio = \frac{Marketing\ Expense}{Total\ Sales} \times 100\%$$

Any business that is looking to grow should know its current Marketing Expense Ratio. Since (effective) marketing drives sales, investing in marketing can assure continued future growth. There are plenty of books on how important marketing is, so we won't go into that aspect, but measuring marketing as an expense ratio can be an important management tool. Did sales spike last year? If so, perhaps the marketing expense was higher. If our sales are growing more slowly than the competitors' sales, perhaps our marketing expense is lower. It is useful to compare marketing expense over time—particularly to see if and how it impacts sales—and also to compare marketing expense to other companies in the same industry. These kinds of comparisons would be meaningless if we were to compare only the actual dollars spent—but the Marketing Expense Ratio gives us a common-sized percentage, which can be easily and effectively compared across various time periods and even between companies.

We can't say that the Marketing Expense Ratio should be a specific number, or even that it should be higher or lower. But tracking it, comparing it, and targeting a reasonable number can help control growth and expense.

How Good Is Our Location?

Retail businesses and restaurants are particularly prone to over-spending on rent. A great location can make a business, to be sure, but how do we judge whether one space is better than another? There are several ways to measure this (and we will see some other ways in later chapters), but the Rent Expense Ratio is the simplest. This ratio will give us a good idea of whether we are using our space effectively, or perhaps paying too much for rent.

$$Rent\ Expense\ Ratio = \frac{Rent}{Total\ Net\ Sales} \times 100\%$$

Since this ratio appears as part of a common-sized P&L, no special calculation is needed, and we can restate the results in a way that makes intuitive sense: "We spent X% of our sales on rent during the period." For this ratio, lower is always better. If rent is a fixed cost, then a lower number means the location produces more sales per dollar of rent. If rent is tied to sales (as in some retail locations), a lower number could indicate either a better location or a better lease agreement (i.e., "cheaper" rent). In either case, we want the number to be as small as possible, which would mean that we are getting more sales and/or paying less rent.

Even a traditional office-based business should consider this ratio from time to time. Since office rent is often one of our largest single cost items, keeping it low can help us keep our prices low and be more competitive. Conversely, it may be that having the prime location in an uptown office building is symbolic of the power and prestige of a successful business and adds to our customer satisfaction. In this case, a higher ratio result would be expected—but could still be compared to the competition to be sure that the rent was reasonable and appropriate for our level of sales.

Are We Controlling Our Spending?

The common-sized P&L gives us an opportunity to examine any expense—or any combination of expenses. Entrepreneurs and managers will always find spending categories that seem to be out of whack—or perhaps even out of control. Spotting one odd expense line on a P&L, however, is not enough to tell us whether the spending is unusual or even under control. Instead, we use a ratio to let us know for sure. As with the marketing and rent examples above, the Expense Ratio is easily calculated for any expense item on our P&L:

$$Expense\ Ratio = \frac{Expense}{Total\ Net\ Sales} \times 100\%$$

This tells us what percentage of sales we are spending on a particular category. Then, any Expense Ratio can be evaluated by answering two basic questions:

1. Is the Expense Ratio for this expense staying about the same over time?
2. Is the Expense Ratio about the same as other companies in our industry?

> *Tip*: To compare one company to another company in the same industry, look for the Risk Management Association's *Annual Statement Studies*. This well-known book compiles industry averages for P&L and balance sheet accounts from thousands of companies across hundreds of industries. It is generally available at public libraries, bank branch locations, and online at http://www.rmahq.org.

This basic process of calculating the ratio, comparing it over time, and comparing it to the competition will become second nature. The same process can be used on any single expense, or any group of expenses. Comparing the Total Expense line in this way is one of the more useful measures of how effectively we are spending money. As we have said, different companies will want to measure different ratios. Only a close examination of a particular business, industry, or operating environment will help us find the key expenses that should be measured in this way.

THE QUESTION OF BREAK EVEN

The first questions any entrepreneur asks herself are usually about breaking even. Perhaps even before we start a business, we naturally want to know how much we have to sell to cover our basic expenses such as rent, electricity, and office salaries. There are a couple of ways to figure breakeven, and each gives us insight into how to build a better business. The most obvious question about breakeven is this:

How Much Do We Have to Sell to Break Even?

The answer turns out to be—you guessed it—a simple ratio based on factors we already know. This ratio uses gross margin (expressed as a percentage and found on a common-sized P&L such as we have already created) and total expenses (expressed as dollars from the same P&L).

$$Breakeven\ Sales = \frac{Total\ Expenses}{Gross\ Margin\ \%}$$

Tip: Remember that for our discussion, gross profit (GP) is a measure of dollars, while gross margin (GM) is expressed as a percentage of sales. The equation is found in our discussion of "common-sizing": GM = (GP/Net Sales) × 100%.

Note that in this ratio, total expense is a dollar amount, but gross margin is a percentage. Without this ratio we could, of course, compare dollars to dollars by simply looking at gross profit and total expense. (Hopefully, gross profit > total expense!) That's a good comparison, but it will not tell us anything about what sales *should be*. Using this ratio—or fraction—helps us see exactly the amount of sales we need to make so that our gross profit covers our total expenses.

Tip: Entrepreneurs are famous for leaving one thing out of the expense calculation: their own wages! If we ignore our own salaries, then the Breakeven Sales Ratio shows only the minimum sales we must make *before* taking any wages for ourselves! A better practice would be to add your salary to the expenses on the P&L even if you do not take a paycheck. Including all (potential) wages gives a much more honest and complete answer to any question that involves calculating ratios from the P&L.

Let's do an example. If our total expenses are $1,000 each month for office rent, administrative salaries, marketing, accounting, etc., and each sale contributes a gross margin of 50%, then our formula looks like this:

$$Break\ Even\ Sales = \frac{\$1,000}{50\%} = \$2,000$$

This ratio is very helpful when we are talking with the sales team— it's a great way to set minimum sales targets or goals. There's an entirely different way to look at this same question, however, when we want to deal with production costs or pricing. That gives us a new question:

What's the Minimum Gross Margin We Need to Break Even?

Sometimes we have more control over pricing and production costs than we have over sales volume. For example, my friend Carey owns a preschool in a nice building in the suburbs. But the building is only 6,000 square feet, and the state gave Carey a license for no more than 80 students. Once he sells those 80 seats, no more sales are possible. If the business is not profitable with 80 students, then Carey's only solution is to either raise prices or cut costs.

When thinking about breakeven, Cary's real question is about gross margin (GM). What GM is needed to make the preschool profitable (break even or better)? The ratio that answers this question looks like this:

$$Breakeven\ GM = \frac{Expenses}{Net\ Sales} \times 100\%$$

This ratio is one that we can calculate on a monthly or even weekly basis. Keep in mind that this ratio tells us what our gross margin *should be—to break even*. It does not tell us what our gross margin *actually* is. We could be doing better or worse than breakeven—this ratio does not judge how well we are doing, but only what gross margin we must have at a *minimum* to pay our expenses.

To complete this analysis, we should compare the result to the *actual* gross margin (GM). We know from our common-sized P&L that GM is the ratio of gross profit to net sales, expressed as a percentage.

$$Gross\ Margin = \frac{Gross\ Profit}{Total\ Net\ Sales} \times 100\%$$

Comparing the *breakeven* gross margin to the *actual* gross margin will tell us how we are doing. If the actual margin is greater than the breakeven level, we've got a profitable business. If it is less than the breakeven level, then there is work to be done.

QUESTIONS ABOUT WHAT WE OWE

Not every business borrows money from a bank, but it is safe to say that every business owes somebody something. The debts of a company are not always measured strictly in loans—the balance sheet concept of liabilities includes unpaid bills, accrued payroll, credit card accounts, and other nonbank debts. Whether or not we have or need bank loans, however, it is useful to measure our indebtedness in order to keep tight controls on it.

There are three common debt ratios used. We will look at all three, in order from the least strict (most optimistic) to the most strict (most pessimistic). Each one is a "pure" ratio, which means that the results of the ratio are not multiplied by 100% or by any other number. The result is therefore written as a simple decimal, such as 2.5 or 0.739 (how many decimal places is up to you).

Keep in mind that the following three ratios are commonly used by bankers to measure a company's use of debt and its ability to borrow more. It is important that an entrepreneur do the same. While the questions are similar, the three ratios can provide slightly different answers.

Can We Get Through the Next Few Months If Sales Were Interrupted?

Now, *that's* a gutsy question. No entrepreneur wants to think about sales coming to a halt, but it is an important consideration. If our business is cyclical—a seasonal landscaping company or a winter snow-skiing resort—we may well face this tough situation every year! Even in a business with steady sales, the unthinkable could happen: a fire, flood, or death of a key employee could bring the whole operation to a stop for a short period of time, but the company would still be obligated to pay back debts, including credit cards, payroll, and amounts owed to vendors.

To answer this particular question, then, we are interested in how much cash we can generate in the current period and how much debt we have to cover in the current period.

Definition: The term "Current" in accounting means "within the next 12 months." Thus, "Current Assets" are assets that can be converted to cash within 12 months. Likewise, "Current Liabilities" are debts that we must pay within the next 12 months. A credit card is a current liability, because it is a loan we must repay each month. An invoice we have sent to a customer is a "Current Asset" because we expect the customer to pay within a month or two.

Since some businesses have inventory that can be sold quickly—at cost or close to it—our balance sheet includes inventory in the Current Asset category. If our inventory can be liquidated quickly and at a reasonable value, then we can count it among the current assets we use to pay back debt.

Definition: Converting a physical asset like inventory to cash is called "liquidation." Typically a liquidation that is forced or caused by negative circumstances (such as a fire) results in selling assets at a deep discount—perhaps even for less than we paid.

The ratio that takes this into account is called the Current Ratio because it allows us to use all our current assets, in including inventory.

$$Current\ Ratio = \frac{Current\ Assets}{Current\ Liabilities}$$

This is one of the simplest ratios, and it is widely used by banks to judge whether a company can repay debt in a worst-case scenario. Refer back to the balance sheet examples in prior chapters to see that Current Assets includes not just inventory, but things such as cash in the bank and accounts receivable.

This ratio can also be used by services businesses that have no inventory at all. In this case, since there is no inventory to liquidate, the value of the Current Ratio will be the same as the Quick Ratio which we will look at next.

If Sales Were Interrupted, Could We Get Through the Current Period without Liquidating Inventory?

Any business that has a lot of inventory that could not be easily liquidated should use a ratio called the "Quick Ratio." It is quick to calculate and quick to give us an indisputable answer to the question of whether we can cover our debts in the current term.

$$Quick\ Ratio = \frac{Current\ Assets - Inventory}{Current\ Liabilities}$$

Again, this is a simple ratio that requires only a few values from the balance sheet. Since the balance sheet accounts are very easy to verify (by comparing them to actual bank statements, for example), this ratio is quite reliable.

If Sales Were Interrupted, Could We Get Through the Current Period with Only the Cash on Hand Today?

Appropriately named, the Doomsday Ratio assumes the worst. It blatantly ignores any asset the company has except cash (and cash equivalents such as easily marketable securities). Like the Quick Ratio above, the Doomsday Ratio does not consider inventory to be of any real value. Additionally, however, this ratio eliminates accounts receivable—assuming that if worse comes to worst, the company's customers cannot be counted on to pay outstanding invoices. This may seem arbitrary, but it could well be the case for businesses that have long-term relationships with clients. Contracts for continuing technical support or long-term supply agreements, for example, could not be broken without dire consequences: breaking off service suddenly could violate these contracts and give customers reason enough not to pay their current bills. So the Doomsday Ratio looks alarmingly simple, like this:

$$Doomsday\ Ratio = \frac{Cash}{Current\ Liabilities}$$

As the most stringent of these three ratios, the Doomsday Ratio can produce wildly fluctuating results from day to day and from month to month, depending on the balance of cash in the bank. For that reason, no one data point should be considered alone, but rather as part of a continuing effort to measure and monitor this ratio.

Interpreting the Results

Remember that each of these ratios—Current, Quick, and Doomsday—are "pure" ratios expressed only as a decimal. And, although the numerator changes, the denominator of each ratio is Current Liabilities. In every case, therefore, a higher number is better than a lower number. If the result of the calculation is greater than 1.0, the company has a pretty good chance of being able to meet its short-term obligations. In some industries, a ratio of 2.0 or greater is expected, particularly in the less stringent measure of the Current Ratio, since it might include inventory (which is notoriously difficult to liquidate). If the result falls below 1.0, the business does not have adequate assets to cover debt and we should consider cutting some debt or going on a strict savings plan.

Tip: When evaluating the results of these ratio calculations, keep in mind that today's Current Liabilities includes only *some* of what we might owe during the current period (which we previously defined as 12 months). If sales were interrupted for an extended time, new debts would come up, such as continuing payroll and credit card charges. Likewise, we might continue to spend Current Assets (e.g., cash) on expenses like rent. If cash was not replenished by new sales, our ratio results would decline quickly (as would our business in general). So a ratio result of 1.0 from any of these ratios *today* does not indicate that we could survive the *entire* current period of 12 months, but only that we could pay off our *current* debt.

These ratios are important, meaningful, and specific. They should not, however, be relied upon without looking at the results from several periods. Fluctuations in bank account balances, inventory levels, and credit card balances (for example) can create large swings in this ratio, particularly for a small business. To overcome this, we measure these ratios on a monthly basis and compare the results. Over time, we may find that the results all fall within a narrow range of values. In this way, we can also set goals for improvement and chart our progress against prior values.

LOOKING AT OPERATIONAL RATIOS

So far we have used only the data we can get from either the P&L or the balance sheet. These financial statements cover a lot of ground, but they miss some important operating metrics. Neither statement can tell us, for instance:

- How efficient our employees are
- Whether we have a good location for our business
- How much our customers spend on an average order
- Who our best customers are

These kinds of measures require information that is not readily available on the financial statements but is not hard to find. Most entrepreneurs will know off the top of their head facts such as: how many employees we have; how many customers we have; how many square feet of space we rent; and how many orders we process per month. When we *combine* operational facts like these with the operating results from financial statements, we end up with powerful ways to measure efficiency, productivity, and expense.

The insights available by mixing operational and financial data seem more down to earth and will make sense to any entrepreneur who has ever hired employees, run a production shop, or rented a retail space. With operational and finance data, we can answer questions about employees, space, customers, and just about every other resource in our business.

QUESTIONS ABOUT EMPLOYEES

One simple operating fact about a company that will never show up on a financial statement is their number of employees. Measuring and managing employee payroll and productivity is a key concern for most business owners, and there are a number of ratios that help us do just that. Some of the basic questions we can answer with ratios about employees follow.

Did We Hire the Right People?

Having the right people doing the right job can be a real competitive advantage. One way of measuring this is through employee efficiency ratios. These ratios can also help us decide whether to invest in tools and technology to make employees more productive. How do we know how productive our employees are? One simple way is to measure total sales per employee:

$$Employee\ Productivity\ Ratio = \frac{Total\ Sales}{Number\ of\ Employees}$$

Be careful when calculating this ratio to count employees using the convention we call FTE—Full Time Equivalent. Under this rule, two half-time employees would count as just one FTE. If we have a big staff, one way of calculating this is to find the total number of hours worked in an average week and divide by 40 (assuming that a full-time employee would work 40 hours per week).

This ratio also can be very useful for comparing smaller groups of employees (such as teams or divisions), and for deciding when to upgrade equipment. A landscaping company, for example, may have five crews all doing similar work. Comparing sales per crew might reveal that one crew accomplishes only half of what another does. This could be caused by lax attitudes, differences in technique, or even poor equipment. Finding the highest-productivity employees can often inform changes that help elevate the productivity of all the employees.

Are the Employees Doing the Right Things?

At first, this may seem like the same question we just answered, but plenty of companies can make a sale and never deliver a profit. Measuring *profit* per employee can give us a very different efficiency metric to make some important decisions. We might, for example, need a guide for staffing levels in the back office, where additional employees often add expense without contributing to revenue. Is the company maintaining the same (or better) profit per person as it grows? What is the optimal staffing level? We might also look at profit per employee for guidance on compensation issues—year-end bonuses and profit sharing are two easy examples. The formula is straightforward:

$$Profit \ per \ Employee = \frac{Net \ Profit}{Number \ of \ Employees}$$

Note that, as before, the denominator is the number of full-time equivalent (FTE) employees. It should also be an average number for the period being measured. In other words, if we are calculating profit per employee for the *year*, then the number of employees we use is the average FTEs employed during the year.

This ratio can certainly be tracked on a monthly or quarterly basis. If our number of employees changes seasonally (or for any other reason), then this number could reveal some important dynamics hidden in our business model. Perhaps the business is much more profitable *per person* when we deploy only a few highly trained people. Or maybe the whole business is more profitable *per person* when we staff up and run larger projects.

Knowing where the sweet spot is can have a profound impact on how we manage the business. See the story of the Event Company in Chapter 12 for an example of how profit per employee can be used to find the sweet spot in a business.

Are Our Employees Happy and Loyal?

Measuring true happiness is not really a subject for a finance book, but there are some ratios that can give us a hint at the answer. The worst thing about having unhappy employees is that they quit. Managing an employee turnover problem starts with measuring it, which we can do with the following simple math:

$$Employee\ Turnover = \frac{Terminations}{Average\ number\ of\ Staff} \times 100\%$$

This ratio may not really answer the question of whether our employees are happy, but it can tell us whether they are leaving our company at a rate that might indicate a problem. If so, the problem is bigger than a few people with bad attitudes: When an employee quits, she takes with her all of the time and resources we invested in recruiting her, screening and hiring her, training her, and helping her "fit in" and "get up to speed." When we hire a new employee to replace her, we spend more resources to start the process over again. Terminations and replacements can become a very expensive problem—an expense that the company should measure and control by using this ratio.

> *Note*: This is the first ratio we've examined that does not use any inputs from the financial statement. It is a good example of how useful ratios are in almost any situation. I've included it here because turnover is such an important issue to entrepreneurs, and this ratio can help us understand the results from other ratios, such as *employee efficiency* and *profit per employee*.

All businesses have some employee attrition or turnover—people grow older and retire, find more lucrative careers, or perhaps just die. So while this ratio is best if it is zero, that is likely an impossibility. In any event, a lower number is always better, and a large or increasing number signals a problem with management, compensation, or working conditions that will need to be addressed.

What Is the Full Cost of Hiring Another Person?

Employees are one of the largest categories of costs for most businesses. Even when turnover is low, the true cost of an employee is often hidden—and always more than just her wage. Additional expenses include taxes, insurance, benefits, sick time, and other related fees. In HR circles, the nonwage costs of an employee are often called the "burden" or "load." Although we could add up each of these expenses for each employee, it is simplest to express the burden as a percentage of wages or salaries. Most of the expenses are variable (meaning the expense is higher when the wage is higher), so settling on a percentage of wages makes sense. The basic formula for finding the wage burden is:

$$Burden = \frac{\Sigma\ All\ Nonwage\ Payroll\ Expenses}{Total\ Gross\ Wages} \times 100\%$$

The top of this ratio should be read as "the sum of all nonwage payroll expenses" and includes the costs of all employer-paid expenses related to payroll. Specifically, we add up workers comp insurance, payroll processing fees, and the portion of FICA, FUTA, and SUTA (also called Social Security and unemployment taxes) that is paid by the business. We would also add benefits paid by the business, including health insurance, paid time off, bonuses, and other perks. The sum of all of these items forms the top of the ratio (the numerator)—and it can be quite large!

Note that the top of this ratio does not include taxes paid by the employee. This is because the business pays a gross wage to the employee, and then the employee pays taxes through withholding. The business counts only the gross wages, so we avoid counting his tax expense twice.

Once we have used this ratio to calculate a burden percentage, we can use it to estimate the total cost of any employee (or department) and to budget for new employees. Often the burden is as much as 20% of gross wages or more, so including the burden in our budgeting and planning is quite important.

Note that the burden is a percentage of gross wages. That means that the total cost of the employee is his gross wage *plus* the burden. If we pay an employee $10 per hour, and our burden is 20%, then the true cost of that employee is $12 per hour, as shown here:

$$Cost\ of\ Employee = Wage + (Burden\ Rate \times Wage)$$

$$\therefore Hourly\ Cost\ of\ Employee = \$10 + (20\% \times \$10) = \$12$$

We can use this same logic to calculate the true cost of any employee—hourly or salaried—assuming they share the same burden. It would not be fair, however, to say that the same 20% burden we calculate for our salaried executives also applies to a *part-time* hourly worker. Since part-time employees do not qualify for many of the most expensive benefits, like health insurance and paid time off, it is best to figure this ratio twice—once for full-time people and once for part-timers.

> *Tip*: Since part-timers and full-time employees have fundamentally different benefits, businesses that use a lot of part-time help will find it helpful to calculate two burden rates—one for each group.

How Much Does It Cost to Support Each Employee?

Besides paying an employee their fully burdened wage (calculated above), we must also provide for that person in other ways. In an office setting, this means a desk, chair, computer, phone, and other creature comforts such as heat, light, and water (or, in my case, coffee). In other environments, hiring a new employee might mean paying for uniforms, vehicles, tools, licenses, and more. Whatever your situation, having employees nearly always costs more than just the burdened wage.

While we could try to add up each of these costs individually, a faster way to judge the total cost of an employee is to split the total fixed costs of the business between the employees, using this formula:

$$Fixed\ Cost\ per\ Employee = \frac{Total\ Expenses - Wages}{Number\ of\ Employees}$$

This ratio is pretty flexible, and can be adjusted based on the exact situation. We could argue, for example, that hiring more staff will eventually require us to hire more management! In that case, we could adjust the ratio by adding management wages to the numerator (top of the ratio). Whether "Wages" in this ratio includes the burden we calculated early is a similar issue—one we can decide on a case-by-case basis.

Tip: Every ratio can be "tweaked" to make it fit a particular situation. As we have seen, making a standard ratio fit the business facts is usually just a matter of adding or subtracting certain account balances that "don't fit." So long as we always calculate the ratio in the same way, small tweaks are a normal and acceptable way to use ratios. The true value of a ratio comes not from calculating the value one time, but rather from comparing the calculations over time. In those cases, consistently using the same formula is more important than whether the formula captures every expense precisely as we want.

In businesses for which overhead expense is small and focused on supporting employees (such as the example of uniform and vehicle expenses), this ratio takes on particular significance. In any case, calculating the fixed cost per employee is an important component when budgeting for future employees. Fixed cost per employee can be added to the budget in the same way we added "burden" to wages above.

ANSWERING QUESTIONS ABOUT CUSTOMERS

Employees are not the only concern of a business owner, of course. In fact, most entrepreneurs would say that customers are top of mind; understanding our customers is certainly one key to success. Using ratios (and other analytical tools) to evaluate our customers can yield some surprisingly powerful insights, which in turn can help us better serve—and perhaps better select—our customers.

Tip: Knowing and understanding customers requires us to keep good track of them. For the ratios in this section, we will need to know how many customers we have, when they became a customer, and how much they spent while they were a customer. Every business should have a good customer database (also called a CRM system). If your CRM does not have this information, however, your accounting software might. Most accounting software will track (or let you track) the dates that customers start and finish, as well as what they spend in between. If collecting this information sounds like a daunting task, know that it will be worth the effort. Few parts of this book will have as much impact on your business strategy as this one: a complete understanding of customers is invaluable.

Some of the more common questions we want answered about customers are: how much customers spend; which customers are best for our business; and whether our systems are optimized for the customers we serve. Following are some of the ratios that help us find those answers.

How Much Does It Cost to Get a Customer?

Before a customer can spend money with us, we have to first spend money to find them. The cost of finding a customer, called "acquisition cost," includes everything we spend on marketing and sales activities. The ratio looks like this:

$$Customer\ Acquisition\ Cost = \frac{Sales\ and\ Marketing\ Expense}{Number\ of\ New\ Customers}$$

This ratio is deceptively simple looking. The numerator, Sales and Marketing Expenses, can be taken right from our P&L. Nothing to it. In practice, however, the challenge is to more carefully examine which expenses we count toward sales and marketing. The cost of building a website and printing a sign are straightforward marketing costs. What about the annual dues to join a networking group? Or the salary of the marketing manager?

On the P&L we may have multiple categories that capture expenses that benefit the sales and marketing function. If, for example, we join a networking group to find new customers, then that expense ought to get lumped into the Sales and Marketing Expense in this ratio, even though it may be captured in a category called "dues" on the P&L.

Conversely, we may have sent each of our customers a large gift-basket during the holiday season. If that expense went into our P&L account for marketing costs, we might be better off taking that *out* of the equation, since it applied only to *existing* customers and not *new* ones. It is worth a quick look through the expenses included in the numerator to be sure we've captured them accurately and completely.

Why do we care how much it costs to capture a new customer? The cost of acquisition can drive all kinds of management decisions. One decision would be how to allocate our marketing and sales budget in the future. If during one period we find that cheap Internet ads generated a lot of new customers at a small cost, we would certainly prefer that over an expensive ad in a newspaper or magazine, which had been less effective.

Less obviously, perhaps, we should compare how much a customer costs to how much profit that customer will generate. If we spend more to get a customer than that customer will return to us in profits, we will not be in business very long. Let's go on to the next set of questions, then, for a good look at ways to value each customer.

How Valuable Is Each Customer?

We want to answer this question in two ways. First, let's find out how much each customer spends with us, on average. That question then, gives us a shortcut to another question, which is, "How profitable is each customer?" But we're getting ahead of ourselves. Here's the first step: the formula for calculating what the average customer spends.

$$Average\ Customer\ Sales = \frac{Total\ Sales}{Number\ of\ Customers}$$

Note that the result of this is the average customer sales *in a single time period*. Let's take one more step and ask the related question, "How profitable is the average customer?" Since we already have a common-sized P&L, we can quickly calculate the dollar amount of gross profit on each customer. Remember, with a common-sized P&L, once we know the top line (sales), we can figure any other amount, including profit. So in this case, we use the results from above and do one more quick calculation:

$$Gross\ Profit\ per\ Customer = Sales\ per\ Customer \times GM\%$$

Gross margin (or GM% in this formula) is the percentage of gross profit from our common-sized P&L. Gross margin is a percentage of total sales; in this case we're using it to mean the percentage of one customer's sales.

Why is gross profit per customer an important number? With this level of detail, we can now say how many customers we must have to reach breakeven (or to predict any other level of profitability). Note that with a bit of work, we could calculate even the net profit if we had, say, 500 customers. To do this we use the formula above to figure the gross profit, and then deduct fixed expenses.

Note: Using gross profit per customer to calculate net profit only works if our fixed expenses are truly fixed. Certainly our expenses would increase if we grew our customer base from 50 customers to 50,000 customers, for example. To get a more accurate picture of rapid growth, we employ a more detailed financial model, which is a topic in the next section.

Tip: Gross margin is the fulcrum on which nearly every other aspect of our business finances depends. Gross margin tells us whether our products can generate more money than they cost us to produce, but it also tells us whether we will have enough to pay for fixed expenses—and how much we must sell (top line) to generate net profit (bottom line). A business with a great gross margin is likely to be a great business. A business without a healthy gross margin will always have a tough go of it.

What Is the Lifetime Value of a Customer?

So far we have looked only at the sales and profit from a single (average) customer over a single period—a week, a month, a year. When a customer continues to buy from us over multiple periods, however, we can begin to paint a picture of the total value the business gets from the customer. This is often called the lifetime value of a customer and sometimes abbreviated as CLV.

It takes some work to get the numbers we need to calculate our CLV. We need to know how long a customer keeps buying from us and how an average customer spends during that period. Not every business owner knows these numbers, but they are worth finding out. The formula for CLV is this:

$$CLV = Customer\ Lifetime \times Average\ Customer\ Sales$$

Where:

$$Average\ Customer\ Sales = \frac{Total\ Sales}{Number\ of\ Customers}$$

It is important that we measure the inputs (Lifetime and Sales) using the same time value. That is, if our customer lifetime is expressed in years, then the average customer sales should also be measured over a period of one year.

This formula results in a sales amount—how much the average customer spends before leaving. Just as we did in the prior example, however, it is more useful to quickly convert that to gross profit by multiplying by the gross margin percentage:

$$Customer\ Lifetime\ Gross\ Profit = CLV \times GM\%$$

What can we do with this number? Plenty. The lifetime gross profit (LGP) of an average customer helps us determine how much we can spend on key items like marketing and sales. If each customer generates just $100 in gross profit, then there is no sense in sending each customer a $200 holiday gift.

Tip: Now we can compare Customer Lifetime Gross Profit to a prior formula, "Customer Acquisition Cost." Using these two numbers, we can analyze every sales and marketing campaign to be sure that the cost to find a new customer (the Customer Acquisition Cost) is never more than a fraction of what the customer will return to us in gross profit (the Customer Lifetime Gross Profit).

What Is the Average Order Size?

Knowing the average order size can be vital in any business that provides shipping, delivery, packaging, or any other add-on to an order. Online retailers, for example, might be tempted to provide free shipping—adding a few dollars' expense to each order. If the average order size is large enough, the gross margin may be sufficient to cover the cost of shipping. If it is not, then providing free shipping is inviting trouble.

$$Average\ Order\ Size = \frac{Total\ Sales}{Number\ of\ Orders}$$

Using our common-sized P&L, we can again calculate the average gross profit on an order:

$$Gross\ Profit\ on\ Average\ Order = Average\ Order\ Size \times GM\%$$

It is this number that we would compare to the cost of any new marketing offer, such as free shipping. Before we approve the expense, we should at least be sure that the gross profit per average order is more than the new expense. Using the same process, we could also use the gross profit per average order to evaluate sales commissions, rebate offers, or "SPIFs" (Sales Promotion Incentive Funds). In Chapter 12, we will see how knowing gross profit per order and customer lifetime value changed the way one company marketed and sold their products. These numbers should always be considered in any discussion of marketing and sales strategy.

What's Driving the Growth (or Decline) in Sales?

Sales can come from current customers buying more, or from new customers making their first purchase. Knowing which group accounts for our sales (and in what proportion) is a crucial piece of management information. This knowledge can impact every aspect of our business, from marketing to customer service. Encouraging loyalty, for example, is a very different operating strategy from soliciting broadly for new accounts. To understand where our sales come from, we can use the two following ratios.

$$Customer\ Growth = \frac{(Number\ of\ Customers - Customers\ at\ Start\ of\ Period)}{Customers\ at\ Start\ of\ Period} \times 100\%$$

$$Sales\ Growth = \frac{Current\ Sales - Last\ Period\ Sales}{Last\ Period\ Sales} \times 100\%$$

Comparing these two results, we can quickly tell which are growing faster—total sales or number of customers. If we assume that both new and old customers spend about the same amount, then any difference between the customer growth rate and the sales growth rate may indicate that our existing customers are purchasing more, or less.

Note that this comparison can be misleading in businesses that have very different pricing for new and old customers. Charging a new customer a "setup fee" could cause the sales growth to appear larger than the customer growth. Conversely, giving away "one free year" for new accounts could skew the results significantly in the other direction—making it appear that customers were growing even though sales were not. We'll have to take those kinds of pricing variations into consideration when calculating these ratios.

Are We Spending Too Much on Overhead?

A growing business is usually a good thing, but growth can also obscure (*or cause*) a host of problems. When cash is coming in the door and piling up in the bank, it is tempting to go on a shopping spree—hiring more staff, up-fitting the office, or splurging on advertising. Some spending on overhead is unavoidable, of course, but when the rate of new spending is faster than the rate of new income, we can run into problems.

A useful way to measure (and then control) overhead spending is to compare the rates of growth between overhead (OH) and sales. Measure the growth of each and then find the difference between them, as follows:

$$Change\ in\ Overhead = \frac{This\ Period's\ OH}{Last\ Period's\ OH} \times 100\%$$

$$Change\ in\ Sales = \frac{This\ Period's\ Sales}{Last\ Period's\ Sales} \times 100\%$$

Excess OH Spending = Change in Overhead – Change in Sales

If the resulting ratio is positive (greater than 0%), then spending on overhead is increasing faster than sales. Since overhead is a fixed expense (paid out of Gross Profit), overspending in this way will erode our net profit margin (the percentage of net profits).

The danger may not be immediately obvious in a growing company because increases in overhead will not stand out in either the Gross Profit or the Net Profit lines. That is, *the dollar amount of profit may continue to grow, even while the percentage of net profit (i.e., the net profit margin) is shrinking.* Such is the danger of managing rapid growth.

Finally, this basic ratio can be modified to measure the growth of any category of fixed expense—or even the Total Expense line—by substituting those dollar amounts in place of the "Overhead" measures in the equation above.

Do We Have a Good Location for Retail Sales?

Retail businesses have a unique challenge—where a store is located is the single most important decision an owner can make. Retailers tend to assume that paying higher rent will result in better sales. The only way to be sure is to measure the ratio of sales per square foot.

$$Sales\ per\ Square\ Foot = \frac{Total\ Retail\ Sales}{Total\ Retail\ Floor\ Space}$$

This ratio will help to quickly compare two locations, or one location to a benchmark. Further, we can use this ratio in combination with our common-sized P&L to find our gross profit per square foot:

$$Gross\ Profit\ per\ Square\ Foot = Sales\ per\ Square\ Foot \times GM\%$$

Once we know gross profit per square foot, it is a simple matter to look at both rent expense and consider whether the rent (per square foot) is too high relative to the sales and gross profit that the location generates.

Are We in the *Best* Location?

There are a number of ways to judge location—traffic, visibility, convenience, etc.—but none are as straightforward and powerful as measuring profit per square foot.

$$Profit\ per\ Square\ Foot = \frac{Operating\ Profit}{Total\ Square\ Feet}$$

This ratio is useful whether we are in retail, manufacturing, or even a simple office. Because the ratio uses operating profit, it captures the effect of not just rent, but utilities, repairs, insurance, and property tax. If your P&L also captures things like fuel or travel expenses, this ratio might also reflect less obvious expenses like travel time to and from the office.

Where we locate our business is one of the most basic criteria and can have the largest impact on the company's sales and profits. Measuring profit per square foot—and comparing it to similar businesses in other locations—is a good way to judge whether we have settled in the right spot.

Do We Have the Right Equipment? (And Are We Making the Best Use of It?)

Although this sounds like a question for an equipment expert, we can quickly tell how well our equipment is performing just by looking at our financial statements. The Return on Assets Ratio can tell us how well we have selected and deployed our equipment by showing us how much profit we make for each dollar we spend on these assets.

At its root, this is an "efficiency" question. Efficiency ratios look at the business as a whole and help us compare our business to other businesses—and to other uses of capital in general. In this case, we want to know if the money we have invested is giving us a reasonable return. Return on Assets is the first way to measure efficiency (which we also call a "rate of return" and express as a percentage). In a business with few assets, like a consulting practice, for example, this ratio may not be very helpful. For those businesses that need a lot of fixed assets, like a manufacturer, Return on Assets can be a very important ratio. As this ratio increases, it indicates that the firm is able to generate more profits from fewer assets (less investment).

$$Return\ on\ Assets = \frac{Net\ Profit\ after\ Tax}{Total\ Assets} \times 100\%$$

All efficiency ratios can be adapted slightly to better fit a particular circumstance or industry. For example, we might want to compare two printing companies. One uses traditional presses, the other a new digital press. Which one is has a better rate of return on their investment? To make our comparison apples to apples, we would exclude intangible assets like trademarks or patents that do not impact the efficient use of a printing press. The denominator ("Total Assets") thus could be more narrowly defined as "Tangible Assets" by subtracting the balance sheet value of any *intangible* assets.

Should We Keep Investing in Our Company?

Just as the Return on Assets Ratio shows us how much profit we get from buying more equipment (assets), we can measure the return on equity to tell us whether our personal investment in the company is an efficient use of our money.

$$Return\ on\ Equity = \frac{Net\ Profit\ after\ Tax}{Total\ Equity} \times 100\%$$

As business owners, we have many emotional and strategic reasons to invest in our business, but there is only one financial reason to invest (or not): a better return on our capital.

The Return on Equity Ratio tells us whether our business provides a better financial return than, say, a certificate of deposit (CD) at a local bank. If the return on our invested business equity is the same or less than a CD, perhaps we should put our money in the bank instead! (Or, more likely, find a way to make the business more efficient.)

How Healthy Is the Business, Overall?

Most of the ratios we have seen so far tend to describe the current state of affairs or a historical trend. There are ratios, however, that can predict the future—or at least, they can predict certain things about the future, if our business continues down its current path. The most well-known "future-predicting" ratio is called the Altman Z-score.

Edward I. Altman first created the "Altman Z-score" in 1968 to predict bankruptcies at public companies. Since then, Altman has created a version of the model for private companies. Altman is a finance professor at New York University's Stern School of Business (http://www.valuebasedmanagement.net/methods_altman_z-score.html).

The Altman Z-score for private companies is a complex formula of constants and ratios. Let's break it down into its four main components, which we'll simply call A, B, C, and D. Then we'll add those together and analyze the results.

$$A = 6.56 \times \frac{Working\ Capital}{Total\ Assets}$$

$$B = 3.26 \times \frac{Retained\ Earnings}{Total\ Assets}$$

$$C = 6.72 \times \frac{EBIT}{Total\ Assets}$$

$$D = 1.05 \times \frac{Stockholder's\ Equity}{Total\ Liabilities}$$

$$Altman\ Z\text{-}Score = A + B + C + D$$

The key to using the Altman Z-score is putting the numeric result into one of three ranges, which Dr. Altman called the Danger Zone, the Gray Zone, and the Safe Zone. According to Altman's book on this subject, *Corporate Financial Distress* (John Wiley & Sons, 1983), there is a strong likelihood of default (bankruptcy) when a private company scores less than 1.1. The company is likely safe from default with any score greater than 2.6. In between these values, a prediction is hard to make.

How Fast Can the Business Grow?

A marketer might well believe that a company's growth is limited only by the size of the market or how quickly it can acquire customers. A finance person, however, knows that there is a natural limit to how fast a company can *afford* to grow. The financial ratio called Affordable Growth Rate (AGR) presumes that sales can only grow as fast as our assets grow. Based on that, we can calculate the Affordable Growth Rate as follows:

$$Affordable\ Growth = \frac{Net\ Profit\ after\ Tax}{Beginning\ Shareholder's\ Equity}$$

How do we use this result? Affordable Growth Rate is primarily a budgeting and planning tool—particularly for sales projections. A company's AGR is the percentage that sales can grow year over year. If sales are projected to grow faster than the company's AGR, we immediately know that new sources of outside capital are needed. Knowing that it takes profits to fuel sales, however, we might take a more cautious approach. Rather than taking in new investors or expanding our borrowing to fuel projected sales, we might wish to grow profits first and ramp sales later. The more cautious approach helps us avoid excessive borrowing.

Note that AGR contains two important assumptions: First, that profits are kept in the company to fuel growth and not distributed to owners; second, if debt was used in the prior year, then debt will continue to be available in the same *proportion to equity* going forward.

How Long Can the Business Survive without New Sales?

There are hundreds of reasons why a business's sales might suddenly skid to a halt. Regulatory problems, distribution snags, natural disasters, or the death of a key employee are simple examples of situations that could stop sales in a hurry. To measure the impact of such situations, we use a ratio with a very holistic view of the business. Called the Basic Defense Interval (BDI), this ratio measures the number of days that a business can survive without income (or new debt).

$$BDI = \frac{Cash + Accounts\ Receivable}{Operating\ Expenses + Interest + Taxes} \times 360$$

Calculating the BDI may seem morbid, but it's a good measure of a company's staying power. Life is full of surprises, and a business should be prepared to weather a few storms. Keeping track of our BDI is a good reminder that having a bit of excess cash on hand can be a very good thing.

CASH CYCLE RATIOS

We have already discussed the cash cycle in Part 3 of this book. There are three primary ratios used in the cash cycle (see Chapter 10 for a complete description of the cash cycle): each describes how efficiently we use our money. Let's look at the math behind each part of the cash cycle.

For each ratio in this group, it is important to use figures from an annual P&L and the corresponding end-of-period balance sheet. This allows us to create a ratio (through division) that represents a fraction of a year. Multiplying the ratio by 360 (days per year) converts that fraction to a number of days. Let's look at each one again briefly:

Days Receivable Outstanding (DRO)

DRO, also called the Collection Period, is a measure of how long we allow our customers to hang onto invoices before they pay us. The longer we allow customers to take, the longer we go without that cash. Naturally, a shorter period of time (thus a smaller number) is desirable.

$$DRO = \frac{Year\ End\ Accounts\ Receivable}{Total\ Net\ Sales\ during\ the\ Year} \times 360$$

> *Note*: Did you notice how we multiply by 360? Have you already figured out why? This number (360) represents the total number of days in a year. Yes, there are 365 days in a year (or 366 in a leap year), but 360 divides nicely into 12 months of 30 days each. Using 360 is a convenient fiction that accountants and analysts use to ignore complications such as leap years and 28-, 30-, and 31-day months. Of course, 365 works, too, as long as we apply it consistently. Either way, this equation converts a pure fraction (dollars divided by dollars) into days by multiplying by the number of days in the period being measured. Likewise, when measuring monthly ratios, it's generally prudent to standardize on 30 days.

What if we wanted to measure just January's DRO? This requires only two small changes: (1) Use the financial statements from January; and (2) multiply the result by 30 instead of 360. The result would look like this:

$$DRO = \frac{\textit{Jan. 31 Accounts Receivable}}{\textit{Total January Net Sales}} \times 30$$

Because customers pay at different speeds, DRO is most accurate when the period captures many payments from many customers. The longer the period, the more accurate DRO becomes, so DRO is ideally measured over several months or quarters. It is an important number to watch, however, and the change of DRO from month to month or from quarter to quarter can indicate how well a business is collecting its invoices.

By the way, we can safely ignore the fact that January has 31 days. It is just simpler to standardize on 360 days in a year, or 12 equal months of 30 days each.

Days Payables Outstanding (DPO)

DPO is the way to judge how long, on average, we take to pay our vendors. Since we want to hold onto cash as long as possible, this ratio can be said to improve when it increases. There might come a time, of course, when the number grows too large. This would indicate that we are dragging out payments simply because we do not have enough cash in the business to cover our bills. The danger is that the number could grow so large that vendors start to cut us off, or slap us with unreasonable fees.

$$DPO = \frac{Year\ End\ Accounts\ Payable}{Total\ Cost\ of\ Sales\ for\ the\ Year} \times 360$$

Or more generally, as we saw above, we can calculate this for any period as follows:

$$DPO = \frac{Accounts\ Payable\ at\ End\ of\ Period}{Total\ Cost\ of\ Sales\ during\ Period} \times Number\ of\ days\ in\ period$$

DPO can be done over any period, but it will produce the most accurate results when the inputs come from a longer period—a quarter or a year. If a business pays its bills on a very specific and regular schedule, such as invoice date plus 60 days, then the DPO should be the same regardless of which period we look at. A DPO that never changes is a sign of very disciplined management.

Days Sales of Inventory

The third ratio we need to capture for the cash flow cycle measures the value of our inventory—not in dollars, but in days. Just as DRO and DPO tell us the number of days in the collection or payable cycle, Days Sales of Inventory (DSI) tells us how many "days' worth" of inventory we have at current sales levels. The formula for DSI is:

$$DSI = \frac{Year\ End\ Inventory}{Total\ Cost\ of\ Sales\ for\ the\ Year} \times 360$$

This is an interesting and helpful way to look at inventory. It is one thing to say, "We have $20,000 worth of inventory," and quite another thing to say, "We have six months of inventory." The base numbers might be the same, but knowing how long inventory will last helps us plan ahead (maybe way ahead, as in this example).

Since inventory can be very expensive, keeping a minimum amount on hand is essential. If our inventory is, for example, fresh spinach, then of course it would be ridiculous to find ourselves with six months of spinach on hand! For that reason, DSI is a key ratio to keep an eye on.

Note: For convenience we divide by the total Cost of Sales (the denominator) in this formula. To get an even more accurate picture of inventory, we could use the total cost of inventory as the denominator instead. If our COS included a lot of labor or noninventory costs, then using the cost of inventory as the denominator would be more accurate and meaningful. The most important thing, however, is to be consistent. When looking for trends, it is vital that the ratios be calculated in the same way from month to month or from year to year.

The three ratios above can be added together to estimate the cash cycle, which was covered in Part 3 of this book. This is a useful tool for understanding where and how cash is used in our business. Refer back to Chapter 10 for more on the cash cycle.

SUMMARY

☑ Financial ratios can be used to answer many common (and not-so-common) questions about a business.

☑ Ratios can be used to measure employees, customers, operating efficiency, financial performance, and more.

☑ The most common ratio calculations are called "common-sizing," and these show the standard financial statement results as a percentage of a common number (usually as a percentage of total revenue) rather than as dollars.

☑ Anything that can be measured in a business can become part of a ratio, even another ratio. If the thing being measured is important to the success of the business, then it helps to track the ratio results over time.

☑ A company's cash cycle can be calculated using a specific set of ratios. This is a key metric for every business.

12

Analysis in Action

It is one thing to read a book about financial statements and ratios; it is something quite different to apply those ratios in a way that gives us meaningful data and actionable information about our business. In this chapter, we'll meet entrepreneurs who used a combination of financial statements and ratios to identify weaknesses in their business and to solve specific problems. These stories are based on real situations faced by real entrepreneurs, and while the solutions are specific to their situation, the methods they used can be applied to numerous situations.

Before any analysis can be useful, of course, we must have a very deep understanding of the business and our desired business model. It does not make sense to calculate ratios and draw conclusions without a clear understanding of where the business is and where we wish to take it. The solutions worked out by the entrepreneurs in this chapter fit their particular vision for the company they wanted to build. You or I might use the same ratios and analysis to reach very different solutions based on our own vision for our future business.

Ratios can be used to compare strategic alternatives (which business model will return a better profit per employee?), or to fine-tune tactical decisions. Ratios are not, however, a substitute for strategic planning, market research, or innovation. By their nature, ratios describe what is and what has been, far more than they predict what will be in the future. To be useful, ratios and analysis must be guided by our own vision of what *should* be!

With the following stories as an introduction to the power of ratios to diagnose and fix problems in small business, we hope to spark ideas about how ratios can be used in our own businesses.

STORY #1: FINDING NEW OPPORTUNITIES FOR PROFIT

Carey is an accomplished teacher and administrator, so it was no surprise when she opened her own preschool. Within about a year, Carey was able to fill the school with wonderful children from the surrounding neighborhoods. Now, however, the school is at its legal maximum number of students and the building is full. Unfortunately, Carey's P&L is showing a troubling pattern of losses. Since she can't add more students in the current building, Carey decided to look at her pricing. She needs to know what price she should charge students per week in order to turn a profit.

Carey's first effort was to use the Breakeven Gross Margin Ratio to calculate the minimum gross margin needed.

$$Breakeven\ Gross\ Margin = \frac{Total\ Expenses}{Total\ Net\ Sales} \times 100\%$$

Let's look at an example calculation. Here are the key numbers from the weekly financial statements of the Preschool Company:

- Price per student per week: $97.50
- Weekly Net Sales (80 students × $97.50) = $7,800
- Total Expenses = $5,500

Carey's expenses every week run about $5,500. And with 80 children paying $97.50 per week for classes, Carey's net sales are $7,800. In this case, the breakeven gross margin for the preschool looks like this:

$$Breakeven\ Gross\ Margin = \frac{\$5,500}{\$7,800} \times 100\% = 70.5\%$$

Notice that the result tells us gross margin. From our work with common-sizing a P&L, we already know that gross margin is a percentage: gross profit expressed as a percentage of net sales.

$$Gross\ Margin = \frac{Gross\ Profit}{Total\ Net\ Sales} \times 100\%$$

So let's restate the ratio in simpler language. We know that gross margin should be at least 70.5%, so we can also say that gross profit should be at least 70.5% of total sales. Remember, gross profit is total sales less cost of sales.

$$Gross\ Profit = Total\ Net\ Sales - Cost\ of\ Sales$$

The great thing about common-sizing a P&L as we did in previous chapters is that we can now substitute percentages for dollars whenever we want to talk about items on the P&L. In this case, we want gross profit (margin) to be 70.5%, and we know that total net sales is always 100%, so we can quickly see that the cost of sales must be 29.5%.

$$70.5\% = 100\% - Cost\ of\ Sales$$

$$\therefore Cost\ of\ Sales = 100\% - 70.5\% = 29.5\%$$

Now we see that our cost of sales has to be 29.5% of net sales in order to break even—and it must be less than 29.5% of net sales if we want to make a profit. In this case, the preschool can spend just $28.76 on each student each week.

$$29.5\% \times \$97.50 = \$28.76$$

Remember, this tells us what our gross margin *should be*. In order to reach breakeven (or better), we must adjust our *actual* gross margin. That means changing either the price we sell at or the cost we put into each sale.

If this calculation shows that Carey's gross margin is not high enough, what can she do? Plenty. It could be that her particular building is not large enough to house a profitable preschool, or that the market price for preschool care is too low. It could also be that her teachers' wages are too high or she's spending too much on lunch. This one ratio has exposed a host of options for Carey to improve profitability.

STORY #2: DECIDING WHICH CUSTOMERS TO KEEP—AND WHICH TO FIRE

Over the last 20 years, Sandy has built up a nice business managing large events. As often happens, success breeds success. Each job Sandy completed lead to another larger job, and within the last few years, Sandy's average job size has grown quite large. To handle the extra work load, Sandy began hiring more and more people. One aspect of his services includes hiring temporary workers to provide security, vending, ticketing, cleanup, and other duties. Lately, the number of part-time workers needed has grown so large that Sandy has had to add a significant number of full-time staff just to handle the burden of hiring and managing part-time workers!

Adding more full-time staff has really changed Sandy's business, and Sandy's role within the business. The more staff he adds, the less time Sandy spends doing the kind of work he really enjoys—designing and managing events.

Sitting with his financial statements, Sandy decided to do some quick calculations. He wondered if all these extra employees were making the company more efficient or less efficient. His first calculation was the Employee Efficiency Ratio, or simply sales per employee:

$$Employee\ Efficiency\ Ratio = \frac{Total\ Sales}{Number\ of\ Employees}$$

For accuracy, Sandy used monthly financial statements, and calculated the number of full-time equivalent staff members in the office each month. To keep it simple, he ignored all the part-time event staff and looked only at the permanent employees. He ran this ratio for a number of months, during the period that he was adding full-time staff, and he was happy to see that the ratio continued to increase. He wrote down his results as follows:

- January: $65,400 sales/FTE
- March: $69,300 sales/FTE
- June: $78,800 sales/FTE
- August: $122,000 sales/FTE

Great news! Sandy's sales per employee had almost doubled in just eight months, even while he was adding employees. The extra staff clearly allowed him to take larger and larger jobs, generating larger and larger sales. Not only were the jobs larger than before, but the size of the jobs (measured in dollars of sales) was growing faster than the size of his staff (measured in number of FTE employees). With this key piece of information, Sandy began to think that he should continue to add staff and take on bigger jobs.

Before he signed up for more work, however, he ran one more ratio: Profit per Employee. To be sure he was comparing apples to apples, Sandy used the same number of FTE employees and the same monthly results as last time. The equation is this:

$$Profit\ per\ Employee = \frac{Net\ Profit}{Number\ of\ Employees}$$

This time, the results surprised Sandy. His P&L clearly showed that both sales and profits had been increasing over the course of the year. Yet this ratio produced the following results:

- January: $4,300 profit/FTE
- March: $4,200 profit/FTE
- June: $3,800 profit/FTE
- August: $3,700 profit/FTE

According to these results, Sandy's net profit per employee was falling! Sandy realized that this meant his headcount was growing faster than profits could keep up. If he continued to add staff without thinking about profitability, he might eventually overspend on staffing and not have any profits at all.

This started to make more and more sense as Sandy considered his business model. The recent hires had been quite expensive. Larger events required more sophisticated managers, so he had brought on people with advanced project management certifications and graphic design skills as well as executives in human resources, information technology, and accounting. The complexity of his business had exploded—and along with it, the salaries of his office staff. This additional overhead expense was beginning to deteriorate profitability in a big way.

Sandy wanted more information. He wasn't going to just fire all these new staff people because one ratio said profits were slipping. He decided to look at the kinds of jobs he was running. This time he ignored his office staff and looked only at the events themselves—how many part-time people did he have to hire to get the job done? How profitable was each job *per person*?

He ran the same ratios again for each job. Sandy had only the basic financial results of each job: the total price of the job and the gross profits (what was left after all the job-related expenses were paid). Although his ratios called for slightly different numbers, he recognized that for just one job, *price* is the same as sales, and gross profit can substitute as a measure of profits. Moreover, the number of temporary employees needed for each job was a nice way to measure the size of the job. So, pen in hand, Sandy modified the ratios to look like this:

$$Employee\ Efficiency\ Ratio = \frac{Job\ Price}{Number\ of\ Temp\ Workers}$$

And:

$$Profit\ per\ Employee = \frac{Job\ Gross\ Profit}{Number\ of\ Temp\ Workers}$$

When he ran these ratios for each job, he found that the biggest jobs were the least efficient and the least profitable, when measured per employee. His notes looked like this:

EFFICIENCY:
- Smallest Job = $65,400/Temp Worker
- Medium Job = $40,300/Temp Worker
- Biggest Job = $15,600/Temp Worker

PROFIT:
- Smallest Job = $400/Temp Worker
- Medium Job = $300/Temp Worker
- Biggest Job = $250/Temp Worker

There it was, in black and white. The largest jobs required Sandy to hire hundreds of temporary workers, but generated far less in both sales and profit *per person*. Even though the large jobs made it seem as if the company was growing, it was also growing less efficient!

Sandy knew that many of his new office employees were hired to manage the part-time workers on these large jobs. The HR team was constantly recruiting low-wage workers. The IT team struggled to keep each worker connected with an iPhone and a scheduling app. The payroll alone for one large event required the work of three full-time staff just to collect tax forms, proof of citizenship, and time sheets. Keeping up with the large teams of temp workers was going to be a constant drain on Sandy's office staff and might require more and more full-time employees.

Like many entrepreneurs, Sandy started his business to make his own life more fulfilling and more fun. Managing a giant staff, pushing paper around, and worrying about profits were not the reasons he started the Event Company.

With that insight, Sandy decided that "enough is enough." He began turning down the biggest jobs, even when they seemed like a good fit. Over the next few months, Sandy trimmed the staff a bit where needed, and found that he had more time to do the work he enjoyed. As a result, both sales and profits fell back a bit, but the company was far more efficient. In the end, as Sandy focused on efficiency, he began to see profits rise to new levels while he also enjoyed more time off and more satisfaction with the company he had built.

STORY #3: COMPENSATING SALESPEOPLE USING CUSTOMER LIFETIME VALUE AND AVERAGE GROSS MARGIN PER ORDER

We met Chris early in this book. She owns a fast-growing canine services studio where she trains and grooms dogs. Her advanced methods have produced highly specialized working dogs for dozens of people with various disabilities. But her bread-and-butter services are for those people who are passionate about taking their dogs to dog shows and other competitive events. She has over 1,000 customers who show their dogs at various events and come to her for expert grooming and training.

Chris would like to incent her employees with a sales commission for bringing in new accounts. She decided to look at the average order size in order to see how much commission she could pay. She prepared a P&L for the prior 12 months and plugged the numbers into the formula:

$$Average\ Order\ Size = \frac{Total\ Sales}{Number\ of\ Orders}$$

When she was done, she found that the average order was just $47.50. That wasn't very much money to split with the employee who made the sale—a $10 or $20 sales commission did not seem like enough to get people excited.

$$Average\ Order\ Size = \frac{\$774{,}250\ in\ Sales}{16{,}300\ Orders} = \$47.50$$

To make things worse, Chris knew that her young business had a pretty low gross profit per order—just $12. She confirmed this by using her common-sized P&L to calculate the average gross profit on an order:

$$Gross\ Profit\ per\ Order = \$47.50 \times 25.2\% = \$12$$

Even if she paid her employees 100% of the gross profits, she could only afford to pay $12. She needed a new way to look at things.

Chris decided to look at the lifetime value of a customer instead of just the value of a single order. She knew that most of her customers continued to come back month after month—it can take many months of practice to teach a dog to compete at the highest levels, and of course, nothing can stop a dog's hair from growing, so grooming customers were particularly loyal. In fact, some of her clients had been coming to see her every month since she started the business four years prior.

With that in mind, Chris decided to run a lifetime value of a customer (LVC) calculation.

$$LVC = Customer\ Lifetime \times Average\ Customer\ Sales$$

Looking over her list of customers, she found that most had been with her for two years. There were some new customers of course, and there were unfortunate cases when a longtime customer had moved away or their pet had died. Overall, however, she could clearly identify when most customers started working with her and how long they stayed, on average.

Next, all she needed was the average customer sales. Looking back at the P&L she created, she saw that her sales ($774,250) came from 1,450 active customers. Quick math told her that her average customer was spending $534 per year on her services.

$$Average\ Sales\ per\ Customer = \frac{\$774,250\ sales}{1,450\ customers} = \$534$$

Chris was starting to see the bigger picture, and it changed her whole outlook on paying sales commissions. She looked at what she knew:

- The average customer spends $534 per year
- The average customer stays for two years
- Gross margin is 25.2%

With these calculations in hand, Chris now knew both the LVC and the lifetime gross profit of a customer (LGP).

$$Lifetime\ Value\ of\ a\ Customer = \frac{\$534}{year} \times 2\ years = \$1,068$$

$$Lifetime\ Gross\ Profit = \$1,068\ LVC \times 25.2\%\ GM = \$269$$

Now it was clear. Although the first sale only generated $12 in gross profit, the real value of bringing in a new customer was $269 (over two years). Chris decided to offer her people a "$50 bounty" on any new account that they brought in. To make it even more fun, any employee who brought in five new accounts would receive an additional $50 gift card, making the total reward $300.

Under this new plan, Chris was paying $500 for five new customers—but those same customers would contribute approximately $1,068 in sales *each*. Chris was confident that every $500 investment in sales commissions would result (on average) in more than $1,345 gross profit to the business. That's a 4-to-1 return on her money in just two years. Her employees thought it was a great incentive, and the harder they worked to bring in new accounts, the more the business—and the profits—grew.

STORY #4: PRICING FOR PROFIT

We met Pat, who owns a landscaping business, in Chapter 4. Although many landscapers work alone or in small crews, Pat has quickly grown to a $5 million business with 10 crews in the field working every month of the year. Pat's ultimate vision is to double in size. To get there, Pat's crews are installing custom patios, masonry, and swimming pools, along with beautiful lawns, gardens, and other residential landscaping services. The problem Pat has encountered is pricing: he knows that he must include some charges for overhead costs in his bids, but he's not sure how (or how much).

As Pat's landscaping business grows, the problem of pricing only gets worse: the larger the company gets, the more overhead it takes on. Pat already supports an office and office manager, bookkeepers, designers, and crew managers plus a fleet of vehicles, insurance, and all the normal costs associated with running a company. This left Pat with a number of questions:

- How much should I mark up materials?
- Should I use more subcontractors or fewer?
- How much should I mark up subcontractors?
- How do I recover the cost of cars, trucks, and other equipment?

After considering all these questions, Pat tried working out a spreadsheet that would help him to bid on each job. The spreadsheet captured a large number of operational variables, including: how many trip the crews would make to a job site, the gasoline expense to get there, the amount of materials used, delivery charges, and even the cost of hauling off waste. The resulting spreadsheet was accurate, but large and complicated.

Growing tired from having too much data (and not enough information), Pat ditched the big spreadsheet and took a different approach. Instead of worrying about materials, waste, subcontractors, or even gasoline, Pat took a big-picture approach to the problem. His chief goal was to keep his crews busy and the company profitable. Allowing for a few rain days, Pat knew that with 10 crews of three landscapers each, he had about 3,000 man-hours per month of available labor to sell.

$$Total\ Hours = 30\ People \times 100\ Hours\ per\ Month = 3,000\ Hours$$

During those 3,000 hours, the business would have to generate enough money to pay the labor (their salaries) plus all of the overhead. Pat quickly calculated the average hourly price he'd have to charge to recover all his overhead:

$$Minimum\ Hourly\ Rate = \frac{(Monthly\ Labor\ Cost + Fixed\ Costs)}{3,000\ Hours\ per\ Month}$$

Using this ratio, Pat quickly discovered that the price per hour he would have to charge his customers was $97—almost twice the market rate of $50! Clearly he could not keep everyone busy if he could not price the jobs competitively. (Further, if Pat was not able to sell all 3,000 hours, then the price per hour would actually increase to make up for the loss.)

Fortunately, most landscaping jobs called for a mixture of labor and materials, which gave Pat a new way to make money: markup on materials. Any dollars that labor could not make would have to come from markup on materials. This meant that some jobs that did not have enough materials might not be a good fit—Pat's bid would still come out too high to get the job unless he could spread the profit he needed across a large order for materials.

The formulas Pat put together looked something like this:

$$Unrecovered\ Cost = (Minimum\ Hourly\ Rate - Bid\ Rate) \times Hours$$

$$Markup = \frac{Unrecovered\ Costs}{Material\ Costs}$$

For a 100-hour job on which Pat could bid $60 an hour, for example, he would have unrecovered costs of $3,700.

$$Unrecovered\ Cost = (\$97 - \$60) \times 100\ hours = \$3,700$$

In this case, the markup on materials would have to make up the difference. If the job called for only $10,000 of materials, the markup would be 37%.

$$Markup = \frac{\$3,700\ Unrecovered\ Costs}{\$10,000\ Material\ Costs} = 37\%$$

Knowing the markup made it easy for Pat to put together estimates and invoices for customers. Each brick or yard of cement or roll of sod would show up on the invoice at the full value—Pat's price plus 37%.

Finally, when Pat rolled this information together with the more complex spreadsheet, three things happened:

- The calculations became simpler because overhead such as vehicles, equipment, interest, and office expenses were all included in the single number—$97 per hour
- Pat could focus on recapturing other unusual expenses, like the cost to rent unusual equipment or special delivery charges
- Every job became profitable, and so did the company as a whole; since overhead was covered by each job, there was enough money to pay all the bills

The technique Pat used is sometimes called absorption costing, because it spreads all the fixed expenses over the total earning potential of the company. Said another way, the total costs to run the business are "absorbed" into the total potential sales. This is an excellent way to be sure that the business as a whole can be profitable.

Tip: Absorption costing is related to the concept of breakeven gross margin, which we calculated in Chapter 11. Absorption costing turns gross margin on its head: calculating what total price (and therefore margin) we must sell at in order to cover expenses (which is the definition of breakeven).

In this chapter we've met several entrepreneurs who have used financial and operating ratios in various ways to solve real problems. Now let's turn our attention to people outside the business—investors and bankers—and see how they might use these tools to answer their own unique set of questions.

SUMMARY

☑ Financial ratios can be used to solve real-world problems and answer important business questions.

☑ Financial ratio analysis can lead to better strategic decisions, but ratios by themselves do not create strategy—they merely help an owner or manager measure results and identify strengths and weaknesses of various business systems.

☑ Calculating a single financial ratio is often not enough. Complex business problems often require using the results of one ratio to feed the inputs of another.

☑ Ratios can expose problems and measure the impact of decisions. Tracking results over time is an important way to know whether business management decisions are helping or hindering the business.

13

How Bankers and Investors Evaluate a Business

We've focused so far on evaluating our own business by using ratios. Business owners, however, are not the only ones interested in the health and prospects of their business. Outsiders, especially bankers and investors, will have an interest in evaluating our business, too. Whenever an entrepreneur seeks outside capital, it is useful to see the business from the view of a financier and be able to talk about our business in a way that they will understand and appreciate.

Fundamentally, there are only two sources of financing: debt and equity. Debt includes any kind of loan, whether from a bank or any other lender. Equity includes any investment that includes stock or ownership of the company. Understandably, lenders and equity investors are looking for very different things: Lenders are looking for strong cash flow that will enable easy repayment of debt; an equity investor, meanwhile, may be much more interested in how fast the company can reach profitability—even if cash flow is poor.

Both lenders and investors rely on financial ratio analysis, but for very different reasons: when a bank evaluates financial ratios prior to approving a loan, they are looking for indications of financial strength or weakness; an equity investor may use financial ratio analysis to find out where and how much capital should be spent. Both types of investors care deeply about risk, and financial ratio analysis can tell them a great deal about the type and degree of risk inherent in a business.

A well-prepared entrepreneur will use the appropriate financial ratios for each group, describing the business in the way the lender or investor needs and expects to see it. Let's look at how we do that, beginning with lenders.

LENDERS AND THE FOUR Cs OF CREDIT

Although it may seem like bankers do a lot of financial analysis before approving a loan, most lenders worry about just a few criteria. The four Cs of credit are the primary thing every banker looks at:

- *Capacity*: Does the business generate enough cash to repay the loan?
- *Collateral*: If the business fails to repay the loan, what asset will the business forfeit? (For example, a house is collateral for a home mortgage.)
- *Capital*: In addition to the collateral, where else can the bank look for payback? Does the entrepreneur have personal assets or savings that could be used to repay the bank?
- *Character*: Is the business owner trustworthy and reliable—and is this evidenced by a good personal credit score?

Capacity: Debt Service Coverage Ratio

The first of the four Cs of credit (above) is capacity, and the primary measure of a company's capacity—or ability to repay a loan—is the Debt Service Coverage Ratio (DSC). The DSC is the key formula a bank uses to determine if the business generates enough cash each month or year to safely make the needed payments. To find your DSC, use the following formula:

$$DSC = \frac{Cash\ Flow\ from\ Operations}{Total\ Loan\ Payments\ during\ Period}$$

Remember, the numerator (Cash Flow from Operations) is a number you can get directly from the statement of cash flows. Most banks say that a DSC of 1.25 is sufficient to qualify for a loan. A DSC of 1.25 means that there is at least $1.25 of cash available from operations for each $1.00 of loan payments to be made.

Collateral and Capital: What We Give Up

There is not much analysis involved in these two Cs. For the small business, collateral and capital are simply the assets owned by the company and the entrepreneur, respectively. It is common—almost universal, really—that a bank uses everything we own to secure the loan. If we purchase a piece of equipment, that equipment may be the collateral; but in addition, a bank will ask for a "blanket lien" and a "personal guarantee," which mean simply that everything the business owns, and everything the entrepreneur owns, could be seized and sold to make good on the loan.

For mortgages, construction, and equipment loans, the only ratio used to calculate collateral is the Loan to Value (LTV). That ratio is:

$$LTV = \frac{Loan\ Amount}{Value\ of\ Collateral} \times 100\%$$

Bankers will want to know that the collateral behind the loan is worth at least as much as the loan. In most cases, bankers expect this ratio to come out at 80% or less. There is no other calculation associated with "capital"—it is simply everything else that could be used to guarantee the loan.

Character: Know the Business, Know Ourselves

It is vital that we go further in our understanding of how a loan will impact our business and how we will repay it. With a deeper understanding we also have the chance to create a great "loan package" for the bank: a written financial analysis of the loan repayment and a credible story of how the loan will be used and repaid. Showing the bank that we possess a deep understanding of our own business, our finances, and our ability to repay the loan—even for a small loan—demonstrates good character (the second C from the four Cs above). It is true that character is judged by more than a single loan application (for example, building a solid relationship with the bank over time can weigh heavily in our favor), but a great loan application demonstrates that we care about the fundamentals of our business—financial, operational, and strategic.

Part of a complete analysis (for the bank or for ourselves) might include one or more of these three other ratios: Times Interest Earned; Fixed Charge Coverage; and Total Debt to EBITDA. Let's take a look at each of these.

Times Interest Earned and Fixed Charge Coverage

Interest on a loan and lease payments are two types of "fixed charges"—the amounts a business is obligated to pay on loans and leases. We want to be sure that our business has plenty of cash flow to cover these known expenses on a month to month basis, so we first calculate the Times Interest Earned.

$$Times\ Interest\ Earned = \frac{EBIT}{Total\ Interest\ Expense}$$

Note that this ratio should be used as a *forecast*. That means the denominator (interest) is the total interest expense the company will have after the new loan is made. To be conservative, EBIT is usually assumed to be the actual EBIT from the most recent period. Since we are "telling a story" for the lender, however, we might project an EBIT that takes into account having used the loan money in the business. In any event, a banker is hoping to see that the company has earned quite a bit more than enough to cover the interest expense on all its loans. The larger TIE is, the more buffer the company has to weather problems while still making minimum payments on debt.

Knowing we can cover interest payments is one quick way of judging whether the company has taken on too much debt. There are other types of debt, including leases, which do not generate interest expense, however. If our business has substantial lease payments that must be made each month, a better ratio to use is the Fixed Charge Coverage. This is essentially the same equation, with lease payments added to both the numerator and the denominator.

$$FCC = \frac{EBIT + Lease\ Payments}{Interest + Lease\ Payments}$$

Note that by convention, we use EBIT (Earnings Before Interest and Tax) as a simple substitute for cash flow. Unlike the narrow margin allowed in the Debt Service Coverage ratio (above), we hope that the FCC ratio shows a higher multiple. Multiples of 3 to 5 might be expected in a healthy small business.

Total Debt to EBITDA

One of the largest dangers to a small business is to take on too much debt. Bankers call this being "over-leveraged." The ratios above measure our ability to pay the absolute minimum from our cash flow.

Those three ratios (DSC, TIE, FCC) give us a good idea of how easy it will be to meet our debt obligations and whether we can continue to do so even if our business runs into trouble.

A different—and perhaps better—way to look at debt is to compare the total debt to our profit and/or cash flow. The Total Debt to EBITDA Ratio does just that:

$$Total\ Debt\ to\ EBITDA = \frac{Total\ of\ All\ Loans\ and\ Leases}{EBITDA}$$

Note: Recall that EBITDA (Earnings Before Interest, Taxes, Depreciation, and Amortization) is a measure of profitability. Additionally, because EBITDA is free from noncash factors (depreciation and amortization are means of accounting for the cost of assets, but do not reflect actual cash used), EBITDA is commonly used as a stand-in for operating cash flow.

Comparing total debt to EBITDA gives a business owner (and a banker) a look at the bigger picture. We can think of this ratio as answering the question, "How many years would it take to pay off all our debt?" That's a poignant way to think about debt!

Working with Lenders

These three ratios are generally grouped together under the label "liquidity ratios" because they tell a lender how easily a company will be able to repay debt. The more liquid a company is, the more cash is available for loan payments and the less likely the company is to default.

Ratios alone, however, are not nearly enough to justify taking on (or making) a loan. A good manager or lender wants to know the story behind the loan. Any loan application or discussion with a lender should answer qualitative questions like: What will the loan pay for? How will the loan change or improve the business? Will this particular loan be enough to accomplish the business goals, or are we also looking for other sources of funding?

Keep in mind that lenders are naturally conservative animals—they want to know that the company will benefit from the loan, but also that it is not being used in a high-risk way. Lenders are looking for clear, well-reasoned answers to these questions, along with ratios that demonstrate a good level of liquidity.

EQUITY INVESTORS AND CAPITALIZATION

We've seen how lenders look for liquidity. Equity investors, on the other hand, are not looking to be repaid (at least not immediately). For an equity investor, payback comes when the business is successful, grows rapidly, and/or shows increasing profits. Growth (and profits) make the equity of the company more valuable, so an equity investor will use financial ratio analysis to look for signs of past growth and opportunities for (or limits to) future growth. Equity investors are owners after all, so their goals are going to be in line with our goals. Any analysis that we find interesting is likely to also be of interest to an equity investor. The ratios in Chapter 11 cover most of the issues that an equity investor will want to discuss, so let's review them just briefly here.

Sales Ratios as an Indicator of Growth

Since growth means increasing sales, an equity investor will spend time looking at various sales ratios. Of particular interest will be: the *cost of customer acquisition*, *lifetime value of a customer*, and *average sale size*. An equity investor is likely to calculate these ratios for the company's historical results and project them into the future. It is up to us to show investors how their capital can be used to significantly improve the company's performance as measured by these key growth ratios.

Efficiency and Return

More sophisticated investors will turn to the company's balance sheet and calculate our efficiency ratios, including the *return on assets* and *return on equity*. Since an investor's money is additional equity, the Return on Equity Ratio is going to be of particular interest. Can the business use his equity efficiently to create more sales? How much growth can he expect from his contribution to equity? If the money is used to purchase assets, what return might that produce? These are all questions that can be answered with the efficiency ratios we explored in Chapter 11.

Calculating Ownership

There are two investor questions that cannot be answered by standard financial ratios: "How much of the company do I own now?" and "How much will I own later?" These questions are not as straightforward as they may appear. Answering accurately requires that we know how much equity (stock) others already own, and how much more equity will be sold in the future. With that information, we can create a capitalization table and calculate the answers (or likely answers). Let's take a look at what a capitalization table is and how to make one.

THE CAPITALIZATION TABLE

Capitalization, in this case, means the value of owners' contributions to the company. In other words, how much money has been paid into the company by stockholders, and what percentage of the company does each own? A capitalization table, or cap table, is the standard way of listing the owners of a company and their relative contributions. A cap table is not a financial statement, per se, but it is an important document that entrepreneurs should maintain at all times. Company ownership is an important consideration in many situations, so an up-to-date cap table is vital.

What a Cap Table Contains

At its simplest, a cap table is a list of owners and their contributions. See the example in Table 13.1. The minimum column heading should include: Name, Shares Owned, Investment, Percentage Ownership, and Current Value.

More complex capitalization tables demonstrate the effect of employee stock ownership plans, future rounds of investment, and multiple "classes" of stock. Table 13.2 is a much more sophisticated capitalization table showing the effect of two rounds of investment. Notice how the founder has the same number of shares, but his ownership percentage has declined as other investors buy in. This effect is called "dilution."

> *Note*: Company stock gives the holder certain rights. A company can choose to issue different classes of shares, each of which gives the owner different rights. As an example, class "A" shares may have the right to vote on corporate resolutions, while class "B" shares may not. Class "B" shares may, however, have a guaranteed dividend rate, while "A" does not.

The calculations that are going on inside a capitalization table are not difficult. In fact, many of them resemble the work we've done with fractions, or ratios. Let's build a cap table from scratch so we can see what happens. Table 13.3 is a blank cap table that we can fill in together.

1. Start by listing the names of all investors down the left-most column. The list should be chronological, with the founder listed first and the most recent investor at the bottom of the list. If any person invested more than once, include each purchase as a separate line.
2. After each person's name, put the total number of shares each person bought (column 2) and the dollar amount invested (column 3).
3. At the bottom of columns 2 and 3, total up the number of shares and dollars.
4. Under the "Percentage Ownership" heading, we'll calculate the percentage of the company controlled by each person today. To do this, we need a simple calculation: the number of shares held by the individual, divided by the total number of shares held by everyone on the list (X% = my shares / everyone's shares).
5. Finally, go to the "Current Value" column. This is trickier. The current value changes each time someone makes a new investment, so look at the most recent investor. Calculate how much that one investor paid per share (price per share = dollars invested/shares purchased). Multiply the latest per share value by the shares held for each person on the list, and enter the result in the Value column.
6. Total up the Current Value column to see the total value of the business.

We've just created a basic capitalization table that describes our company's current ownership structure. With this knowledge, we can tell both current and potential equity investors what percentage of the business he owns or will own. Let's look at an actual example of how this works.

Tip: For multiple rounds of capital, things get tricky. Download a much more complex capitalization table at http://bit.ly/W8bP36.

Table 13.1. Simple Capitalization Table

CAPITALIZATION TABLE		
Owners	**Initial Shares**	**Initial Ownership**
Common Stock		
David Smith	50,000	29%
John Jones	50,000	29%
Steve Johnson	10,000	6%
Employees Options	10,000	6%
Charlotte Angel Capital Fund	5,000	3%
Monterey Venture Partners	5,000	3%
Preferred Stock		
Charlotte Angel Capital Fund	15,000	9%
Monterey Venture Partners	15,000	9%
Global Venture Fund	15,000	9%
Total Shares	175,000	100%

Table 13.2. Complex Capitalization Table

<table>
<tr><td colspan="10" align="center">CAPITALIZATION TABLE</td></tr>
<tr>
<th>SEED</th>
<th>Initial Shares</th>
<th>Initial Ownership</th>
<th>New $ Invested</th>
<th>New Shares</th>
<th>Total Shares</th>
<th>SEED Owner-ship %</th>
<th>SEED Voting %</th>
<th>"A" Owner-ship %</th>
<th>"A" Voting %</th>
</tr>
<tr><td>Common Stock</td><td></td><td></td><td></td><td></td><td></td><td></td><td></td><td></td><td></td></tr>
<tr><td>Partner #1</td><td>50,000</td><td>50%</td><td></td><td></td><td>50,000</td><td>35%</td><td>35%</td><td>26.3%</td><td>26.3%</td></tr>
<tr><td>Partner #2</td><td>50,000</td><td>50%</td><td></td><td></td><td>50,000</td><td>35%</td><td>35%</td><td>26.3%</td><td>26.3%</td></tr>
<tr><td>First Round VC Investor</td><td>0</td><td>0%</td><td>$6,000,000</td><td>42,857</td><td>42,857</td><td>30%</td><td>30%</td><td>22.5%</td><td>22.5%</td></tr>
<tr><td>Employees Options</td><td>0</td><td>0%</td><td></td><td></td><td>0</td><td>0%</td><td>0%</td><td>0.0%</td><td>0.0%</td></tr>
<tr><td>Total Common</td><td>100,000</td><td>100%</td><td>$6,000,000</td><td>42,857</td><td>142,857</td><td>100%</td><td>100.00%</td><td>75.00%</td><td>75.00%</td></tr>
<tr><td>Imputed Share Price</td><td>$140</td><td></td><td></td><td></td><td></td><td></td><td></td><td></td><td></td></tr>
<tr><td>Post $ Value = $20,000,000</td><td></td><td></td><td></td><td></td><td></td><td></td><td></td><td></td><td></td></tr>
<tr><td>"A" ROUND</td><td></td><td></td><td>New $ Invested</td><td>New Shares</td><td>Total Shares</td><td></td><td></td><td></td><td></td></tr>
<tr><td>Preferred Stock</td><td></td><td></td><td></td><td></td><td></td><td></td><td></td><td></td><td></td></tr>
<tr><td>Angel</td><td></td><td></td><td>$1,000,000</td><td>4,762</td><td>4,762</td><td></td><td></td><td>2.5%</td><td>2.5%</td></tr>
</table>

(continued)

Table 13.2. (Continued)

CAPITALIZATION TABLE

SEED	Initial Shares	Initial Ownership	New $ Invested	New Shares	Total Shares	SEED Owner-ship %	SEED Voting %	"A" Owner-ship %	"A" Voting %
Corporate Partner			$2,000,000	9,524	9,524			5.0%	5.0%
VC			$7,000,000	33,333	33,333			17.5%	17.5%
Total Preferred			$10,000,000	47,619	47,619			25.0%	25.0%
Total, Fully Diluted	100,000				190,476			100.0%	100.0%
Imputed Share Price	$210								
Post $ Value =	$40,000,000								

195

Table 13.3. Fill-in-the-Blank Capitalization Table

1 Stockholder Name	2 Shares Purchased	3 Dollars Invested	4 Percentage Ownership	5 Current Value
——	——	——	——	——
——	——	——	——	——
——	——	——	——	——
——	——	——	——	——
——	——	——	——	——
——	——	——	——	——
——	——	——	——	——
——	——	——	——	——
——	——	——	——	——
——	——	——	——	——
TOTAL		$	100%	$

Slicing the Pie

Tracey was an engineer and product designer. When he invented a revolutionary new medical device, he formed a company with 100 shares of stock and found a group of doctors that were anxious to invest. Together, a group of doctors contributed $1 million and owned 40 shares, or 40% of the business. Tracey kept 60 shares, or 60% of the business, for himself. Knowing just this much, we can take a shortcut to valuation of the business as a whole:

$$Total\ Business\ Value = \frac{Last\ Investment}{Last\ Percentage\ Purchased}$$

$$\therefore\ Total\ Business\ Value = \frac{\$1\ million}{40\%} = \$2.5\ million$$

$$\therefore\ Price\ per\ Share = \frac{\$2,500,000}{100\ shares} = \frac{\$25,000}{share}$$

After a few years, the company had grown and needed more capital. Tracey found one angel investor who was willing to invest $500,000 into the business. To start the negotiations, Tracey offered the new investor stock at the same *price per share* as prior investors: $25,000. At that rate, Tracey would issue the new investor 20 new shares ($500,000 / $25,000 = 20), and the investor would have owned 16.6% of the business.

$$New\ Ownership = \frac{New\ Shares}{Old\ Shares + New\ Shares} \times 100\%$$

$$\therefore New\ Ownership = \frac{20}{100 + 20} \times 100\% = 16.66\%$$

After some negotiation, the investor said she would invest only if she could purchase 20% of the company. Since the investor was not willing to pay any additional money, her terms meant a reduction in the price of the shares and selling more shares to the investor. To figure how much the new valuation was, and how many shares to issue, Tracey had to go back to our first equation and do some quick math:

$$Total\ Business\ Value = \frac{\$500,000}{20\%} = \$2.5\ million$$

Ouch. Tracey realized that although the investor was contributing a half-million dollars in cash, the actual value of the business did not change!

Note: When considering an equity investment, we talk about the value of the business before the investment (*pre-money valuation*) and after the investment (*post-money valuation*). The difference is simply the amount of money invested. That is, pre-money valuation + cash invested = post-money valuation.

Without an increase in the business valuation, the *current value* of each (old) investor's shares would go down. That is, they would own the same number of shares, but they would own a smaller percentage of the total business—and their ownership was worth less than it was before the new investor.

Now Tracey was worried about his first investors—the doctors—and exactly how much this transaction might affect their ownership (and his own). By issuing 20% more stock, everyone's share of the business declines. (This is called dilution.) Tracey needed to know how many shares to issue to the new investor, and what the percentage ownership would be for each current investor. Tracey started by calculating the new total number of shares needed in order for the new investor to own 20%. He did this by dividing the current number of shares by the percentage that current investors would own after the new shares were issued. Since the new investor wanted 20%, he knew that together, he and the old investors would own 80% of the new total. The equation looks like this:

$$Total\ Shares = \frac{Total\ Current\ Shares}{(100\% - Percent\ Sold\ to\ New\ Investor)}$$

$$\therefore Total\ Shares = \frac{100\ shares}{(100\% - 20\%)} = 125\ shares$$

$$\therefore New\ Shares = 20\%\ of\ 125 = 25\ shares$$

> Note that the investor's ownership is always calculated using the post-money valuation. That means that if the investor wants to buy 20%, she gets 20% of the business after the transaction. New shares have to be issued from the company to the investor. (That is, the investor is *not* buying 20% of the *existing* stock, but rather 20% of the *total* ownership.)

The new investor would receive 25 new shares. The total number of shares after the transaction became 125, and the old owners held 80% of those (or 100 shares) collectively. Everything was working out.

Now, however, there were 125 shares where there had only been 100 before, so each original investor owned a smaller percent of the whole. Tracey's ownership was now 60 of 125 shares, or just 48%. The original investors still owned 40 shares, but now those shares represented just 32% of the outstanding stock. Tracey calculated this dilution as follows:

$$Diluted\ Ownership = \frac{Shares\ Held}{New\ Total\ Number\ of\ Shares} \times 100\%$$

$$\therefore Doctors'\ Diluted\ Ownership = \frac{40}{125} \times 100\% = 32\%$$

In the end, Tracey took the investor's offer. Happily, Tracey was able to grow the business substantially by using the investor's money to build an international sales team. Once the medical devices began to sell in Europe and Asia, the company became quite profitable and the value of the business increased dramatically. Tracey began paying small dividends to all of the stockholders, and hoped to soon sell the entire business for $25 million. If that happens, the stockholders will truly have made a great return on their investment.

SPEAKING THEIR LANGUAGE

Financial ratio analysis is truly the first language of investors and bankers. More than any concern for an entrepreneur's character, and no matter how much an investor likes us or wants to help, the company must demonstrate solid financial fundamentals.

Speaking to an investor or banker without a well-prepared set of financial statements is like venturing into a foreign country without a dictionary—we're not likely to get very far. A complete understanding of the language of finance is not necessary, of course, but knowing the basics is absolutely vital to building a relationship with a banker or investor. When we head to the banker's office, there is no substitute for being prepared with a complete, accurate, and up-to-date set of financial statements, along with a few of the financial ratio calculations we've explored above. Once the basics are out of the way, a banker will want to talk about our plans for the future; this is the subject of the next chapter, where we will cover how to see into the future using a business dashboard.

SUMMARY

☑ There are only two kinds of capital in a business: debt and equity.

☑ Lenders and equity investors will use financial ratio analysis to learn more about our business.

☑ Although they are both trying to minimize risk, lenders and equity investors have fundamentally different goals and will want to know different things about the business.

☑ Lenders are concerned with liquidity and cash flow, which is an indication of how easily a company can repay a loan.

☑ Liquidity and cash flow ratios include the Debt Service Coverage Ratio, which most lenders say should be greater than 1.25.

☑ Lenders also look at the "Four Cs of Credit"—Capacity, Collateral, Capital, and Character. A small business owner's personal finances are as important as those of the business.

☑ Equity investors are more concerned with growth, which may eventually lead to a higher value for the business (and their ownership share).

☑ A capitalization table is a supplemental financial statement that describes who owns the company and how much it is worth.

☑ A capitalization table can be a very simple list of investors, or a very complex spreadsheet that can calculate future ownership scenarios.

☑ Dilution is the current owner's reduction in percentage ownership that results from adding new shareholders (and new shares).

Part 5

MANAGING BY THE NUMBERS

14

Dashboards

So far we've discovered hundreds of ways to look at the results of operating our business—measuring, recording, and calculating the financial outcome of our work. By themselves, however, measurements and mathematics are not going to improve our business. Financial statements and ratios are important signposts along the road to a bigger, more profitable, and more sustainable business—but what an entrepreneur really needs is a map.

Financial statements alone tell us only where we've already been. A map tells us two things that are even more important: where we are now, and where we are going. There are three fundamental ways to make historical financial statements into something more forward-looking: dashboards, forecasts, and budgets. We'll cover each of them and discuss how to use them to guide the management and development of our business. In this chapter, let's start with dashboards.

Like the dashboard in a car, a business dashboard is a tool that tells us how things are going. If we are worried about the engine overheating, we have a temperature gauge. If we want to know whether we are likely to get a speeding ticket, we glance at the speedometer. All the car's vital systems can be displayed on the dashboard—oil, water, gasoline, RPM, distance, and even the direction of travel. A well-constructed business dashboard can likewise tell us a great deal about the function and health of our business.

DASHBOARD BASICS

In past chapters and examples, we've seen how to use financial results and ratios to understand what is going on beneath the surface of our business. The next step in any serious analysis of a business is to chart results over time. A dashboard is the perfect way to report financial results over multiple periods. Although there are complex dashboards driven by powerful software (which we will explore later in this chapter), a simple dashboard might be nothing more than a bar chart. The point of a great dashboard is not to introduce complexity or confusion, but rather to show the key metrics in a business and how those metrics change over time.

TIGER—THE CHARACTERISTICS OF A GREAT DASHBOARD

- *Time*—results are shown over several periods
- *Impact*—the metrics displayed can be controlled through management decisions
- *Goals*—results are shown relative to a business goal
- *Ease*—the metrics must be easy to measure and to understand
- *Relationships*—interrelated metrics are shown in a way that their relationship becomes obvious

There are five characteristics of a great dashboard, which are easy to remember by using the word TIGER, as shown in the list above. Let's look at how to create a dashboard that includes these five qualities.

> *Tip*: A great dashboard should be simple, be easy to read, and capture only the most important and controllable metrics of a business. It must also show how these metrics change over time and how they are related to each other. Remember the word TIGER: Time, Impact, Goals, Ease, Relationships.

Time

Imagine printing our financial statements at the end of each month (a good practice, by the way). Now imagine comparing each line of those financial statements across the entire year. The top line, *Sales*, for example, is an important metric to measure on a regular basis. If we can chart our sales—make a simple bar chart by comparing monthly results side by side—we end up with a simple dashboard that actually tells us a lot about our business. Figure 14.1 shows how one business has a very seasonal income—higher in the summer and over holidays, but lower in

Figure 14.1. A Simple Seasonal Dashboard

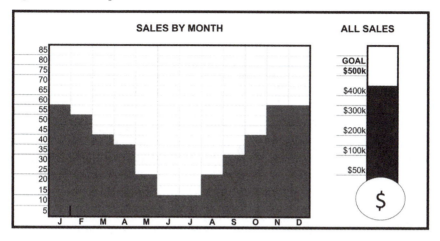

the fall and winter. This simple dashboard shows both month-to-month sales and a goal-driven thermometer graph of the same information. Just knowing that the business is seasonal can help us make important management decisions. No single financial statement can show us this seasonality, but this key piece of information becomes glaringly obvious when our dashboard plots a single metric on a regular basis over multiple time periods.

Monthly sales figures are a good example for a bar chart because we are used to talking about total sales per month. Keep in mind, however, that a dashboard can reflect changes in conditions over any time period we choose. Just as the car dashboard is continuously monitoring the state of the engine, our dashboard can measure figures monthly, weekly, or hourly if that is practical and necessary. A manufacturer might measure hourly output, while a homebuilder may choose to plot quarterly home starts. Whatever periodicity we choose, it is important to stick to it. Regular reporting is key to getting reliable results.

Impact

So far, our simple dashboard has only one figure—monthly sales. Eventually it may have many more (and we'll discuss how to select them later in this chapter). Whatever metrics make their way onto our dashboard must meet the impact test: can we affect the metric through our action as managers? If we have no hope of ever impacting the metric, then it may not be appropriate to chart it.

It would not make sense, for example, to chart our monthly office rent if that expense is fixed by a long-term contract. No amount of good management will impact rent on an ongoing basis. Likewise, measuring arbitrary figures like "miles employees drive to work" will simply distract us from the more important issues.

Goal Driven

Besides showing actual results over time, a dashboard can also serve as a reminder of our larger business goals, such as total annual sales. Notice that the last illustration has both a bar graph of sales and a "thermometer" graph, showing the total sales for the year accumulating toward an annual goal of $500,000. Adding a goal-driven component to a dashboard puts the results into perspective, creates a greater sense of progress, and keeps us focused on the bigger picture. Remember that our analogy was that of a map: Plotting goal-driven metrics is a great way to make a simple dashboard that reminds us of where we are now *and* where we are going.

There are many ways to depict goals within our dashboard. By nature, dashboards are visual, so the more obvious the goal appears, the better. The thermometer is a common way to show how results accumulate over time. Sales goals could also be charted for each month—as either a flat-line average or a seasonally adjusted goal for each month. In that way we would better be able to see whether each month's results were getting us closer to our goal.

There's no rule that says a dashboard has to be dry and serious. Other goal-focused visuals include a race track or "reach the moon" pictorial representation of progress toward a goal. By picturing an annual goal (for example) as a race around a track, we can continuously update our position on the track relative to competitors, to each other, or just to our expected performance. Unlike a thermometer, the race track analogy might even show us moving backward when we've had especially poor results. Not everything in business moves us forward!

Easy

Nobody wants to be saddled with a dashboard that is complex, time consuming to update, or difficult to understand. Our financial statements already give us so much information; we are not trying to create more, but rather to interpret what we already have. The inputs for a great dashboard will come from one of three sources: (1) directly from the financial statements; (2) from the kind of straightforward financial ratios we have calculated in this book; or (3) from measures of productivity, which are easily observable. Where ever they come from, dashboard metrics should be easy to retrieve, and easy to understand.

Examples of "Easy" Dashboard Metrics

- Sales
- Accounts Receivable
- Accounts Payable
- Days Sales Outstanding
- Number of Units Sold
- Number of Errors, or Error Rate
- Number of New Customers Signed Up
- Website Visitors
- Total Overhead Expenses
- Net Profit

Relationships

When a dashboard contains many metrics or ratios, it is important that interrelated metrics are shown in a way that their relationship becomes obvious. Sales should be shown in proximity to accounts receivable, for example, and expenses should be on the same page as the expense ratios they drive.

Those examples are metrics (raw results) that drive ratios. We can also flip that concept on its head and show ratios along with the metrics they drive (or that we hope they drive). Plotting a marketing expense ratio alongside a sales metric might reveal a very interesting relationship.

Just be careful not to confuse an interesting relationship with a business fact. Remember the saying, "Correlation does not a causation make." In other words, the fact that sales go up when we spend more on advertising does not, in itself, mean that increased ad spending is causing the increase in sales. It's important to show the relationship, and equally important to keep asking questions about those relationships.

Putting It All Together

We've seen in the examples and stories in this book how financial ratios can be interrelated and used in combination. Accounts receivable, for example, is a ratio that is directly affected by sales. As sales increase, we also expect AR to increase. If we were plotting AR without plotting sales, our dashboard would only be telling half the story—and not the very useful half.

A great dashboard shows *all* of the data we need to tell the whole story. The more obvious the relationship is, the more careful we should be to show it. Look at Figure 14.2 for an example of how we might draw AR and Sales on the same graph. If our job is to control AR, we'd certainly want to see the data presented in this way so we would know whether increases in AR were due to our lack of collections or simply higher sales. Additionally, the ratio of AR to Sales shows an interesting fact—even though AR is rising rapidly, the percentage of our sales that go into AR is declining!

The key to discovering related metrics is to show a mixture of ratios, raw financial results (from), and operational results. If accounts payable (AP) is a particular concern for our business, then we should track

Figure 14.2. Tracking Sales and Collections

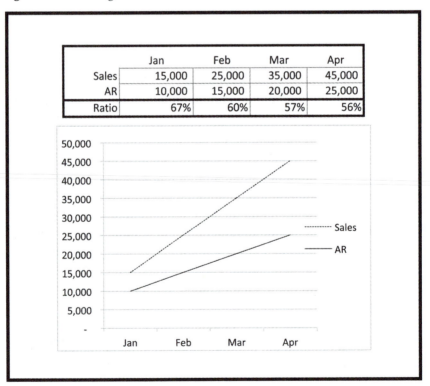

both AP (a ratio) and the expenses that drive AP (a financial result). Likewise, since we can choose to pay our bills more quickly or slowly, the number of days payables pile up becomes an operations issue. To track how well we are managing those operations, measure the days payable outstanding, or DPO (an operational result).

CHOOSING METRICS

It is easy to start recording metrics on a dashboard, but often difficult to know when to stop. There are certainly some companies that are more difficult to control than others, and it's likely that complex companies would require larger, more complex dashboards. There is more danger however, in overcomplicating things than there is in making them too simple. Imagine trying to drive a bicycle while looking at the hundreds of dials and gauges on the dashboard of a 747 jetliner. Even the simple task of riding a bike can be made impossible by confusing the issue with too much information.

How Many Variables

There is an interesting theory to keep in mind as we design a dashboard. The theory—maybe a rule of thumb is a better description—says that humans can best manage no more than seven different data points at once. This is a slight oversimplification of a study by psychologist George A. Miller, published in the journal *Psychology Review* in 1956. Nonetheless, the article, and our rule of thumb, serve to remind us that people do not deal well with complexity (George A. Miller, "The Magical Number Seven, Plus or Minus Two: Some Limits on Our Capacity for Processing Information," *Psychological Review* 101, no. 2 (1955): 343–52, http://www.psych.utoronto.ca/users/peterson/psy430s2001/Miller GA Magical Seven Psych Review 1955.pdf [accessed February 22, 2013]).

Let's forget business for a moment: imagine a dashboard that would help us in our day-to-day lives. If our goal is to lose a few pounds and eat better, what should we measure? Weight is the obvious first pick. But then we want to focus on the controllable inputs, like food and exercise. Within food, however, we have hundreds of variables to choose from. Should we measure sodium, fats, calories, protein, vitamins, cholesterol, fiber, etc.? The number of possible variables could be dizzying, and measuring too many might make it impossible to pick any food that fits our criteria at all! Instead of worrying about every food factor, successful dieters focus on a few key things that they can easily recognize and control, such as total calories, grams of protein, or some kind of arbitrary "points" system.

Now then, back to business. Allowing ourselves to find as many as seven items to measure in the business is a great start. The perfect number may be a few more or a few less, but starting with seven exposes the inner workings of our business without drowning us in the detail. Keep "Miller's Rule of Seven" in mind and much of the complexity will drop away.

Deciding What to Measure

As we've seen, the choices of what to measure are numerous. Prior chapters in this book have offered dozens of metrics, and there are certainly dozens more. Knowing which ones matter can be a trick. Fortunately, we don't have to get it right the first time, and there is no deadline for having the right mix. Plenty of business dashboards morph and change over time—as they should.

The right dashboard metrics are those that will discover weakness in vital systems, evaluate activity, or predict disaster. In other words, a dashboard should answer the following questions:

1. What's always important?
2. What's effective now?
3. What's ahead?

What's Important?

What is important in a business may not be obvious at first, even to the entrepreneur. It's easy to say "sales"—and every owner's dashboard should track sales—but let's go deeper. What is the real "engine" of sales? An online retailer's sales engine is far different from that at a lumber mill or real estate office. Different business models have different key ingredients.

- The online retailer can sell only when people come to the website, so the key metrics might be traffic, number of ads running, or click-through rate
- The lumber mill can sell as much wood as they can cut, so the key to sales might be the tons of wood processed or the board-feet produced

- The real estate brokerage makes money when sales close, but that is driven by the number of homes under contract, or the total value of pending transactions

By identifying the underlying drivers of sales, we can measure and monitor those operational items that we can actually impact or control through careful management. Plotting "sales" is important, but not all that helpful by itself. (Unless we are primarily engaged in direct sales!) A business that drives sales should observe and record the factors that result in sales as well as the sales themselves.

When we correctly identify both the key drivers of sales and measure sales, we get a nice bonus—the ratio of the two. For example, the real estate broker may track the number of houses under contract, and commissions earned. By calculating and tracking the ratio of these two numbers (dollars earned/houses contracted), she can get a feel for how fast houses are closing, how efficient her agents are at finding buyers, and for how much her houses are selling. Tracking each of those specific numbers every month would be arduous. By tracking just the ratio of houses to dollars, the experienced broker can spot trends or anomalies which can direct further investigation. Can you spot the point in Figure 14.3 where the real estate broker might pause to investigate?

The whole purpose of plotting the most important metrics (sales and sales drivers, for example) is to gain deeper insight into the external market and a clearer understanding of the inner workings of our own business. Trends, opportunities, and dangers are hidden by average financial statement, but become crystal clear when we plot a few metrics on a dashboard. By identifying key drivers, the results, and the ratio between them, we will have our thumb on the pulse of the business.

What's Effective Now?

No business strategy lasts forever. As market conditions change, our management response must keep pace. From month to month or from year to year, every business will adjust priorities and direction. The dashboard is the ideal place to monitor the effectiveness of management decisions and their implementation.

If this year's strategic priority is to promote our business through trade shows, the dashboard could measure the number of trade shows we attend (the input) and the number of leads or customers that come from that effort (the result). As above, we can also get the bonus ratio

Figure 14.3. A Real Estate Dashboard

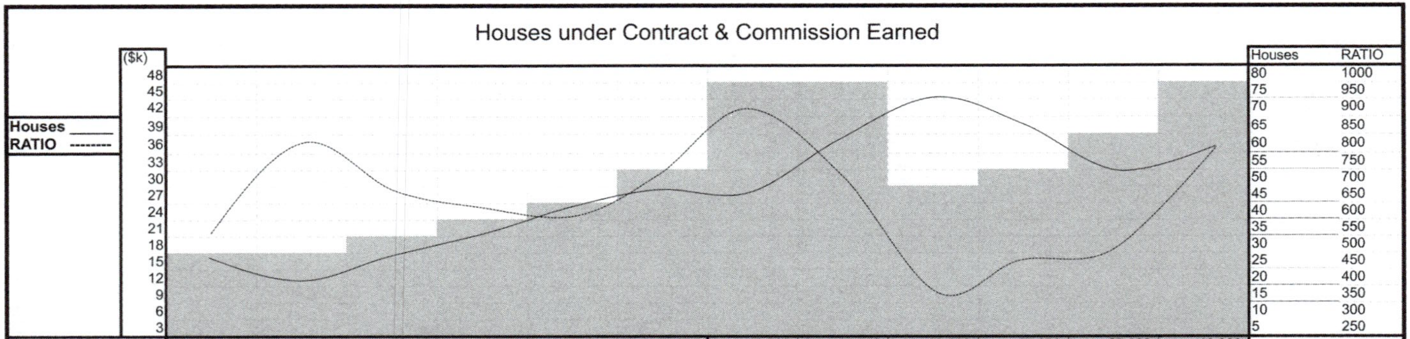

Houses under Contract & Commission Earned

	JAN	FEB	MAR	APR	MAY	JUN	JUL	AUG	SEP	OCT	NOV	DEC
Comm	15,000	17,000	20,000	22,000	26,000	33,000	44,000	44,000	29,000	33,000	27,000	48,000
Houses	27	22	29	35	43	48	47	62	75	68	54	60
RATIO ($ per house)	556	773	690	629	605	688	936	710	387	485	500	800

of these two items to tell us how efficient we are at converting trade show attendance to new leads.

When tradeshows prove to be inefficient at driving sales, perhaps we shift our focus to billboards. The dashboard can shift, too—measuring the total number of cars that pass by our billboard ads and the number of inbound phone calls we receive as a result. (Yes, and the ratio!)

These examples are promotional goals, but a dashboard could just as easily track strategic initiatives for hiring (job ads versus applicants), manufacturing (total units versus defect rate), retail operations (hours open versus net profit), and any other aspect of the business that corresponds to a management initiative.

Part of the fun of owning a business is the ability to experiment with various strategies and find the best fit. Will longer hours increase profit? It's impossible to say for sure, but by trying it out while tracking the metrics—and the ratio—on a dashboard, we'll soon find out.

What's Ahead?

The single most important use of a dashboard is its uncanny ability to predict the future. Next to a crystal ball, a dashboard is the best tool we've got to warn of impending doom. What kind of doom? Let's look at a couple examples.

A cash flow crisis is one flavor of doom that every business faces and every dashboard could predict. There are only a few things that we need to track in order to project a future cash flow crunch: cash on hand; accounts receivable; accounts payable; and sales. The key is not just to know what these values are, but to track the trends. When cash on hand is diving, and accounts payable is increasing, a storm is brewing. If accounts receivable is stagnant or decreasing, we may not be able to bring in more cash in the short term, and the storm is upon us. Finally, if sales are also decreasing, then we have little hope of replenishing either the cash or the AR, and the storm could continue for a long while.

Tracking cash by itself is almost useless. When it's gone, it's too late to do anything about it. Tracking cash *and payables* will give us a little warning—maybe a week or two. We might even have enough time to delay some payments and fix the problem. Tracking cash, payables, *and receivables* will let us see the storm coming three or four weeks away. That's enough time to clamp down on spending, speed up collections, or borrow some money. Finally, when we add sales to the mix, we may be able to see three or six months out (though admittedly, for some businesses the crystal ball gets a bit fuzzy). With that kind of advance warning, we can change course and avoid the storm altogether.

Another crisis that could be avoided by using a dashboard would be backlogs or backorders that result when orders exceed supply. By tracking production or inventory (or both, if that is relevant) alongside unit sales, we can see potential shortfalls coming well before they happen. Measuring sales and inventory monthly may not be often enough if our production or sales environment is highly dynamic. Measuring weekly, daily, or even hourly could be required. That sounds like a lot of work, but running short of stock could shut down an entire manufacturing process, delay sales, or force customers to go elsewhere. The cost of measuring and projecting is nothing compared to the potentially devastating cost of the operation running short of a vital part or supply. A dashboard that tracks units on hand and units sold might be enough to avert disaster far in advance.

Finally, consider a company that uses estimates, sales orders, and invoices. Every new job starts life as an estimate. When the customer agrees to the purchase, the estimate is turned into a sales order. Finally, when the work is completed, the sales order is "closed" and an equivalent invoice is created. This process neatly mirrors what some companies call the "sales pipeline," and can be captured completely within the financial or accounting software.

> *Tip*: Even moderately priced accounting software packages (like QuickBooks Premier) support the use of estimates and sales orders. It's an invaluable tool!

If we then take the amount of business currently in each of these stages, and plot the results over several periods, our dashboard can tell us a lot about the future of our sales. Since every sale starts with an estimate, a decline in estimates now might signal a decline in sales later. Not only can we predict whether sales are going to move up or down, but it is even possible to predict (quite accurately) what the actual dollar value of sales will be in the future. How? By plotting the ratio of estimates to sales. If we have a reasonably steady ratio over time—sales dollars per estimate dollar—then knowing what today's estimate value is can easily translate into a prediction of tomorrow's sales.

This is an example of a "pipeline" situation, and a dashboard can be used to measure inputs and outputs in any similar pipeline. Other pipelines might exist in how we turn parts into finished products, or pay-per-click ads into prospects. There are even pipelines on the expense side: more inventory purchases might cause us to borrow more money, which increases the interest expense. Wherever there is a series of events that leads directly and inevitably to a known conclusion (over time), we can build a dashboard that shows the pipeline's status and gives us a prediction of its future.

The only tricky part about pipeline situations is knowing *when* to take the measurements that we will use in the *ratio*. Let's go back to the estimates that become sales. Since today's sales started as yesterday's estimates, we really want to tag the two numbers at different points in time. Each business will have a different sales cycle (the period of time between creating an estimate and making a sale). When the sales cycle is known, we can create two simple formulas to apply to our dashboard:

$$Sales: Estimate\ Ratio = \frac{End\ of\ Cycle\ Sales}{Beginning\ of\ Cycle\ Estimates}$$

$$Future\ Sales = Today's\ Sales\ Estimates \times Ratio$$

In this case, "Future Sales" is the value of sales that we'd expect to see at the end of a sales cycle starting today.

Tip: Don't let math override business judgment. Every projection should be tempered by our knowledge of what is going on in the rest of the business or marketplace. No input or ratio can capture all the complexities of a business, so it is important that we keep an eye on the "big picture" even as we calculate specific details.

The Magic of Writing It Down

There is something magical about a well-constructed business dashboard. The act of creating a dashboard forces us to find, examine, measure, calculate, and record those things that are most important to our business success. If we update the dashboard often enough, then that process alone should be enough to shape the decisions we make in the day-to-day business operations. The dashboard not only makes our priorities obvious, but also provides a feedback loop so we can see the results of the decisions we've made.

There is one more step that can make the magic of a dashboard even more powerful—printing it out. Ignore the temptation to keep a dashboard file on a PC or website. Instead, print it out. Carry it. Tape it to the wall. Update it with a magic marker. Share it with others. Make it obvious!

Just as a car dashboard is always right in front of us, our business dashboard should be within our field of view as much as possible. The process of creating a dashboard and keeping it in front of us commits us to work on the priorities we've measured. It is amazing what our focused attention can accomplish—and the dashboard is the lens that can focus us on those things that matter most.

SOFTWARE AND WEB-BASED DASHBOARDS

So far we have focused primarily on the Do It Yourself (DIY) version of business dashboards. For charting simple financial results and ratios, there is rarely a need for anything much more than a spreadsheet. As businesses get more sophisticated—and as entrepreneurs grow increasingly comfortable with technology like tablet computers, cloud-based systems, and software as a service—there are many opportunities to leverage technology to create bigger and better spreadsheets.

Following is a quick survey of software and online tools that attempt to serve the entrepreneur who needs more and more powerful dashboards. This is a rapidly changing landscape, however, so we'll stick to the most well-established names and focus on how to evaluate them.

Small Business Accounting Software: QuickBooks, Xero, and Wave

Accounting packages—both desktop versions of the software and those that live predominantly online—have increasingly sophisticated built-in dashboards. These tend to be only moderately customizable: users can select between a few (or as many as a few dozen) preformatted reports. Each report opens in a separate mini-window, with the effect being that the dashboard resembles a mosaic of lists and simple charts. For purely financial purposes, these dashboards can be quite effective. A finance manager, for example, can easily use the dashboard in QuickBooks to monitor accounts receivable, accounts payable, and the checking account balance. More sophisticated calculations (such as using accounts receivable to monitor Days Sales Outstanding) are not possible.

Add-Ons: Bill.com, Profitsee, Etc.

For companies that have already committed to an accounting package and want something that seamlessly integrates accounting information into a useful (but more flexible) dashboard, add-ons such as Bill.com and Profitsee are good choices. Many of these add-ons do a lot more than parse accounting data and make pretty pictures. Bill.com, for example, adds payment processing (for paying bills and for getting invoices paid by customers), plus a cash flow calendar. Sophisticated and interactive tools like that calendar can add serious value to a company's operations and allow the tech-savvy entrepreneur to see weeks into the future. These tools generally charge a monthly membership fee.

Larger Accounting and ERP Systems

Moving upmarket from the small business accounting packages, we'll find well-known names like Microsoft Dynamics competing for the accounting function and offering more sophisticated enterprise resource planning (ERP) tools, along with dashboards that can monitor any system connected to the network. InterAcct and NetSuite are two other leaders in this area, often called "accounting and management software." The dashboards available through these systems are far more sophisticated but could well require a great deal of support to define, implement and maintain.

Dedicated Systems: Birst, Domo, Etc.

There has been an explosion of useful data available to entrepreneurs recently. So-called "big data" and "social graphs" are both private and public treasure troves of market data that can be culled together to help create amazingly useful dashboards. Imagine cross-referencing your customer's email addresses with social data that tells you their age, gender, zip code and Twitter handle. Not only can a company harvest important demographic information, but also exceptionally detailed information about key customers. To enable this type of dashboard requires committing to larger, more powerful software. Birst and Domo are two large brands that allow users to tie together internal and external sources of data—not just mining knowledge from existing systems but actually creating new information by combining the various data in new ways. These tools are more expensive (though often not prohibitively so) and require significant implementation and maintenance support. Companies that have an IT staff or a dedicated finance department should have no trouble getting value from such systems.

SUMMARY

☑ Dashboards combine data from our financial statements, financial ratios, and operations to unlock new insights and knowledge.

☑ Dashboards should inform and empower management decisions.

☑ When creating a dashboard, use the "TIGER" acronym: Time, Impact, Goals, Ease, Relationships.

☑ Dashboards should measure enough information to answer three key questions: What is important? What is effective? What is ahead?

☑ Once we've decided what to measure, we should select several metrics that show various aspects.

☑ The process of creating a dashboard focuses out attention on what is most important to our business. This focus is important to successfully building a financially stable business.

☑ Great dashboards can be built using nothing more than paper and pencil—or a spreadsheet.

☑ New software and online tools are helping entrepreneurs make and use more and more sophisticated dashboard tools.

15

Models, Forecasts, and Budgets

It is fitting that this book concludes where so many entrepreneurs begin: imagining the future, planning how to build a company, forecasting the great success that lies ahead, and building a budget for how to get there. Entrepreneurs are natural optimists—looking to the future and believing that we can create something that does not yet exist. We want to believe that we can not only define the future, but also control it. Models, budgets, and forecasts are the best tools we have to paint a picture of that future—a picture that will help us define it, communicate it, and ultimately build it in a controlled and profitable way.

So why have we left models and budgets until the end? Because a reasonably complete understanding of financial statements and ratio analysis is important for building models, budgets and forecasts. We've already seen examples of how financial statements describe the past and present, and how ratios and operating metrics can predict the future. Models, forecasts, and budgets take the same building blocks and combine them in ways that peer deeply into the unknown and produce conclusions that, if not perfectly accurate, can at least be used to guide long-term planning, strategy, and decisions.

Is there a difference between models, forecasts, and budgets? Not necessarily. We may build one or two general projections that fit our need and never bother with the detail of a formal budget or the complexities of a giant model. Small businesses have no need to complicate the present by overanalyzing the future!

It is useful, however, to understand what is meant by these three terms and the different functions that each serves. Let's define these terms as follows:

- *Models* describe how we make and spend money. Models start with the big picture—external market conditions and available resources—and attempt to distill *the size and scope of a business that could be built within those parameters.*
- *Forecasts* start with a known size and scope of business and project how the business might change over time. Forecasts are *predictions of future results that are rooted in past experience.*
- *Budgets* take the predictions of a forecast and describe in as much detail as possible exactly *what income and expenses are likely to result.*

Entrepreneurs who are concerned with the future will want to use these tools (or pieces of them) at different times and for different reasons. One day we may settle for a quick forecast based on current conditions; another day we may need a model to look at an entirely new line of business. Let's look closely at how to best create and use each tool.

MODELS

Of all the topics we have covered in this book, models are potentially the most complex. Wall Street is full of MBAs that do little more than design and maintain new financial models—trying to predict everything from stock market fluctuations to next year's profit potential of giant global corporations. A professionally built model can span hundreds of pages and contain tens of thousands of calculations. These models are often made using nothing more than Microsoft Excel, yet their sophistication is such that only the person who actually created the model is capable of fully understanding and maintaining it.

> *Note:* The newest versions of Microsoft Excel can handle up to one million lines of data, making its use for model building virtually unlimited.

A million-line model is not the kind of model that will be of much use to a small business owner. It is, however, good to understand the potential for spreadsheet models to consolidate vast amounts of data and produce meaningful results. We can use this point of reference to make our tools as sophisticated as we need them to be (and not more).

Start Simple

A small business model might be as simple as four lines in an Excel spreadsheet. (Or a spreadsheet from Google, Open Office, or Apple Numbers, for that matter.) Those four lines, however, should be chosen carefully to capture the market conditions and resources that are most important to the scope and scale of the business (now or in the future). These first "inputs" become the foundation from which we will calculate all manner of business attributes.

> *Tip*: For this discussion of business modeling, we will use specific terminology. "Inputs" are measurable facts, such as how many people live in a city. "Variables" are the calculated values that we will use in our business, such as how many stores we will open or how many sales we will make.

Let's take the example of a grocery store looking to open a new location in a rapidly growing city. The entrepreneur knows that there are certain rules or assumptions that will drive his future business:

- Total sales will increase as population increases
- The square footage of the store may have to increase as population grows
- The number of different products in stock could increase as population expands
- There must be at least 5,000 people in a three-mile area to support one store, and 12,000 to support two stores

Knowing that his basic business is so dependent on the population around his store location, one of the model inputs will have to be that population.

Then, using the input and the assumptions together, we can calculate any number of variables, such as how many staff work at the store, how many cash registers are needed to serve customers efficiently, what hours the store is open, and how much working capital the store needs. A simple model can calculate each of these variables based solely on the number of people who live within three miles of the new store location. Table 15.1 shows what the grocer model might look like.

Table 15.1. Grocery Store Expansion Model

	Grocery Store Expansion and Sales Model				
	INPUTS	**2014**	**2015**	**2016**	**2017**
a	Houses in Three-Mile Area	7,000	9,000	12,000	14,000
b	Houses Needed to Open a Store	5,000	5,000	5,000	6,000
c	Monthly Grocery Budget per House	200	225	225	250
d	Total Stores (Us + Competition)	1	2	3	4
	CALCULATED VARIABLES				
A	Stores We Should Have (a / b)	1	1	2	2
B	Groceries Purchased Monthly (a x c)	$1,400,000	$2,025,000	$2,700,000	$3,500,000
C	One Store's Monthly Income (B / d)	$1,400,000	$1,012,500	$900,000	$875,000

Identifying Inputs

The number of possible customers is an obvious input for a retailer, but the grocery store owner could also have chosen to count the number of cars that pass by a particular location, or the number of new houses built. Each of these might yield substantially the same results, so the choice comes down to how easy it is to find the numbers and how reliably accurate they are.

No matter how we calculate it, population density is a good input for a retailer. Other types of business might have very different concerns. A trucking company might track how many grocery stores open in a particular region in order to judge how many trucks they will need to service customers. A farmer's model is likely to be based on how many acres of land are available. Every business has inputs that are critical to its ability to expand—inputs that either impose natural limits to growth or reveal the inherent potential.

There is no right answer for which inputs to use. Some will make more sense, be easier to identify, or be naturally more accurate than others, but few will be perfect. Still, anchoring a model to one or more "facts"—inputs that can be verified—is a necessary starting point. When a business attempts to create a model that does not include any fact-based inputs, the model loses credibility and is more accurately called a "wild guess"!

Internal versus External

The first inputs into a model should be a mixture of external (market) and internal (company) facts. The number of people in a city is a great example of an external variable that can have a big impact on our success. An internal input may be the amount of money we have available to build new stores or to buy inventory. The best selection of inputs will be in a natural state of tension. Population and capital are good examples of this tension: even if the population grows, we may not have enough money to keep pace. Likewise, we might have plenty of money to build new stores, but no people moving to the area.

Internal Inputs
- Current number of customers or employees
- Capital available for expansion
- Size of region served (square miles or states)
- Number of square feet in our store
- Hours available for operation
- Likely down time or inefficiencies
- Gross margin or markup
- Advertising opportunities or budget
- Maximum number of sales per hour or day

External Inputs
- Population in the area we serve
- Number of competitors
- Cost of raw materials
- Number of distributors serving our industry
- Total web searches on a key term
- Price of web hosting, bandwidth, gasoline, or any other input
- Number of certain events per year (trade shows, hurricanes, satellite launches, etc.)

In general, anything that drives demand, supply, or price of our product or service should be considered as an input. We are looking for variables that impact our ability to produce, sell, or profit from the goods and services we sell. Consider all possible customers, competitors, and costs when collecting possible inputs. Then keep those that are most directly related to the success of the business and can be most easily verified.

How Many Inputs and Variables

Accurate modeling may call for several fact-based, measurable inputs. More is not always better, however. Like a dashboard, however, we need to keep the model simple enough to be meaningful and easy to understand, so a page full of inputs is rarely helpful.

The number of inputs will naturally increase as we increase the number of calculated variables that we want to predict. If the grocery store owner wants to model his growth for the next 25 years, showing everything from the number of stores to the price of bread, we might end up with input variables for inflation rates, economic growth, the price of gas, changing consumer preferences, global climate change, and 10 other factors. That kind of complexity will not yield helpful or meaningful results. Even as a model is used to set the scope and scale of a business, the business owner must first set the scope and scale of the model. In general, small business models are most useful when they use fewer than 10 inputs to calculate fewer than 25 variables over a period of five years or less. As we said, much more complexity is certainly possible, but it is rarely useful for a small business to guess what its situation will be 10 years from now; business is simply too dynamic.

Turning Dashboards into Models

The last chapter described how to make a "business dashboard" to guide management decisions within our business. We created this useful tool by selecting environmental variables—inputs, really—that impact our business results. For a real estate brokerage, we saw how measuring the number of houses under contract could be an important indicator of future sales, business growth, and the state of the market in general.

A model might rely on exactly the same inputs. In fact, the relationships and ratios we discover while making a dashboard (which plots events as they happen), might become the inputs and calculations for a very powerful and accurate model. If we have an operating business, and we can build a dashboard that measures meaningful and

Table 15.2. Real Estate Commission Model

REAL ESTATE COMMISSION REVENUE MODEL & PROJECTION				
INPUTS	**Jan**	**Feb**	**March**	**April**
a	Houses under Contract	100	110	120	130
b	Key Ratio - % of Houses Sold	13.7%	14.2%	14.5%	15.5%
c	Commission Rate	6%	6%	5.50%	5.50%
d	Average House Price	$100,000	$110,000	$125,000	$150,000
CALCULATED VARIABLES				
A	Number of Sales / Month (a x b)	13.7	15.6	17.4	20.2
B	Commission per Sale (c x d)	$6,000	$6,600	$6,875	$8,250
C	Projected Commissions (A x B)	$82,200	$103,092	$119,625	$166,238

predictive ratios, then that work will flow naturally into a model that can be used to predict the future and to play "what if" with the business inputs we select. For example, the real estate broker could use a simple model to discover: What if I get twice as many homes under contract? What if I sell only higher-priced homes? What if I raise my commission rate? Table 15.2 might be the kind of model our broker uses to answer these questions.

Everything Is Custom

The downside to using a business model is that we have to build it from scratch. No one model can predict the business results for every business. In fact, although there are generic models that apply to particular industries, each business should create a model that specifically and uniquely captures its own operating inputs and variables. Most business owners find it helpful to work with a financial analyst or

CFO to create a model. Once created, however, we'll use it over and over to answer key questions and adapt our strategy to the changes we see coming in the future.

FORECASTS

While a model tells us what may be possible, a forecast defines what we want to accomplish. Beginning with the parameters set by a model, a forecast adds layers of specificity and moves our management discussion from "what could be" to "what we are building."

As the name suggests, forecasts are projections of what we believe *will* happen in the future. It is a necessary step between modeling what *might* happen and budgeting for what *must* happen.

Tip: Think of the four tools as looking at the same situation from four different viewpoints:

1. Model: "What could happen"
2. Forecast: "What we believe will happen—within the model"
3. Budget: "What must happen to reach the forecast"
4. Dashboard: "What actually happened"

Starting Simple

Since the scope and scale of a business depends entirely on how much we sell, every forecast starts with an estimate of what sales will be. Within the parameters set by the model (and perhaps using the mathematical relationships established by the model), we must look into the future and set a reasonable and attainable goal for sales. From that sales goal, every other aspect of the business can be forecast: prior to sales, we need advertising and awareness; after sales, we need production and product support; and those functions must be backed up by administration and overhead.

The forecast begins to fall in place when we answer five questions:

1. How much will we sell?
2. What is needed to attract those sales?
3. What is needed to complete those sales?
4. What else will customers need?

5. How big must the other parts of the company be in order to support all of that activity?

Writing It Down

A forecast can be as simple as a few bullet points, or as complex as an entire P&L statement. Large companies will forecast every income and expense item for multiple periods or years. At that level of complexity, however, a forecast starts to look more like a budget (which we will cover in a moment) and becomes too big to adjust quickly. Entrepreneurs will want to keep forecasts simple and nimble.

A "rolling forecast" is quite useful for small businesses. Rolling forecasts have two important attributes: (1) they predict results over a specific, constant period of time; and (2) we update them regularly and often. In practice, a 12- or 15-week rolling forecast, updated weekly, is a powerful tool. Twelve weeks—about three months—is enough time to start and complete significant projects and to see their impact on business. Projecting sales (and related needs) for three months into the future allows a business to anticipate critical issues like the need for cash and personnel, without looking so far into the future that critical factors get inadvertently exaggerated or minimized.

> Remember, a forecast is a prediction—it should be firmly grounded in reality, so looking too far ahead can be counterproductive.

How we record a forecast is really a function of who will act on the information. Generally, a forecast is a table of future values for key data—for example, number of orders, units of sales, number of people needed, or the remaining inventory. Notice that this list does not include any income or expense dollars, only operational needs or goals. To the extent that these numbers drive other specific activities or expenses in the business, a forecast might include additional calculations. The real value of a forecast is not to calculate every detail, but instead to put a target on the wall that all members of the team can shoot for. Forecasts set direction, scale, and timing expectations for every part of the business operation. Even when a forecast includes some dollars and cents, the majority of income and expense details are best left to the budget.

BUDGETS

With a complete forecast in hand, a manager should be able to esti-mate—calculate, really—the amount of money that will be made and spent in every part of the business.

Established businesses have the advantage of using a current P&L as the basis of a budget. Since the P&L already lists every income and expense account, a budgeter can estimate every detail. Further, by com-paring forecast numbers to actual historical data, she also has impor-tant information about the relative size of each income or expense account for a given level of sales.

Breaking It Down

Budgeting is simple when we follow much the same pattern as we did with forecasting—begin with sales and work "down" the P&L. A forecast that shows total units of expected sales converts easily into a sales budget. That's the top line. Progressing down the P&L means that the next section we tackle is the cost of sales. In many businesses, COS (or the equivalent, cost of goods sold) is a relatively stable percentage of sales. Budgeting for the cost of sales can lead to inventory budgets and labor budgets. And finally, a budgeter must make adjustments to fixed expenses that would be needed to accommodate the growth or contraction of sales.

> *Tip*: The budgeting process starts in the same way as forecasting—looking first at sales. It then moves down a historical P&L, making changes based on the forecast sales volume.

The Budget Cycle

In large companies, budgets are famous for being annual projects that take weeks and sometimes months to prepare at the beginning of the year—and become terribly outdated by the end of the year. An entrepreneur's budget should be much more spry. Like the forecast, an ideal budget will be updated at least monthly (weekly is better, if possible), and it should project financial results for a rolling period of 12 to 16 weeks. The benefit of this practice will be a budget that is always fresh, deadly accurate, and top of mind.

> *Tip*: Budgeting is as much about discipline as it is about adding up income and expenses. Find the discipline to refreshing the budget every week: it will take very little time and the budget will stay deadly accurate.

For a little more rigor, a budget cycle can include a look at how closely the budget matched the actual results. When this is done weekly (or perhaps monthly), the results ought to start to be closely in line with projections. When results do not meet budget, the manager ought to explore exactly why, what impact that will have on the rest of the organization, and whether the future numbers must also be adjusted accordingly.

Finally, this process of comparing actual to budget can correspond to recording the results onto the dashboard. Armed with both a dashboard and a budget, we can increase the accuracy of both by comparing past results and future projections from each tool. If the dashboard indicates a near-term crisis, or a possible shortage of cash, does the budget agree? In the near term of 12 to 16 weeks, these two tools should at least point us in the same direction.

For most small businesses, a finished budget will be indistinguishable from a P&L, except for the dates—the P&L describes the past, while a budget will reach into the future. On a budget, it is often useful to keep a few periods of actual results to refer back to. A slightly more complex budget will fold together the actual results with budgeted results so that each month (historical and future) is represented by two columns: budget and actual. This forces the budgeter to keep historical budgeted numbers intact as a reminder of what we thought would happen and what actually happened. Table 15.3 shows a budget that combines historical and actual data. Notice the dark line that separates past from future—it's a good reminder of where we are and an easy visual queue to prevent readers from becoming confused.

Delegating Budget Duties

If our company is large enough to have departments, then each department can be responsible for its own budget. Frankly, any employee who has spending authority should also have the

Table 15.3. Six-Month Budget

	ACTUAL				BUDGET		
	Jan	Feb	Mar		Apr	May	Jun
Income							
Product A	20,000	22,500	23,000		24,000	25,000	26,000
Product B	15,000	14,500	14,000		13,500	13,000	12,500
Product C	5,000	4,000	3,000		3,000	2,500	2,000
Returns	(1,000)	(1,000)	(1,000)		(1,000)	(1,000)	(1,000)
Total Revenue	39,000	40,000	39,000		39,500	39,500	39,500
Operating Expenses							
6275 Professional Fees	3,591	3,346	3,952		3,591	3,591	3,591
6290 - Rent	2,887	2,887	2,887		2,887	2,887	2,887
6320 - Utilities (electric, phone, fax)	1,441	1,435	1,260		1,441	1,441	1,441
6400 - Software	1,905	1,750	1,865		1,905	1,905	1,905
6330 - Travel & Entertainment	477	525	-		477	477	477
6155 - Subscriptions	1,000	1,000	1,000		1,000	1,000	1,000
6140 - Cleaning/Janitorial	700	700	700		700	700	700
6810 - Property Taxes	623	623	623		623	623	623
6180 - Insurance	641	641	641		641	641	641
6270 - Professional Development	144	144	144		144	144	144
6238 - Marketing & Advertising	2,860	2,860	2,860		2,860	2,860	2,860
6310 - Office Supplies	185	185	185		185	185	185
6115 - Bank Service Charges	130	130	130		130	130	130
6160 - Automobile Expenses	146	146	146		146	146	146
6120 - Business License & Fees	25	25	25		25	25	25

(*continued*)

Table 15.3. (Continued)

	ACTUAL				BUDGET		
	Jan	Feb	Mar		Apr	May	Jun
Total Non-Payroll Expense	16,755	16,397	16,418		16,755	16,755	16,755
Payroll							
John	3,000	3,000	3,000		3,000	3,000	3,000
Don	3,000	3,000	3,000		3,000	3,000	3,000
Cathy	3,000	3,000	3,000		3,000	3,000	3,000
Kelly	3,000	3,000	3,000		3,000	3,000	3,000
Jack	1,500	1,500	1,250		-	-	-
Bonuses	2,085	2,145	2,078		8,488	1,875	1,875
Commissions	400	800	600		500	500	500
Total Payroll Expenses	15,985	16,445	15,928		20,988	14,375	14,375
NET PROFIT FROM OPERATIONS	6,260	7,158	6,655		1,758	8,370	8,370

responsibility of keeping a budget. This is an excellent way to reinforce the need for frugality and reduces the budgeting burden on the business owner at the same time. We shouldn't forget, however, to roll up the departmental budgets into one consolidated company budget.

Zero-Based Budgets

A business does not have to be small to be frugal—managing the expense side of budgets tightly is a virtue for all sizes of companies. Small, entrepreneurial companies have a special capacity for frugality, however: the ability to operate under so-called "zero-based budgets." From the perspective of a zero-based budgeter, no expense is assumed to be mandatory and every dollar spent must be treated like an investment.

It may not be possible, of course, to treat some fixed expenses (like rent or water, for example) in this way. Nevertheless, zero-based budgets assume that each period begins with *no preset level of spending* and any unnecessary expense is cut. It can be a powerful tool for controlling costs and making staff members think critically about purchases.

This approach works well for both very small expenses and for very large ones. In fact, the concept can be applied to all three kinds of expenses in a business: cost of goods, ordinary expenses, and capital expenses.

1. *Cost of Goods Sold*: When applied to the cost of goods sold category of expenses, a zero-based budget will minimize overpurchases and force us to think about efficiency measures that might reduce inputs or waste. Cost of goods budgets must start at zero and be built on actual sales (or at least the forecast of actual sales). If money is spent on these variable costs without tying them to the variable revenue, we will end up carrying too much inventory, which causes other problems as we saw in cash cycles (Chapter 10).
2. *Ordinary Expenses*: Small items, such as office supplies, should never have a standing or fixed budget (i.e., we don't want to name any amount money that "should be" spent on supplies). By eliminating our budget for such things, we challenge ourselves to minimize the expense, work with what we have, and never buy anything that is not absolutely called for. This is true of all items in the Expense category, although, as we've seen some items such as rent, they tend to be fixed in the short term. In the long term, everything is negotiable.
3. *Capital Expenses*: At the other end of the spectrum, capitalized expenses for equipment, machines, vehicles, and leasehold improvements should always begin at zero, and each purchase must be scrutinized carefully. Large purchases are often the easiest to justify—an inexpensive machine that saves labor hours every day will quickly pay for itself; likewise, some expenses are simply required to conduct business such as a computer and a telephone.

Be careful: Zero-based budgeting does not mean that we never bother to do forecasts, projections, or budgets for these items. Foreseeing the expense is a matter of good planning. Approving the expense, however, should require more careful analysis. Zero-based budgeting frames the issues and forces the entrepreneur to recognize and analyze each dollar spent—but it does not relieve us of the duty to make accurate budgets.

COMPLETING THE CYCLE

We've come a long way, from simply understanding basic financial statements to using statements and ratios to diagnose operational issues, to uncover opportunities, and finally to predict future results. Incredibly, we are almost back to where we started. Now that we have a dashboard, model, forecast, and budget, the cycle is nearly complete: the next and last step in the process is actually *doing*. And from the doing comes results—which bring us all the way back to the financial statements.

The Six Steps to the Business Data Cycle

1. Financial statements show results from operations and help us understand weaknesses and opportunities
2. Dashboards unlock the interrelation of financial statements and show how operating results are related to certain other inputs or parameters
3. Models use those relationships to build "what if" and "what could be" scenarios
4. Forecasts take the model results and add a dose of reality, telling us what we think will happen
5. Budgets use the forecast goals to justify and assign financial resources to the business operations
6. The business uses budgeted resources to operate, creating actual results that are presented in financial statements—and the cycle "starts over"

When this cycle is operating correctly, and when the entrepreneur is diligent, this six-step process becomes a virtuous feedback loop, helping the business grow stronger and stronger with each cycle. The data show us opportunities, and we set strategies to capture them. The data show us threats and we set strategies to avoid them. Each strategy brings new results and new data, which can reveal new threats or opportunities. All the while, the owner and managers are learning how the business works and how the market reacts.

When we know how financial statements work, how a few ratios can describe our business, and what externalities we should be watching, we will be rewarded with a new and more complete understanding of our business and where it is going. When we learn the language of finance and data, we will start to hear what our business is telling us. Every business can speak. Every entrepreneur can listen. Together, we can grow a company that is more profitable, more sustainable, and more fun.

SUMMARY

☑ Models are spreadsheets that take inputs from the real world and calculate "what could be" for our business.

☑ Many of the calculations in a good model come from observing how variables and ratios on a dashboard change as the business changes.

☑ Forecasts are our best guess at what will happen in the business. Small business forecasts should focus on top line sales results and the external inputs that shape them.

☑ Forecasts may or may not contain any financial predictions, and are generally not as detailed as budgets.

☑ Budgets describe the financial operating results we expect in the future.

☑ The "data cycle" describes how operating results, financial ratios, and other data about a company starts from financial statements and progresses through dashboards, models, forecasts, and budgets.

☑ Every business owner can manage risks and opportunities more effectively by using the tools in the data cycle.

Afterword

In the dangerous and risky world of small business, success is not an accident. Success comes from making better decisions than our competition; from making decisions that are more in tune with the market; and from decisions that are better informed by business realities.

I believe that these kinds of decisions are possible only when an entrepreneur embraces the financial results of her business and knows how to interpret those results. Understanding concepts like the cash conversion cycle (Chapter 10), for example, can mean the difference between a good try and a screaming success.

Knowing *about* the cash conversion cycle (or any other financial metric) is not enough; entrepreneurs must use the information to shape our actions and management decisions. We must constantly measure and re-measure results to know whether our decisions are leading us in the right direction. And finally, we must be willing to let the results influence our larger strategies even when they take us in unfamiliar or uncomfortable directions.

Exceptional entrepreneurs are able to mix this discipline with their natural creativity to build a business that is not just innovative, but also sustainable and profitable.

It is unfortunate that the term "finance" has become separate from the idea of building and operating a business. So many pundits seem to believe that a great website, a cool brand name, and a well-designed product are enough to assure business success. While these things do not hurt, there are stunning examples of small business successes that have none of these things. Instead, they have a rock-solid business model founded on financial principles such as controlling costs, leveraging capital, and prioritizing cash flow. (My favorite example is the corner dry cleaner, which in my neighborhood generates fabulous returns for its owner without so much as a coupon to promote its services.)

As business owners, we have the amazing opportunity to create companies that support us financially and spiritually. Going to work each day can be incredibly fun when the business we build rewards us for doing the work we love. I hope that some of the tips and techniques presented in this book will help you make your own business more profitable, more sustainable, and more fun.

Dedicated to your business success.

Appendix 1
Calculating Dell Computer's Cash Cycle (Case Study)

Manufacturers are known for having a very long cash cycle: they keep warehouses full of expensive inventory (both raw materials and finished goods) and sell to distributors or wholesalers on long credit terms. Working this way requires a great deal of cash—cash that gets locked away (in inventory or AR) where the company cannot use it. This situation keeps manufacturers cash poor and hampers their ability to fund growth.

Since the 1990s, however, some companies have managed to trim their inventories and collection times with amazing effect. Dell Computer is reputed to be the world leader in implementing lean manufacturing and just-in-time inventory controls. In November 2004, *Fast Company* reported the amazing changes at Dell:

> Eleven years ago, Dell carried 20 to 25 days of inventory in a sprawling network of warehouses. Today, it has no warehouses. And though it assembles nearly 80,000 computers every 24 hours, it carries no more than two hours of inventory in its factories and a maximum of just 72 hours across its entire operation. (Bill Breen, "Living in Dell Time," *Fast Company*, November 2004, http://www.fastcompany.com/51967/living-dell-time [accessed February 10, 2013])

It gets better. Dell's sales model adds even more efficiency. Since Dell builds computers *after* they have been specified, purchased, and paid for by a customer, Dell uses the customer's cash to fund sales costs. Dell's days sales outstanding (DSO) is zero, or perhaps even negative in many cases.

It seems unbelievable, but imagine what all this means to Dell's cash cycle time. In fact, if suppliers give Dell as little as one day to pay (and

Table A.1.1. Calculating Dell's Cash Cycle

From Dell's 12-Month P&L Ending February 1, 2013	
a.	Total Sales	$56,940
b.	Total Cost of Sales	$44,754
From February 1, 2013, Balance Sheet	
c.	Accounts Payable	$11,579
d.	Accounts Receivable	$6,629
e.	Inventory	$1,382
The Formula for Calculating Dell's Cash Cycle	
DSO = (d/a)*360	days
DSI = (e/b)*360	days
DPO = (c/b)*360	days
Cash Cycle = DSI + DSO − DPO =	days

Source: Google Finance, March 2013.

their terms are certainly much better than that), then Dell's days sales in inventory (DSI) also turns negative. That's right; Dell uses money from both customers *and* suppliers! Before it even orders the inventory to build a computer, Dell has received the cash from the customer and credit from the supplier. Dell's entire operations have become a *source* of cash, which the company can use to build new plants, hire new workers, and fuel faster growth. The more they grow, the more cash is available to fuel growth, and the cycle feeds on itself.

Let's calculate Dell's actual cash cycle from 2012, and see how they are doing. Table A.1.1 shows Dell's operating results as reported in their 2012 annual report. Calculate their actual cash cycle days, and then see what this means to Dell in terms of cash used or cash available. For simplicity, the formulas are given, so you can fill in the blanks.

Finally, calculate exactly how much cash Dell uses (or generates). Take the number of days in Dell's cash cycle, divide by 360, and multiply by annual sales. This will tell us how much cash is encumbered or created by Dell.

- Cash Cycle Days (from above) = _____days
- Annual Sales (from 12-month P&L) = $ _____
- Cash Created = (a/360) * b = $ _____

Appendix 2
Other Resources

No entrepreneur builds a company alone. It takes advice and nurturing from mentors, experts, and friends. This is particularly true as we learn to use finance to our strategic advantage. Online and off, there are some great resources available to help entrepreneurs better understand their financial statements, and thus their businesses. Following are a few of the more qualified and helpful sources of small business information available at no cost.

SCORE

Among the best off-line resources is SCORE—the Service Corp of Retired Executives. This not-for-profit organization is part of the Small Business Administration of the U.S. government. SCORE has offices across the United States.

Each SCORE office is staffed by helpful volunteers—most of whom are retired executives, and all of whom are eager to help business owners read and understand their financial statements. A few short hours spent with a SCORE mentor can radically change the way you view your own business—and save you endless hours of frustration. There is no cost and no obligation.

Find your local SCORE office at http://www.score.org. Then call for an appointment, and when you do, ask if your office has anyone who specializes in your industry. If you are a retailer, seek out a SCORE executive with retail experience. Not only will the mentor's advice be more accurate, but their excitement for your business will be genuine, and they will have a much better chance at referring resources from their network.

Like many things in life, the value you get from SCORE comes in direct proportion to your investment of time and energy. Find a SCORE mentor you like, and make regular appointments.

SMALL BUSINESS ADMINISTRATION (SBA)

SCORE's parent organization, the SBA, is clearly focused on helping entrepreneurs. The main website is dotted with detailed, accurate, and helpful articles about everything from business licenses to export strategies. Spending an entire day on http://www.sba.gov would not be enough to take in everything they have to offer.

The real strength of the SBA, however, comes from their off-line presence. The SBA supports hundreds of offices around the country. Each office supports one or more subspecialty areas, including:

- Small Business Development Center (SBDC)
- Women's Business Center
- U.S. Export Assistance Office
- Veterans Business Outreach Center
- Certified Development Company
- Disaster Field Office
- Procurement and Technical Assistance Centers

The last of these, the Procurement and Technical Assistance Center, is worthy of special note. These offices help entrepreneurs identify and qualify for government and military contracts. Many small business successes are built on a foundation of selling to the government, and these offices can get you started.

THE BIG BANKS

Banks and other financial institutions are investing heavily in entrepreneurship, finance education, and online content. Their advice tends to be accurate, concise, and backed up by helpful folks at their branch offices. Of course, these companies also have products to promote, so the content websites are not always easy to find on their home pages. Start with some of these URLs instead.

- Bank of America: https://smallbusinessonlinecommunity.bankof america.com
- Wells Fargo: https://wellsfargobusinessinsights.com
- American Express: https://www.openforum.com
- Visa: http://blog.visa.com/

PUBLICATIONS

There are a number of high-quality publications that support entrepreneurs. Their advice in print and online is unmistakably well written and hard hitting. Magazines tend to focus on telling the personal stories of successful entrepreneurs—case studies that can be very instructive. Start with these resources:

- *Entrepreneur*: http://www.entrepreneur.com
- *Inc.*: http://www.inc.com
- *Fast Company*: http://www.fastcompany.com/magazine
- *Bloomberg Businessweek*: http://www.businessweek.com

BLOGS AND OTHERS

There is so much *bad* information online that finding accurate business information—and meaningful advice—is particularly difficult. It is vital that an entrepreneur understand the source of the information before basing important business decisions on it. Following are a few of the better websites that offer quality content, presented by professional journalists and business owners.

AllBusiness bills itself as the largest website devoted to small business topics—and that could well be true. Check out the excellent resources and in-depth articles at http://www.allbusiness.com.

Intuit, the publisher of QuickBooks, is an excellent resource for anything related to small business finance. Although their home online is dedicated to selling software, the Intuit blog is a hidden gem. Start reading at http://blog.intuit.com.

Jim Blasingame supports a full-featured website that is part news, part blog, and all business. The site is sponsored by Forbes, so it tends to be broad reporting about all aspects of small business and current business news. Start at http://www.smallbusinessadvocate.com/.

Rock Solid Finance is my personal attempt to collect useful finance and strategy advice for small business owners. Join me at http://www.rocksolidfinance.com.

Small Business Trends is one of the most-visited websites for small businesses—http://www.smallbiztrends.com.

Small Biz Daily was launched by former *Entrepreneur* magazine editor Rieva Lesonsky. The site has excellent material from quality writers and is a great way to get inspired to build your next big thing—http://www.smallbizdaily.com.

The *New York Times* publishes an online section just for small business owners called "You're the Boss," which is available at http://boss.blogs.nytimes.com.

Appendix 3
Debits and Credits

Truly mastering your financial statements can be a long journey. Along the way you will undoubtedly meet accountants, CPAs, and other advisers who use terminology that is confusing and new. Some may even use terms we've discussed in this book, but in ways that mean something completely different. There is a complete glossary of such terms in Appendix 4, but two terms deserve special attention: Among the most confusing terms thrown around by accounting professionals are "Debits" and "Credits."

We have purposefully avoided the use of the terms debit and credit in this book because they would have added little to the understanding of how to use financial statements. Nonetheless, it is often helpful to have a handle on these common—but confusing—terms. Use Table A.3.1 to help you remember what is meant by debit (DR) and credit (CR).

Remember, accounting is based on "double entry," which means that every transaction has two sides. Since talking about the "sign" (positive or negative) of a transaction can be quite confusing, accountants decided that we should simply draw the two sides of the transaction and call the left side "credit" and the right side "debit." (We also require that the left and right sides should always be equal, which is how our balance sheet stays in balance!) Personally, I use a short mnemonic device to help remember this: "When you pay for lunch, Don't Ever Call an Accountant." Believe it or not, this phrase—and the acronym DECA—can help you put the debits and credits in the right place. Unscrambled, the phrase is "When you pay for lunch, Debit Expenses and Credit Assets." This is the description of a simple transaction that records paying cash for lunch or any other small expense. In this case the "expense" account is "meals," and the "asset" is cash. The balance of the meals expense account goes up (debit) and the balance of the cash asset account goes down (credit). So just remember that when

Table A.3.1. Debits and Credits

	A Debit Will ...	**A Credit Will** ...
Balance Sheet Accounts:		
Asset Account	Increase the Asset	Decrease the Asset
Liability Account	Decrease the Liability	Increase the Liability
Equity Account	Decrease the Equity	Increase the Equity
P&L Statement Accounts:		
Income	Decrease the Income	Increase the Income
Expense	Increase the Expense	Decrease the Expense

we spend cash, we simply debit expenses and credit assets—but we don't ever call an accountant!

Using "Don't Ever Call an Accountant" can unlock the entire table depicted above. Using DECA, we can work out the opposite relationships as well. For example, since the debit *increases expenses*, then a debit can also be used to *decrease an income account*. Since the credit *decreases assets*, then it can also be used to *increase liabilities* (and, because liabilities and equity are on the same side of the balance sheet, a credit can also increase equity). With this one sentence, we can puzzle out the relationships between each type of account and their relative debits or credits.

Appendix 4
State of Nevada Corporate Filing Fees

The state of Nevada provides a good example of the cost of becoming a corporation (also discussed in Chapter 8). Table A.4.1 shows an example of the fees Nevada charges for corporate registration. Fees are based on the value of the stock—not the market value, but rather the actual written value. Since company founders have complete control to assign a value to shares, this demonstrates why it is usually best to assign a very small value to shares. Many companies assign this "par value" to be less than one-tenth of one cent.

Table A.4.1. State of Nevada Filing Fees

ROSS MILLER	Profit Corporation Fee Schedule
Secretary of State	Effective 7-1-08
202 North Carson Street	Page 1
Carson City, Nevada 89701-4201	
Phone: (775) 684-5708	
Website: www.nvsos.gov	

PROFIT CORPORATIONS *INITIAL FILING* FEE: Pursuant to NRS 78, 80, 78A, and 89 Domestic and Foreign Corporations, Close Corporations and Professional Corporations.

Fees are based on the value of the total number of authorized shares stated in the Articles of Incorporation as prescribed by NRS 78.760:

$75,000 or less		$75.00
over $75,000 and not over $200,000		$175.00
over $200,000 and not over $500,000		$275.00
over $500,000 and not over $1,000,000		$375.00
	OVER $1,000,000	
For the first $1,000,000		$375.00

(*continued*)

Table A.4.1. (Continued)

For each additional $500,000 - or fraction thereof	$275.00
Maximum fee	$35,000.00

For the purpose of computing the filing fee, the value (capital) represented by the total number of shares authorized in the Articles of Incorporation is determined by computing the:

A. total authorized shares multiplied by their par value or;

B. total authorized shares without par value multiplied by $1.00 or;

C. the sum of (a) and (b) above if both par and no par shares.

Filing fees are calculated on a minimum par value of one-tenth of a cent (.001), regardless if the stated par value is less.

The 24-hour expedite fee for Articles of Incorporation for any of the above entities is $125.00 in addition to the filing fee based upon stock.

The 2-hour expedite fee is $500.00 in addition to the filing fee based upon stock.

The 1-hour expedite fee is $1000.00 in addition to the filing fee based upon stock.

PLEASE NOTE: the expedite fee is in addition to the standard filing fee charged on each filing and/or order.

24-HOUR EXPEDITE TIME CONSTRAINTS:

Each filing submitted receives same day filing date and may be picked up within 24-hours. Filings to be mailed the next business day if received by 2:00 pm of receipt date and no later than the 2nd business day if received after 2:00 pm.

Expedite period begins when filing or service request is received in this office in fileable form.

The Secretary of State reserves the right to extend the expedite period in times of extreme volume, staff shortages, or equipment malfunction. These extensions are few and will rarely extend more than a few hours.

Nevada Secretary of State Fee Schedule-NF Profit Pg1

Revised: 2-26-10

Source: https://nvsos.gov/Modules/ShowDocument.aspx?documentid=1050

Appendix 5
Glossary of Accounting Terms

13 Period Calendar is the practice of splitting a standard 52-week year into 13 equal accounting periods of four weeks each, rather than calendar months, which contain a variable number of days.

Absorption Pricing is a way to set pricing such that all costs, both fixed and variable, plus a percentage markup for profit, are recovered in the price.

Accelerated Depreciation is a method of calculating depreciation with larger amounts in the first year(s).

Account is the detailed record of a particular asset, liability, owners' equity, revenue or expense.

Account Aging describes customer accounts in accounts receivable based on how long past due the charges (invoices) are.

Accounting is primarily a system of measurement and reporting of economic events based upon the accounting equation for the purpose of decision making.

Accounting Concepts are the basic assumptions used to prepare financial statements: going concern, accruals, consistency, and prudence.

Accounting Cycle is the sequence of events in each accounting period (usually a year) to prepare for the next period or cycle, including: budgeting, journal entries, adjusting entries, posting to the accounts, financial reports, and closings.

Accounting Equation is the basic formula that states that assets equal liabilities and owner's equity.

Accounting Period is the time period for which financial statements are prepared, usually one month, one quarter, or one year.

Accounting Ratio is the result of dividing one financial statement item by another. Ratios help analysts interpret financial statements by focusing on specific relationships.

Accounts Payable (AP) is the balance sheet liability account that tracks what a company owes to its vendors for goods and services received.

Accounts Receivable (AR) is a balance sheet current asset account that tracks payments due from customers for services performed or merchandise sold.

Accrual Accounting is the recording of income when it is earned, and expenses when incurred, regardless of when cash is received or paid. In order to meet generally accepted accounting principles (GAAP), financial statements should be prepared using Accrual methods. *See also* Cash Accounting.

Accrued Liabilities are expenses which are incurred, or payments that are due, but which have not been paid. An example might be *"ACCRUED PAYROLL TAX LIABILITY,"* which would include taxes withheld from worker's wages, but not yet paid to the government.

Accumulated Amortization is a balance sheet account showing the total amortization charged against intangible assets. This is a "contra" asset account.

Accumulated Depreciation is a balance sheet account showing the total depreciation charged against tangible assets. This is a "contra" asset account.

Acid-Test Ratio is an analysis method used to measure the liquidity of a business by dividing total liquid assets by current liabilities.

Additional Paid in Capital is an equity account on the balance sheet that tracks the amount paid for stock in excess of its par value plus other amounts paid by stockholders.

Adjusting Entries are made in the General Journal to close the books at the end of an accounting period.

Adverse Opinion is an auditor's pronouncement when audit results are unsatisfactory and prevent the auditor from issuing an "unqualified opinion."

Aging of Accounts. *See* Account Aging.

Allowance for Bad Debts is a P&L expense account used to offset customer accounts that will not be paid.

Amortization is an expense account on the P&L which spreads the cost of an intangible asset over the expected useful life of the asset. Another meaning is *LOAN AMORTIZATION*, which is the schedule of repayments by which the principal amount of the loan is repaid.

Annualizing is a way of estimating annual results based on actual results from a shorter period. *See also* Run Rate.

AR and A/R are abbreviations for accounts receivable.

Articles of Incorporation is a corporation's constitution, filed with the state government to create a new corporation.

Asset is anything owned by a business. Assets may be an item (computer, building, etc.) or a claim against others (accounts receivable, for example).

Audit is the inspection of the accounting records and procedures of a business for accuracy, completeness, and compliance with GAAP and other regulation.

Audit Trail is the record of how and when each accounting transaction was recorded. This is useful in uncovering fraud and correcting mistakes.

Authorized Capital Stock is the maximum number of shares of common stock that can be issued under a company's Articles of Incorporation.

Bad Debt is an expense account that reduces loans or receivables are uncollectible.

Balance Sheet is a financial statement that lists what a company owns (assets) and what it owes (liabilities) as well as the historical investments or profits of the business (equity).

Bank Reconciliation is the process of comparing (and matching) internal accounting records of a bank account to a bank statement for the same account.

Basic Tenets of Accounting are four statements about proper accounting practices: (1) Assets = Liabilities + Equity; (2) debits must equal credits; (3) assets are on the left (debit) side; and (4) liabilities and equity are on the right (credit) side.

Basis, generally, is the original or starting value used to compute gain or loss, depreciation, depletion, or amortization of an asset.

Basis Point is 0.01%.

Below the Line refers to any credit or debit that affects the balance sheet accounts rather than the income statement (meaning, "below" the Net Profit line).

Big 4 usually refers to the largest accounting firms: Deloitte & Touche, Ernst and Young, KPMG, and PricewaterhouseCoopers.

Bill is a request for payment received from a vendor. For clarity, "bills" are received from vendors, while "invoices" are what a business sends to its customers.

Bookkeeping is the recording of business transactions into journals or ledgers.

Books refer to the journals or ledgers in which all accounting transactions are recorded.

Bottom Line is slang for net income after taxes.

BOY is an acronym for "Beginning of Year."

Breakeven Analysis is an analysis of the number of jobs or products that need to be sold to reach a breakeven point in a business.

Break-Even Equation is the equation written as [px = vx + FC], where p = unit selling price, v = per unit variable cost, FC = total fixed costs, and x = sales in units.

Budget is a detailed list of all estimated revenue and costs during a given period.

Burden Rate is the combination of all nonwage expenses associated with having employees, including employer taxes, benefits, etc.

Business Entity Principle states that a business is an entity entirely separate from its owner(s). This also means that financial records must be kept separate.

CAGR is an acronym for Compound Annual Growth Rate.

Capex is an acronym for Capital Expense.

Capital is money and other property of a business. Often it is used to mean the money invested into a business to get it started, or to help it grow faster than it could alone.

Capital Budget is the amount expected to be spent on Capital Expenses.

Capital Expense (CAPEX) is any expense or purchase of large assets such as property, plant, or equipment. Capital expense is not shown as an expense item on the P&L, but rather is "capitalized" onto the balance sheet and thus generates depreciation.

Capitalization, or Capital Structure, is the way the business is funded—typically a mixture of equity contributed by owners and debt provided by lenders.

Capital Lease is a lease that is recorded like a (capital) asset purchase, rather than an expense.

Cash Basis of Accounting is the accounting practice of recording revenue and expenses in the period when they are received or expended (in cash). Cash basis accounting is not compliant with generally accepted accounting principles (GAAP) but is often used for income tax reporting because of its simplicity.

Cash Cycle is the length of time (in days) between the date of purchase of raw materials or inventory and the collection of money from customers after the sale of the final product.

Cash Flow is simply the difference between cash received and cash spent.

Cash Flow Statement uses a company's P&L plus changes in balance sheet accounts to reconstruct the actual sources and uses of cash over a specific period of time.

Cash Management is the management of the cash balances of a concern in such a manner as to maximize the availability of cash not invested in fixed assets or inventories and to avoid the risk of insolvency.

Certified Financial Statements are financial statements that have undergone a formal audit by a certified public accountant and usually contain statements of certification by the CPA.

CFO can mean "Cash Flow from Operations" or "Chief Financial Officer."

Chart of Accounts is the list of (ledger) account names that are used in the financial statements. The accounts are listed in the following order: Assets, Liabilities, Owners' Equity, Revenue, Cost of Goods Sold, Expenses, and Other Income and Expenses.

Closing Entry is a journal entry at the end of a period to transfer the period's net profit or loss from the income statement to the owners' equity account on the balance sheet.

COGS. *See* Cost of Goods Sold (COGS).

Common-Size Financial Statement is the use of ratios to make financial statements easier to compare across periods or between companies. The process determines the percentage of one account represented by another account. A common-size P&L shows each account (income or expense) as a percentage of total (net) revenue.

Common Stock is the first or "founders" class of stock, which usually gives the holder a voting right.

Comparative Statement is a financial statement showing results from two or more time periods side by side for purposes of easy comparison.

Consistency Principle sets out the need for businesses to apply the same accounting methods and procedures from period to period.

Contingent Liability is a possible obligation that will be confirmed only by uncertain future events. Pending lawsuits or disputed claims are two examples.

Contra Account is any account created to hold a value that offsets the value of another account. "Returns and Refunds" is a contra account for income.

Contribution Margin (CM) is the gross profit (income – variable costs), which can be said to be "contributed" to cover fixed costs.

Controller or *COMPTROLLER* is the lead accountant at a business, typically responsible for managing cash flow and authorizing payments.

Cooking the Books is when financial statements are fraudulently manipulated to hide or misrepresent accounting facts.

Cost is the amount of money that must be paid to buy something; expense or purchase price.

Cost of Debt is the true after-tax cost of borrowing, expressed as [interest rate x (1 – marginal tax rate)].

Cost of Goods Sold (COGS) is generally the variable cost of raw material and labor required to make a finished product. Cost of sales is a broader term that can include other expenses.

Covenant is a restriction used in a loan contract to say what the borrower promises to do, or not to do, in order to maintain the loan.

Coverage Ratio is a ratio showing the company's ability to meet a particular expense or payment (such as a loan payment).

Creative Accounting is slang for illegal or unethical accounting practices.

Credit is an accounting entry that either decreases an asset or increases a liability.

Credit Memo is a document used to issue a customer a refund.

Credit Sale is the sale of products or services for payment at a later time.

Current Assets are assets that could be converted to cash in a short time, or are expected to be consumed by the business during the normal course of operations (usually within one year). Examples include cash, inventory, and accounts receivable.

Current Liabilities are liabilities (debts) to be paid within one year of the balance sheet date.

Current Ratio is the ratio of current assets to current liabilities, which measures the short-term ability of a company to pay its debts as they come due.

Customer Acquisition Cost is an imprecise but common measure of marketing and sales effectiveness, which shows how much money is spent to bring in one new customer. Because there is no absolute standard equation for calculating this, a business should be careful to be consistent in how it measures this cost from period to period.

Days' Inventory or Days Sales in Inventory (DSI) is a ratio showing how long the on-hand inventory will last at the current rate of sales. A lower ratio generally means the company is more efficient, but could run short of inventory. The formula is [DSI = Inventory/(Net Revenue/360)].

Days Payable Outstanding (DPO) is an estimate of the length of time the company takes to pay its vendors after receiving inventory.

Days Sales Outstanding (DSO), also known as COLLECTION PERIOD (period average), is a ratio showing the average time it takes collect cash from customers.

Debit is an entry on the left-hand side of an account, constituting an addition to an expense or asset account or a deduction from a revenue, net worth, or liability account.

Debt is any money, goods, or services owed to another individual or company.

Debt Ratio is the measurement of the amount of debt compared to the total capital of a company. The formula for this is [Debt Ratio = Total Liabilities/(Total Liabilities + Stockholders Equity)].

Debt Service Coverage is the ratio of cash flow from operations to the payments that must be made against a debt (interest and principal payments).

Deferred Income is that income for which the cash has been collected by the company but has yet to be "earned." This is a liability account and does not show up on the P&L statement.

Depreciation is an accounting convention that captures the "expense" of using a capital asset. Some portion of the expense is booked in each business period over the life of the asset.

Depreciation Schedule is the schedule (timing and amounts) of depreciation and can be either "straight line" (equal values in each period) or "accelerated" (greater values in early periods).

Direct Cost is any expense that can be directly associated with producing a product for sale.

Discounted Cash Flow is a method to evaluate investments that recognizes that future profits (or cash flows) should be discounted by a rate that reflects both the timing and risk associated with those payments.

Dividend is the payment of earnings (profits) to the stockholders. Dividends are never shown as an expense on the P&L.

Doomsday Ratio considers only the cash on hand to determine if a business can cover its current liabilities.

DPO. *See* Days Payable Outstanding (DPO).

DSO. *See* Days Sales Outstanding (DSO).

Earnings means profits, specifically net profits.

EBITDA is an acronym for Earnings Before Interest, Taxes, Depreciation and Amortization. In other words, net profits restated without interest, tax, depreciation or amortization expenses.

Entrepreneur is the person who assumes the financial risk for starting and operating a business.

EOM is an acronym for End of Month.

EOY is an acronym for End of Year.

Equity is a balance sheet item showing the value of ownership of a company.

Expenses are the daily costs incurred in running and maintaining a business.

Extraordinary Items are income or expense items recorded under "Other Income and Expense" in the P&L because they are unusual in nature *and* occur infrequently.

FASB is the Financial Accounting Standards Board, the body that sets accounting standards.

Federal Unemployment Tax Act (FUTA) is a federal tax for unemployment insurance, paid by the employer for the benefit of employees.

FF&E is an acronym for Furniture, Fixtures, & Equipment.

Financial Leverage is the use of loans (or other forms of debt) to increase the expected return on equity.

Financial Ratio Analysis is a way to interpret and understand financial statements. Analysis can answer critical questions about a business and direct management decisions.

Financial Statement is a written report that quantitatively describes the financial health of a company. The income statement, balance sheet, and cash flow statement are usually created on a monthly, quarterly, and annual basis.

Financial Trend Analysis is the process of analyzing financial statements to determine how fast a business metric is changing and in which direction it is moving.

Fiscal Year is the accounting year for a company, which may or may not start on January 1. It should, however, be 52 weeks long.

Fixed Assets are assets that will not be converted into cash during the business cycle. Furniture, land, and buildings are all fixed assets, but inventory is not.

Fixed Cost is any expense hat does not vary based on production or sales levels. Fixed costs usually include rent, property tax, insurance, and interest expense.

Full Charge Bookkeeper is one person who handles all aspects of the accounting function, including AR and AP.

Full Cost Recovery is adjusting prices to cover all operational expenses (as well as cost of sales).

FYE is an acronym for Fiscal Year End.

GAAP. *See* Generally Accepted Accounting Principles (GAAP).

G&A is the group of expense categories known as General and Administrative Expenses.

Gearing or *LEVERAGE* is the ratio of debt to total capital. *See also* Leverage.

Generally Accepted Accounting Principles (GAAP) is a recognized common set of accounting principles, standards, and procedures.

Golden Rules of Accounting are: (1) debits *always equal* credits; (2) increases *do not necessarily equal* decreases; and (3) Assets – Liabilities = Owner's Equity (the Accounting Equation).

Gross is the entire amount of something before any deductions are made.

Gross Margin is the ratio (or percentage) of gross profit to sales revenue.

Gross Profit or Gross Margin Dollars is net sales minus cost of sales.

Gross Sales is the total revenue at invoice value prior to any discounts or allowances.

Illiquid is when cash flows generated by the firm are insufficient to meet the debt service.

Income is value received during a period of time in exchange for labor or services, from the sale of goods or property, or as profit from financial investments.

Income Statement is the financial statement showing income and expenses. Also called Profit and Loss Statement or P&L.

Incorporation is a legal process through which a company receives a charter and the state in which it is based allows it to operate as a corporation.

Indirect Cost is that portion of cost that cannot be directly traced to the production of an item, but is nonetheless included in Cost of Goods (or Cost of Sales) because the expense is closely associated with the production process.

Insolvent is the condition of a business when it is unable to pay debts as they come due.

Intangible Asset is an asset that is not physical in nature, such as a patent, copyright, or goodwill.

Interest Expense is the cost of borrowing shown on the P&L.

Inventory includes parts or raw materials, partially finished items, and finished items available for sale.

Inventory Valuation is the process of assigning a financial value to on-hand inventory, based on standard cost, first-in, first-out (FIFO), last-in, first-out (LIFO), average list price, or other method.

Invoice is a written request for payment sent from a business to its customers. For clarity, an invoice is the document sent to customers, while a "bill" is the document received from vendors.

Job Costing is the process of assigning all identifiable income and expenses to a specific customer or project. When done properly, it provides the ability to track profits and losses on each job.

Journal is the "book" or register where accounting transactions are recorded.

Just-In-Time (JIT) is the practice of having only the needed amount of inventory on hand exactly when it is needed. JIT can eliminate carrying costs and reduce waste.

Leasehold Improvements is a balance sheet account capturing the value of repairs and improvements made to a leased office or facility. The cost is an asset, amortized over the life of the lease.

Leverage is the use of loans to increase the amount of capital available to a business, used to increase returns on equity investment

Liability is any amount owed to another party, including a loan, expense, or any other form of claim on an asset.

Lien is the right to take another's property if an obligation is not discharged.

LIFO (Last-In, First-Out) is an inventory cost calculation convention, in which the last (most recent) goods purchased are said to be the first (next) goods sold. This affects COGS and the ending inventory value.

Line of Credit is a loan that "revolves" or can be used and repaid as needed during an agreed period.

Liquid Asset is cash and any asset that can quickly be converted into cash (e.g., cash, checks, and easily convertible securities).

Liquidation is the selling of all the assets of a business, usually because the business is insolvent or illiquid.

Liquidity is a company's ability to meet current obligations with cash or other assets that can be quickly converted to cash.

Loan is an agreement under which an owner (the lender) allows another (the borrower) to use assets for a specified time period, and for a price (interest).

Lockbox is a service offered by banks by which a company's customers mail payments directly to the company's bank for immediate deposit. This can minimize mistakes, fraud, and the time required to convert accounts receivable.

Long-Term is generally longer than 12 months—e.g., long-term liabilities. *See also* Short-Term.

Loss, in finance, occurs when expenses exceed sales or revenues—i.e., goods or services are sold for less than their total cost.

LTM is an acronym for Last Twelve Months (also called TTM: Trailing Twelve Months).

Managerial Accounting is a system using financial accounting records as basic data to enable better business decisions in the areas of planning and control.

Margin *See* Gross Margin.

Marginal Cost is the additional cost of producing just one more unit of a good or service.

Marginal Profit is the change in the total profit that results from the sale of one additional unit.

Markup is the amount added to the cost of goods in order to produce the desired gross profit.

Matching Concept is the accounting principle that requires the recognition of all costs that are directly associated with the realization of the revenue reported within the income statement.

Negative Cash Flow is when cash spending in a business is greater than cash earnings.

Net is the value remaining after all deductions have been made from the starting, or gross, amount.

Net Profit is the company's total earnings, the same as net income.

Net Revenue is gross revenue less discounts, allowances, sales returns, freight out, etc.

Net 30 is a payment term on an invoice that allows a customer to pay the invoice at face value within 30 days (after which, presumably, interest would be charged).

Nominal Accounts are those accounts that are closed out each period. These include all revenue and expense accounts on the P&L, and dividend and withdrawals accounts found on the balance sheet.

Noncash Expenses are those accounts on the P&L for which the company does not actually spend cash, including depreciation, amortization, and write-offs.

Objectivity Principle states that accounting entries will be based on fact and not on personal opinion or feelings, such that different people observing the facts would reach the same conclusion.

Opening Balance is the balance of an account at the start of an accounting period.

Operating Assets are long-term assets not for resale, including property, plant, and equipment.

Operating Cash Flow (OCF) is the amount of cash used or generated as a result of business operations (and not from borrowing or investing).

Operating Expenses are all selling and general and administrative expenses, including depreciation, but not interest expense on loans.

Operating Income is revenue less cost of goods sold and operating expenses. It excludes financial items such as interest income or expense, extraordinary items, and taxes.

Operating Lease is a short-term, cancelable lease. *See also* Capital Lease.

Operating Profit is gross profit minus operating expenses.

Other Income is income from activities that are not undertaken in the ordinary course of an entity's business.

Outstanding is the amount owed as a debt, an example of which is outstanding bills.

Overhead is the costs associated with the working environment. Examples include rent, utilities, management salaries, and maintenance of the facilities.

Overhead Absorption is a method of assigning overhead and other indirect costs to the product created.

Overleveraged is the condition of having too much debt. The balance sheet will show that the entity is incapable of servicing its debt.

Paid-In Capital is the balance sheet account that records the value received from investors for their stock (capital stock plus paid-in capital).

P&L. *See* Profit and Loss Statement (P&L).

Payable is an amount that must be paid in the future.

Periodicity Concept is the concept that each accounting period has an economic activity associated with it, and that the activity can be measured, accounted for, and reported upon.

Permanent Accounts. *See* Real Accounts.

Personal Property (or Business Personal Property) means tangible or intangible property of any kind except real estate (land and buildings).

Petty Cash is a balance sheet account (and a physical location where cash is kept) used in the business for small purchases or reimbursements.

Petty Cash should be reconciled to actual cash just as a bank account is reconciled to a bank statement.

Physical Inventory is the counting of all merchandise or equipment on hand.

PPE (or PP&E) is the asset account for Property, Plant, and Equipment.

Preferred Stock is stock that has preference over common stock in case of dividends or liquidation of assets. It may have other rights, such as minimum dividends or voting privileges.

Prepaid Expenses is a balance sheet (asset) account representing amounts paid in advance to a vender or creditor for goods and services. Examples may be insurance premiums, software licenses, or maintenance contracts.

Principal is the amount of a loan, excluding interest.

Profit is the excess of revenues over expenses during any given period of time.

Profitability is company's ability to generate revenues in excess of the costs incurred in producing those revenues.

Profit and Loss Statement (P&L) is a financial statement showing revenue and expenses during a specific period of time.

Purchase Order is a written authorization for a vendor to supply goods or services at a specified price over a specified time period. Acceptance of a purchase order constitutes a purchase contract and is legally binding on all parties.

Quick Assets are equal to current assets minus inventories.

Quick Ratio is a ratio showing the ability of a company to pay its current debts as they come due. This ratio counts *only* cash, cash equivalents, and accounts receivable as current assets (not inventory).

Real Accounts, also called permanent accounts, are the balance sheet accounts (assets, liabilities, reserve and capital) that are *not* reset to zero balance at the end of an accounting period, but are carried over to the next period.

Recast Earnings is a recalculation of a P&L to reflect the assumption that certain expenses could or may change under different (future) conditions.

Receivable is an amount awaiting receipt of payment.

Reconciliation is the adjusting of the difference between two items (e.g., balances, amounts, statements, or accounts) so that the figures are in agreement.

Reserve Accounts, generally, are those balance sheet accounts where retained earnings are set aside to pay future dividends, fund improvements, contingencies, retirement of preferred stock, etc.

Retained Earnings is the balance sheet account in which profits from prior periods are "retained" or allowed to accumulate (if the profit has not been paid out to the owners as dividends).

Return on Investment (ROI) is any measure of profitability that evaluates the performance of a business or investment.

Revenue is any income (or asset or reduction of liability) gained from selling goods and services to customers.

Revenue Recognition is the process of assigning revenue to the appropriate accounting period such that all related expenses are in the same period.

Reversing Entry is a special type of adjusting entry made to perfectly reverse a prior entry. The reversing entry is written by simply reversing the position of all debits and credits from the prior entry. The first entry can assign values to certain accounts at the time financial statements are printed—while the second entry restores the proper balance to the operating accounts after statements are printed.

Run Rate is the projection of an annual result from current (shorter-term) results.

Sales is income (at invoice values) received for goods and services over a period of time.

Sales and Marketing Expense is a group of P&L accounts often grouped together, including: salaries, commissions, and benefits to sales and marketing staff; allowances to customers; advertising; warehouse costs; and shipping costs.

Sales Discount is a P&L account that records any reduction in price meant to induce a sale.

Sales Order or Sales Contract is a contract by which buyer and seller agree to the terms and conditions of a sale.

Share (of stock) is one unit of ownership interest in a company.

Shareholder is an individual or company (including corporations) that legally owns one or more shares of a company.

Shareholder Loans include any loans between a corporation and any of its shareholders. If these loans are not kept current, they should be counted instead as equity.

Shareholder's Equity is the total value of the company due to the owners. Mathematically, it is Assets less Liabilities.

Short-Term is 12 months or less.

Short-Term Asset is an asset expected to be converted into cash within the normal operating cycle, such as accounts receivable and inventory.

Short-Term Liability is a liability that will come due within one year or less.

SOP is an acronym for Standard Operating Procedure.

Statement of Cash Flows is a financial statement that specifies and measures how cash was received by, and used by, the business.

Stock is a certificate documenting the shareholder's ownership in a corporation. Sometimes "stock" is also used to mean "inventory."

Stock Certificate is a certificate establishing ownership of a stated number of shares in a corporation's stock.

Straight-Line Depreciation Method allows an equal amount of depreciation to be taken as an expense during each period of an asset's remaining useful life.

SUI is an acronym for either State Unemployment Insurance (tax) or State Unemployment Income.

SUTA is an acronym for the State Unemployment Tax Act. *See also* Federal Unemployment Tax Act (FUTA).

T-Account is the basis for all journal entries in accounting. T-accounts split the transaction into a left side (debits) and a right side (credits) so that it becomes easier to see when a transaction is in balance.

T&E is a P&L account for recording travel and entertainment expenses.

Technically Bankrupt means that the company has, at least temporarily, run out of cash to pay its bills and is, at the moment, bankrupt.

Tenor (of a loan) is the length of time allowed for repayment of a debt.

Top Linie of a company is its gross sales, or revenue.

Total Assets is the total of all assets, both current and fixed.

Total Current Assets is the total of cash and equivalents, trade receivables, inventory, and all other current assets.

Total Current Liabilities is the total of notes payable—short term, current maturities—LTD, trade payables, income taxes payable, and all other current liabilities.

Trailing, in time periods, is the most recently completed time period. For example, trailing 12 months would be the 12-month period that ended on the final day of the last month.

Trend Analysis is the analysis of changes over time through the use of analytical techniques, such as time series analysis, to discern trends.

Trial Balance is a listing of the accounts in your general ledger and their balances on a specific date (usually the last day of an accounting period or year). Changes are made to close a period or adjust balances between the accounts.

Unearned Revenue/Income. *See* Deferred Income.

Variable Costs are those costs associated with production that changes directly with the amount of production—e.g., the direct material or labor required to complete the build or manufacturing of a product.

Variable Expenses are those business expenses that usually fluctuate dependent upon production or sales volume. Contrast with Fixed Expenses.

Vendor is the party in a transaction that sells goods or services for money.

Vet, Vetted, Vetting is to make a careful and critical examination of someone or something, e.g., a person prior to employment.

WIP is an acronym for Work in Process. Often this is a balance sheet account showing the value of inventory which is currently being assembled or completed for sale.

Worker's Compensation is a state or privately managed insurance fund that reimburses employees for injuries suffered on the job.

Working Capital (WC) is current assets minus current liabilities; also called net current assets or current capital. WC measures the company's ability to finance current operations.

Write-Down or Write-Off is the reduction in the book value of an asset.

YTD is an acronym for Year to Date. On a P&L, for example, YTD is the period beginning on the first day of the year (or fiscal year) through the date of the report.

Zero-Based Budget is a budget based solely on careful projections rather than by building on prior years' experience. (Each expense category starts from zero.)

Z-score or Altman's Z-score is a formula that uses financial ratios to accurately predict insolvency (bankruptcy).

Bibliography

There is so much information available online these days that the most difficult and important part of learning is knowing what to read. Throughout this book I have made occasional reference to sources that I have found useful. Some are new and thoroughly up to date; others are more timeless. (The fundamentals of finance—and of a well-run business—do not change that much over time.) Following are a few of the best sources I have found for rock-solid advice on finance and the art of running a small business.

Seldon Gates deserves credit for inspiring me to learn more about financial ratios in general. His book, *101 Business Ratios* (Scottsdale, AZ: McLane Publications, 1993), is a handy list of ratios for every business situation. Further, Gates does a great job of standardizing the variables and how we feed financial results into ratio calculations. Using his book, we can create an entire spreadsheet full of ratios that could be updated with each new month or period end. Personally, I combined Gates's book on ratios with another book on using Excel to create metrics. Conrad Carlberg, PhD, wrote *Business Analysis: Microsoft Excel 2010* (Indianapolis, IN: Que Publishing, 2010), which is the latest of his many fine books about spreadsheeting for finance wonks.

When you are ready to really make a business dashboard that drives every aspect of your company forward, check out the classic book *Keeping Score*, by Mark Graham Brown (New York: Productivity, Inc., 1996). This is an easy-to-read bedside book that you'll polish off quickly, but refer back to time and again.

Finally, every business owner needs a few hardcore finance reference books. I found the following while studying for a financial analyst certification exam and have kept them handy ever since. Although I don't pull them out often, I'm always impressed when I do: These two books are thorough and clearly written, and they have great indexes that pinpoint just what you need. The first is *Fundamentals of Financial Management*, by Eugene F. Brigham and Joel F. Houston (8th ed., New York: Thompson Learning, 1998), and the other is *The Analysis and Use of Financial Statements* by Gerald I. White, Ashwinpaul C. Sondhi, and Dov Fried (3rd ed., New York: John Wiley & Sons, 1986–2001).

Index

About the Author

DAVID WORRELL is an award-winning entrepreneur and small business expert. His insights and advice about small business growth and finance have appeared in *Entrepreneur*, *Success*, AllBusiness.com, and dozens of other business publications, both in print and online. Worrell learned about finance and financial statements the old-fashioned way—with a notebook full of green ledger paper and a sharp pencil—as he guided his first small business through multiple years of 100%+ annual growth and ultimately to a successful sale and exit. Using the lessons learned from growing and selling several companies, Worrell founded Rock Solid Finance. There, as a CFO, consultant, and speaker, he helps his clients make their businesses more profitable, sustainable, and enjoyable. Worrell is a graduate of The Ohio State University and now serves clients around the country from his home in Charlotte, North Carolina, and online at http://www.RockSolidFinance.com.